D0975630

A MEMOIR

A TOUCHSTONE BOOK
Published by Simon & Schuster
New York London Toronto Sydney

LATE, LATE AT NIGHT

RICK SPRINGFIELD

Touchstone

A Division of Simon & Schuster, Inc.
1230 Avenue of the Americas
New York, NY 10020

First Touchstone hardcover edition October 2010

TOUCHSTONE and colophon are registered trademarks of Simon & Schuster, Inc.

For information about special discounts for bulk purchases, please contact Simon & Schuster Special Sales at 1-866-506-1949 or business@simonandschuster.com.

The Simon & Schuster Speakers Bureau can bring authors to your live event. For more information or to book an event contact the Simon & Schuster Speakers Bureau at 866-248-3049 or visit our website at www.simonspeakers.com.

Designed by Joy O'Meara

Manufactured in the United States of America

1 3 5 7 9 10 8 6 4 2

Library of Congress Cataloging-in-Publication Data
Springfield, Rick, 1949–
Late, late at night : a memoir / Rick Springfield.
p. cm.
1. Springfield, Rick, 1949– 2. Singers—United States—Biography.
3. Television actors and actresses—United States—Biography. I. Title.
ML420.S766 A3 2010
782.42166092 B—dc22 2010025074

ISBN 978-1-4391-9115-6
ISBN 978-1-4391-9181-1 (ebook)

All photos not otherwise credited are from the author's personal collection.

For Barbara, my true love

CONTENTS

A NOTE FROM THE AUTHOR

When I turned fifty, I wrote a song about my life so far, to see if I could fit it into a three-minute pop tune.

I could.

My Depression

Born in the Southern Land where a man is a man
Don't remember too much, warm mama, cold touch
Postwar baby boom, fifty kids in one room
All white future bright but living in a womb
Got a TV receiver Jerry Mathers as the Beaver
No blacks, no queers, no sex. Mouseketeers
Daddy kept moving round, I can't settle down
Always the lost new kid in town

Mannlicher lock and loaded, JFK's head exploded
Dark figure at the fence, end of my innocence
Hormones hit me, chew up, spit me
Get stoned, get plastered, always was a moody bastard
Guitar fool, kicked out of high school
Joined a band, Vietnam, Mama-san, killed a man
Daddy gets real sick it's too intense I can't stick it
Buy myself a ticket to the U.S.A.

Oh my God, it's my life. What am I doing kicking at the foundation?
That's right, my life. Better start thinking 'bout my destination

Hollywood sex-rat, been there, done that
Jaded afraid I'd never get a turn at bat
Last in a long line, finally hit the big time
Gold mine, feeding time, money/fame, I get mine
Use it, abuse it, Daddy dies, I lose it
Get a wife get a son, beget another one.
Head said "God's dead," motorcycle body shred
Midlife crisis rears its ugly head

Prozac, lithium, could never get enough of 'em
Last wills, shrink's bills, sleeping pills, sex kills
Edge of sanity, my infidelity
Looking in the mirror and thinking how it used to be
Don't like the skin I'm in, caught in a tailspin
Honest-to-God vision, spiritual transmission
Climb aboard the life raft, looking back I have to laugh
Take a breath, don't know if I'm ready for the second half

Oh my God, it's my life. What am I doing kicking at the foundation?
That's right, my life. Better start looking at my destination

My life, my depression, my sin, my confession,
my curse, my obsession, my school, my lesson.

For anyone with a short attention span, that should cover the major details of my life, so you can put this book back on the bookstore shelf. For those of you who want to hear the deeper cut, many thanks and read on . . .

—RS

LATE, LATE AT NIGHT

PROLOGUE

A SWINGIN' TEENAGER

So here I am, seventeen years of age, feeling as ugly as the ass end of a female baboon at mating season, unloved, very much in need of a good caressing by some attentive young woman and, right now, swinging by my neck at the end of a very thick twine rope like some pathetic B-Western movie bad guy. I'm thinking to myself as I lose consciousness, "Wow, somehow I thought it would all end so differently."

Thank God I haven't succeeded at a lot of the things I've tried, like this suicide attempt for instance. But thank God I *have* succeeded occasionally. Because in a furious flash-forward, of the type that can only happen in the movies or in this book, I am thirty-one years old and standing onstage with a very expensive guitar strapped around my very expensive suit, playing a rock-and-roll song that I wrote. The audience of this sold-out show is clamoring for more. A bevy of young girls is waiting backstage for me, and there's a middle-aged bald guy standing on the side of the stage, smiling at his healthy profit, ready to hand me a big, fat check when I'm done.

Wait . . . Wait, wait, wait, wait! Just a second here . . . So if I'd succeeded in offing myself back in my teenage years of staggering angst, I would have missed all this? Evidence, I think, that when we are at our lowest and ready to give in and go belly-up forever and for always, we should take a step back and say, "Is this the absolute *best* move I can make right now?" And then give ourselves an extra year or two or three.

I am walking, breathing, living proof that, considering how depressed and full of self-loathing and self-pity I am right now, swinging by my skinny, teenage neck three feet off the ground, thinking that I am worthy of not much more than the gig of pre-chewing hay for a horse with bad teeth, good things can still happen. It's just the law of averages, and the law is on our side, losers. Yay us! So to those who are at the bottom of the emotional heap—and it's crowded down here—there is still reason for hope! Not that the teenage idiot I was (who is, by the way, still swinging freely from a crossbeam and turning a lovely shade of blue) would have believed that dopey, feel-good phrase anyway.

Although by nature I tend to gravitate toward the bleaker side of things, I have been open to and have received signs throughout my life that have given me hope when I'd thought there was none. A part of me believes that these signs are directives from the gods. I've stayed surprisingly receptive to them, even though part of me thinks I'm full of shit to take them as any kind of actual, meaningful omens.

Another furious flash-forward—damn it, I wish there were cool sound effects in this book . . . whoooosh!—it's 1979. I'm living in Glendale, California, with a girl named Diana. Playing guitar in a house band at a local restaurant bar. This is not where I'd hoped to be in my music career by the age of twenty-nine, but then again I also thought I'd be dead by now, "strung up," as it were, by the neck, so it's just as well that not all my expectations are met. One night there's a party at someone's house in Glendale after my bar gig, and I go there by myself while my girlfriend waits at home.

A tarot card reader is in attendance. I love these people. They let us pretend to possible bright futures, even when we have none, and right now, I have none. At least not any future I'd want to celebrate. So I pull up a chair and shuffle her cards. Bad disco music is playing in the background and I think to myself, "Is there *good* disco music?" She deals my hand. The Emperor. The Two of Swords. The Hanged Man. The Star. She looks up from the array of archaic cards and locks eyes with me from across the table. She wants me. Wait . . . no, that's not it.

"That's the most incredible card spread I've ever seen," she whispers breathlessly.

"Yeah?" That's pretty much it from me.

"Something big is going to happen in your life . . . and soon," she answers as if definitively.

"Could you be more specific?" I ask. I want dates. Names. Exact amounts of cash. Truly, you can never nail these people down.

"Something . . . really . . . amazing," she replies.

It will have to do. And it does.

As a seeker of encouragement and affirmation all my young life, I've become accustomed to positive if self-servingly vague prophesies from a range of "experts": numerologists, astrologers, phrenologists (I do have a shitload of bumps on my head, so phrenologists have a party when I show up for a reading), tasseographists (look it up), and just plain seers. A year before the encounter with my disco tarot card reader, I'd gone to see a young Romanian with a brain tumor. It was widely believed that the unwelcome "visitor" in this man's head had given him a special view of the future. Everyone in my acting class had consulted this guy, desperate to hear him say, "Yes, I see you in major motion pictures. You are successful . . . wealthy . . . deeply, deeply loved . . . and your likeness is being carved into Mount Rushmore along with those four old dead guys because you are just *so* fucking special."

Honestly, I think that we're all—every one of us—constantly and hungrily searching for signs that we are singular, unique, chosen. And that an equally singular, unique, choice future awaits us. Actors are the neediest bastards in this way; don't ever let us pretend otherwise. Maybe we artist-performers need this kind of affirmation more than most, hence our career choice. I know that a strong, defining element of my character is the five-year-old inside me jumping up and down, demanding, "Hey, Poopypants, look at ME!!!" This need to be noticed and thought of as "special" has, to a large degree, charted my unholy course through adulthood. Dammit.

So when it's finally my turn to see the brain tumor guy, this future-seeing Romanian looks at me and says, "I see gold around you—here." He motions to my throat. I think, "Does he see bling? Am I going to be a pimp?" But he continues, "It's glowing, your voice. Are you a singer?"

"My mum thinks so," I answer. But I am actually heartened by what he apparently sees. Again, I put this "sign" in my back pocket against the times when someone will look at me and say, "You? I don't think so, asshole."

What is that *sound*? Whhhhooooosssshh!!! Yes, if this were a movie there would be amazing visual shit and music and sound effects and all. Use your imagination . . . we are now going *back* in time. Don't sue me for your whiplash; I'm trying to keep this thing interesting.

Okay, I'm going to drop a name, watch your feet. There will be several warnings throughout this book so you can protect your toes. Here's the first one: Elvis. But this is not the truly significant Elvis of my story. The most important Elvis in my life has four legs and black-and-white fur, barks, and is at the center of my heartache. No, this Elvis is the one you guys all know. I'm on a plane from Los Angeles to Australia via Hawaii in 1972, and Elvis (the two-legged, non-furry, singer version) is onboard too. My manager at the time is Steve Binder. Steve directed the Elvis comeback TV special in 1968, so I talk with him for a while about our common link. He's a sweet guy and signs an autograph for my then-girlfriend in Australia, who's a fan.

I get off the plane in Honolulu feeling oddly anointed by this small audience with the King. And as I'm walking down a side street, taking in the island's frangipani-scented sights with Kohilo blowing gently across my face, I walk by a young lady standing in a doorway who's wearing almost nothing and offers to tell my fortune. I say to her that I think my fortune is to get laid for a nominal fee, but she assures me she is an authentic seer and only wants to serve the Great Spirit she channels. She takes my hand gently and assures me I will be "successful in my chosen field." Hahahahahaha. She adds that my "successful" future also includes a "*very* successful happy ending" in the back room for an extra $150. See, I was right! Honey, I'm twenty-two years old. Call me when I'm seventy. I pass. But just like my chance meeting with Elvis, I take this encounter as a sign that big things are afoot for me, career-wise. Always such a positive boy. Except when famous rock-and-roll icons and skimpily dressed fortune-tellers aren't there to make me feel good.

Okay, another "Whhhhoooosssshh." It's 1979 and we're back in Glendale, California, again. Just minutes before I'm to head to the party and the tarot card mystic whose reading will presage a change in my life and my world.

"Aren't you Rick Springfield?" the pretty young girl holding a Long Island iced tea is asking me at the bar. I smile a shit-eating grin. "I loved 'Speak to the Sky,'" she continues, alluding to the hit song I'd had in 1972.

"What a trip you're playing in a restaurant now," she adds with a smirk, and I take that one in the gut. Do I really need her to point out to me that bugger-all has happened since then, it being 1979 now? I wonder if, despite my loser status in her eyes, she's up for a fucking, but she disappears soon after and I am left to my dark feelings. Yes, I *am* a loser. Yes, I had a shot in 1972. Yes, I blew it. Yes, I am playing cover songs in a bar in Glendale. Yes, my life is about to change. Yes, I'm . . . wait. What was that last thing? Amongst the litany of shit? Was there some positive word? Hey, maybe all those oracles I've visited over the years, seers whose "visions" gave me hope, were worth the price of admission after all! Maybe thanks to them (as well as a serendipitous meeting with an insurance guy—more on that later) I harbor some faith in myself yet.

Disco sucks ass! Other than the Bee Gees, disco is a wasteland and in 1979 it is at its worst. Radio is ready for a change. The great and almighty electric guitar is about to make a comeback, thank Christ. AC/DC's "Highway to Hell" is getting heavy radio play. Pat Benatar's "Heartbreaker" looks as though it could actually be a radio hit, and Elvis Costello has just brought some serious, much-needed songwriting and playing credibility to punk with his inaugural album, *My Aim Is True*.

I, on the other hand, am playing Top 40, instead of my *own* music, in a bar and am making stained glass in my garage. But I am *listening* to all this new music on my radio, and I have actually started writing some solid songs again after a hiatus of almost two years. I'm excited by the new movement in music and am getting the itch to take a chance and start playing original songs again. I've spent the last seven years drifting in and out of near-poverty and missed every time I've made a grab for the brass ring. Mainly out of absolute boredom I've signed up for this stained-glass class with the desperate and rather bizarre fantasy of becoming a professional stained-glass master, such is the state of my musical ambition after years of nothing but unfulfilled dreams. How capricious and unexpected the fates are. And you never know where the "nod" will come from.

I meet a couple at this glass class in the middle of nowhere in Pasadena. The girl is petite, dark haired, and really interesting looking, and she grabs my attention if not my loins. I write a song about the two of them. "Gary's Girl" doesn't have enough of a rock-and-roll ring to it so I rename him "Jessie," misspelling the male version of the name because of the Los Angeles Rams' Ron Jessie T-shirt I'm wearing at the time. I toss the finished song onto the heap with the rest of my unheard music.

My thirtieth birthday is fast approaching, and as far as the general public is concerned, my music career—what there was of it—has come and gone. I've had my shot: a Top 10 hit, some teen magazine coverage, a famous girlfriend, and the whole pop-idol-for-fifteen-minutes thing. In the eyes of the world (or at least those who even noticed), I'd shot for the David Cassidy throne and missed.

So I take a hard look at where I am now in 1979. In many ways I seem to be a happy man. I have a beautiful girlfriend, Diana, an ex-model who is artistic and loving; we rent a quiet suburban home with a flock of chickens (each individually named) in the backyard. We attend big Sunday dinners at her parents' house; her brother Doug is my best friend; we share art projects and her very much loved dog, Sasha. You cannot be far from a dog or life is meaningless. Our friends and every busybody with a fucking opinion are sure Diana and I will marry. I assume we will. I guess this is what marriage feels like. I don't know. I've never done it before. I love her dog, I know that much. Can I marry her dog? Is that legal?

My momentum is slowing. I've grown a beard and taken to wearing suspenders and flannel shirts. I'm settling down. But inside my head, a small, clear voice is rising. It is saying it's time to save myself, my dream, my life. It's getting louder and more insistent as the days pass.

I know in my heart that it's time to run.

CHAPTER ONE

THREE WISHES

GLENDALE, CALIFORNIA
1980

I tell the small, clear voice in my head to please shut the fuck up. I've heard its haranguing tone before. This voice is what has gotten me into the predicament I now find myself: almost fifteen years into a life in the music business with nothing to show for it but a handful of unrecorded songs, a few guitar licks, two albums that went nowhere, and as much groupie sex as my road-worn penis could handle. That last one being the biggest benefit so far, in my humble opinion. But I am driven. Compelled by a force that still refuses to take no for an answer. I have always had a deep, restless desire to push myself to have a successful career in music—to have it be my life; it already is my love. Ever since I first touched a guitar and it touched me at the tender age of eleven, I have wanted this. Wanted to be a part of music, the world of the musician, and everything it heralds and promises. But making a living at it has been like trying to suck pregnant goats through a garden hose. Difficult, to say the least.

Diana and I (and her very charming dog) have been together for three years, and we're living in Glendale in a small house we rent from an overzealous missionary who is at present in the Philippines fighting a losing battle to convert the local heathen bastards to his particular brand of Christianity. But he's giving us a killer deal on the house, so I encourage him to remain abroad for a while to fight the good fight. Diana and I have carved out a quiet suburban existence here in the smoggy hills. She has helped me emerge from some pretty dark days after my second album (*Comic Book Heroes*) came and went and I was unceremoniously dropped by Columbia Records with a cursory letter that had one word next to my name: DELETED. The subsequent black depression I fell into was because of more than just not having a record deal: it was because I was literally alone in America. Every person I'd befriended here—business and music associates alike—had deserted me like flies from a burning corpse with the 1973 failure of that record.

I owe Diana so much. Her family took me in and treated me like a favored son when I was at my lowest and most forsaken. Her mother Corinne especially was an ally and would remain so until the day she died. She and her husband, Don, had championed my budding acting career, cheering me on when I landed my very first paid acting role as a Roller Derby skater on the '70s show *The Six Million Dollar Man*, where I'd told the director that "Yes, I can absolutely roller-skate," though I'd never been on a pair of skates in my life. And of course on the first day of shooting I'd tripped all over the fucking things and had given myself a monstrous shiner that made it necessary for the extremely pissed-off director to film me from the left side only, in order to avoid my very discolored and swollen right eye.

Diana has stood by me, even when I appear to be nothing but a big doofus (see first acting gig, above), and she has always been a cheerleader for my musical aspiration. She has given me the connection of family again, supported me in every way, loved me well, and let me and Doug make up some extremely rude songs about her dog Sasha. Now I'm thinking of leaving this girl? I can't tell whether this is a real desire to break out from the complacency I've settled into, essentially living a "family life" with her, or just my old reckless need to play Russian roulette with my life again. I suspect it's a bit of both. I miss the edginess and the promise of sudden opportunity that comes with hanging by the skin of my teeth over the precipice—not knowing where the next meal or the money for the light bill will come from. And I am certainly not feeling *that* here in Glendale, California, in the preacher's house.

There's a creativity and a powerful energy that invades me when I'm not feeling secure in this world. It's part of why I became a musician in the first place: to get away from the steady, mundane existence I perceived my parents and all their friends lived. Now I feel like I'm headed toward that same predictable end: the gentle, sheltered, small life. I'd rather be fighting for something I believe in and living in the gutter with all the other freaks and misfits than disappear quietly into the woodwork of a house like the one I'm now living in. Sex between Diana and me is, at this point, infrequent and obligatory. My dreams, ambitions, energy, and libido are slipping down the drain of a muted, safe, white-picket-fence existence.

I began to pursue an acting career a while ago, and, along with the previously mentioned "Six Million Dollar Skater" role, I've been guest starring on some of the other prime-time '70s TV shows as well. But now the roles seem to have dried up, and my agent, Mike Greenfield, hasn't called me in over a year. I can't say I'm missing acting, although I am missing the money; I feel that the small success I was having in my actor's life was pulling me away from what I really want—music. The dissatisfied voice of ambition and desire for more in this world, which lives inside my head, has somehow gotten hold of a microphone and a rather large PA system. He is screaming at me to do something about my safe, soft life before it's too late. He is so loud that I'm wondering if the neighbors can hear him. It must have been that waiter's gig I applied for the other day that pushed him over the edge.

But there is another voice in my head as well. And this one isn't quite so gung-ho for me to wake up and aim higher. I know him as the Darkness, and he is the voice of my lifelong depression. While the guy with the microphone is encouraging me to get off my ass and do something, the Darkness is whispering a sentiment that is altogether different. "What's the point, Sport?" he says. "You don't have what it takes, and you know it." And goddamn it, part of me does believe that. But I am still young. Even at twenty-nine years of age I have the unbridled energy of the adolescent I will never truly cease to be. On this occasion I'm feeling strong enough to tell the Darkness to sit on a hairbrush, and I head back to my old acting class in Hollywood with the vague idea of doing something productive and artistic, even if I am paying for the privilege. But in class I meet a pretty young actress named Jennifer. Uh-oh. In this case, all things considered, my sexual issues work in my best interests and I latch on to this girl with the tenacity of a deer tick in summer. After class we head to her apartment and sit up all night sipping wine and discussing the theory of Cartesian dualism and its effect on the mind of twentieth-century man. No, not really. I fuck her brains out. And she, mine.

As I head back to Diana and my Maryland Avenue home at 3:30 the following morning, I'm pretty sure I have made a step, if a somewhat cowardly and self-serving one, to terminate this three-year relationship. Annihilate the ant colony with a nuke. It's an ugly, meretricious way to go about ending our live-in affair, but it is quick and effective. I am filled with a mixture of elation and remorse as I walk through the front door for the last time as Diana's boyfriend. She is waiting up with swollen eyes and accusations. I waffle and hedge for a while and then admit what she knows to be true. She understands exactly what this means to our relationship. She is humiliated, angry, and heartbroken, and I realize with guilt and some amazement that I am free. I will not settle down, become a househusband in Glendale, and play my guitar in my bedroom. For better or for worse, I'm on my way to another destiny.

Unfortunately, I don't know exactly where that is, I have no money to get there, and my shit is far from together. Due to a severe lack of finances and the speed at which this all went down, Diana and I agree to coexist under a precarious truce at Maryland Avenue for a while until I can find another place to live. Our swift breakup soon turns into a ragged and prolonged war of attrition. We try to stay out of each other's way, but our conversations are tense and curt and they sometimes turn into screaming matches and entreaties from her for reconciliation. I think to myself, "There was probably a better way to handle this than the path I took." My Darkness runs the video by me of the life Diana and I will never live: the kids we will never have, the family I will no longer be a part of, the road I have forsaken forever. It makes me miserable. But I confess that my biggest regret is leaving Diana's dog, Sasha, who I love like she's my own.

Miraculously, serendipitously, and I know all you proponents of the "it's-meant-to-be" theory will cheer when I tell you that one morning (shortly after the self-serving fornication with my classmate) out of a bright blue sky, an orphaned black-and-white bull terrier mix—filthy, starving, and half-wild—is picked up off the street by my ex and dropped off in our garage, where he proceeds to take a large poop on the cement floor. A short, one-sided turf war follows, in which this headstrong mutt and I draw our respective lines in the sand—mine are wishy-washy because I love all dogs, his are firm because he's a bull terrier—and come up with a game plan for living our lives together. At the end of two days, the quirky pooch and I are inseparable and "Lethal Ron" (so named because of his staggeringly bad gas), the future "Working Class Dog," is now front and center and fast becoming my hair-shedding soul mate, just when I need one the most.

I have made a decisive, life-changing move, and the Universe responds. I take the arrival of Lethal Ron as a good omen, and I am right. Suddenly my destiny opens before me like a flower to the morning sun. The gods smile. The genie pops momentarily out of the bottle and the formerly tortured, starving artist is granted three wishes. Four, if you count the dog. I most certainly do. And this all happens within the space of a month. After years of living in a music wasteland, I am staggered by the speed and force with which this all unfolds.

Wish one: The long-awaited record deal

I'm sitting in the soon-to-be-vacated-by-me Maryland Avenue house one morning, holding my breath as Lethal Ron basks in his own feral stink, feeling despondent over my meager cash reserves and the resulting absence of any prospects of a new pad, when the phone rings. It's my manager, Joe Gottfried, a sweet man with not a mean bone in his body but unfortunately not a lot of managerial savvy either. I love Joe. He rescued me and took me in when no other manager was interested in my future—if any even thought I had one. Joe owns Sound City, a successful recording studio that's part of a hideously ugly industrial complex in the ass end of LA's San Fernando Valley. Joe's only claim to artistic managerial fame is that he once handled Teresa ("Music! Music! Music!") Brewer. He has no business sense whatsoever, a penchant for talking with his mouth crammed with food, and, at age fifty-five, reminds me very much of the comic strip character Charlie Brown all grown up. But Joe is, God bless his sweet heart, a firm believer in me.

And he is calling to tell me that RCA Records, a struggling label with no one on its roster who's selling records except the now-dead Elvis (the two-legged one), wants to talk to me. I am floored. So, quite honestly, is Joe. He tells me that Ed DeJoy, the head of A&R at RCA, would like to hear some of my new songs. It happens that Ed, almost inconceivably, is a fan of my second and most miserable failure of an album, the aforementioned *Comic Book Heroes*.

I have a lot of homemade demos of my new songs. A real *lot*. Despite the primitive state of home recording in the late '70s, my song demos are intricate affairs. I have the basic "songwriter's four-track" tape machine: a TEAC 3340 that I purchased after my ex-girlfriend Linda Blair reclaimed the one she bought for me as a present so she could give it to her new boyfriend, Neil Giraldo. Neil, who is now dating and playing guitar with Pat Benatar and having some major radio success, will further figure in my life in the not-too-distant future.

The demos I am about to take into RCA are all made on this extremely heavy, hernia-inducing tape machine. I begin each new song with a drum track. The drums are not so much drums as cushions. A big fat Indian pillow, which I furiously pound with the tip of a sawed-off broom handle, is my kick drum, and a Naugahyde ottoman that I drag in from the living room and whack with the business end of a wooden spoon approximates the timbre of a snare for a reasonable backbeat. It's close enough to the sound of a real, if badly recorded, set of drums to fool drummers, so I am okay with the extremely laughable visual of me sitting on my music room floor, flailing away at house furnishings with wooden kitchen implements. I then add bass, played on a "pawnshop special" I picked up for $35 at a gun store on Santa Monica Boulevard. I load on guitars, bouncing down tracks to open up new ones so I can add keyboards and a lead vocal, and finally all the vocal harmonies. I leave nothing to chance or imagination in case a record company should ever express a desire to hear these songs. And now one actually has. Fuckin'-A.

I gather up some demos in my arms, like a mad artist picking a few precious paintings, and head to the meeting at RCA. After much consideration I've chosen three songs: "Easy to Cry," a '70s-excess-type rock tune; "Television," a sing-along faux-reggae thing; and "Love Is Alright Tonite," a new, edgier song I've just finished that's full of punk-inspired energy and three-chord thrashing. It's a disparate batch. A diverse, mixed bag to be sure. I don't know what they want to hear, so I'm bringing them choices. I feel not unlike Elvis (again, two legs, no fur), who used to wear a cross, a Star of David, and an Egyptian ankh around his neck so all the bases were covered when he went to meet his maker. I wonder which one got him through the Pearly Gates?

I sit fidgeting in Ed DeJoy's office while he plays the three songs I've brought with me. Joe is next to me, noisily munching potato chips. Ed taps along and nods now and then but says nothing. In the nine minutes it takes to play my songs I run the gamut of his possible responses from "These songs suck duck shit through a straw" to "Yea, verily, the Beatles themselves could learn a thing or two from this young and gifted lad." He lands somewhere in the middle.

"These are all good, but they're very different styles. Which direction do you see yourself heading in?"

Wait . . . did a record executive just ask me an *artistic* question? Well, yes he did.

"'Love Is Alright Tonite' is the newest one. That's the type of stuff

I've been writing lately," I reply, not sure if he's leaning more toward the cross, the Star of David, or the ankh.

"Yeah, that's the direction I was hoping you'd say," says Ed. "When do you think you'll be ready to go into the studio?" asks this angel in a three-piece suit.

Bells go off, the audience cheers, Vanna White smiles a *Wheel of Fortune* smile and opens the curtain, and there on the dais is a brand-new recording contract with yours truly's name on it.

"Wha . . . ?" is all I can manage. After *five* previous record deals have come and gone for me, am I really getting one more shot? A stunned silence settles over the room. Joe stops munching; I blink unbelieving, like a schoolboy in a whorehouse; Ed smiles; and this incredible moment is fleetingly frozen in a glorious tableau.

I have a deal!

Back at Maryland Avenue I jump into overdrive and begin writing songs frenetically, working long hours into the night while Diana tries to sleep, adding more tension to our already tenuous coexistence.

RCA pays me a $5,000 advance to record the album that I will eventually name *Working Class Dog*. I've never seen my name next to so many zeros on a check before. So I decide to do something really "grown-up": I buy a house with it. Obviously it's only a down payment; even in 1980 houses aren't *that* cheap. My new main man Lethal Ron and I go to check out a small homestead in La Crescenta, a working-class neighborhood that's a step or two down from Glendale in social standing. The split-level backyard looks out onto the parking lot of the bank across the alley, and I could throw a dead gerbil from here and hit the restaurant where my old Top 40 bar gig was. I find this kind of weird but also oddly satisfying. I check to make sure Lethal Ron approves of the backyard. He proceeds to take a poop. I take that as a yes.

I now have a $90,000 mortgage hanging over my head like a two-bedroom sword of Damocles, emphasizing the fact that I had better start hitting some career home runs or there will very shortly be a large fiscal train wreck in my future. This RCA deal is my "last shot." I know it, and I am determined to make the most of it. The Darkness, the voice of my lifelong depression, assures me that I will not only look this gift horse in the mouth, but I will kill it, cook it, eat it, and choke to death on a piece of gristle. He is a dick.

Lifespring is a New Agey, est-type self-awareness program that a friend of mine has recently turned me on to. I sign up for the weeklong intensive course and the timing is perfect for where I am in my head—free, open, and ready to take on the world. I don't realize it, but I have neglected my spiritual path over the "lost years" in Glendale and there are quite a few devotional reawakening exercises in this program that are exactly what I need at this point. There is also a lot of hugging, sharing, and uncovering the wounded child, as well as other assorted hippie-dippy shit, but it's all new to me and I suck it up like a brand-spanking-new Hoover. I meet a girl named Sylvia at Lifespring and I write the final song for *Working Class Dog* about her. "Inside Sylvia" confirms my suspicion that classes are an awesome source of writing inspiration.

Bursting with confidence when the week is over, I feel like I'm finally back on the right track. I'm so high on the possibilities for the future that I do something I would never have had the balls to do before: I pick up the phone and call Barbara Porter, the incredibly hot receptionist at Sound City, the recording studio my manager Joe owns. I've had my eye on this girl ever since she started working as a receptionist there—and I'm not the only one. Every horny musician who enters the premises makes a beeline for my girl. They just don't know yet that she is my girl. And for the record, neither does she.

Wish two: The girl of my dreams

Barbara Porter looks like a teenage Brigitte Bardot. She's only eighteen, but I'm pretty sure I would risk a lengthy prison term for her if she were underage and her dad were a cop. She is astonishingly beautiful. I have never seen a more breathtaking face, body, or smile in my life. And I have seen a lot of movies.

I dial the studio number. I know she will answer . . .

"Sound City?"

"Hi, is Joe there?"

"Yes, just a minute."

. . . .

Joe says, "Hello?"

"Joe, it's Rick . . . I'll call you right back."

Click.

Dial again . . . ring, ring.

"Sound City?"

"Hi—Barbara?"

"Yes?"

"It's Rick Springfield."

"Do you want to speak to Joe?"

"No, I just . . . would you like to go out with me?"

. . . . ?

"Hello? Barbara?"

"Yes, I'm here."

"Would you want to go out with me?"

"Yes, I . . . what about Diana?"

"I've broken up with her . . ."

"Okay."

And the deal is done. Set in stone, or at least wet cement. My penis thinks that it's just another potential weeklong romp in the sack, but my heart and my soul suspect that this relationship might last a little longer. Possibly a lifetime. And that I could maybe learn a thing or two about life and love from this young Midwestern girl. I quickly understand that she is a sharp, tough, no-bullshit person. She is the product of a twice-divorced mother and an absent father. Fortunately for me, when she was fourteen, she convinced her mother and her younger sister, Kathi, that they would all have a far better life if they were to pick up their meager belongings, pack them into a small U-Haul trailer, and head for the certainly bright lights and possibly hot boys of Southern California.

On our first date, she makes it pretty clear that her original impression of me was that I was a snotty, stuck-up, and possibly gay older man. Her "snotty, stuck-up" take on me is a fair cop. At this point if I am attracted to a girl, I feign indifference. That way I can't get hurt. I can't get laid either, but I've learned to take the good with the bad. She is, however, smarter than I am and sees through my pathetic proto-teenage shit. The truth is that I'm prone to being painfully shy, self-conscious, and awkward around girls I'm attracted to, and cannot, for the life of me, strike up a real and meaningful conversation if there is anything even remotely sexual between us. That is the big, fat, pink, and glistening banana that always positions itself between me and the object of my hot desire. Barbara is innocent and open enough to not accept this. Thank God.

I have always had a tremendous fear of failure in the sexual arena. The anonymous sex of one-offs on the road has served as a successful way around this fear. I have been as promiscuous as women have allowed me to be in my life. And I thank the worn-and-torn skin of my weary dick that they want it as much as I do. But all the one-offs have not built my self-confidence in this area at all. The Lifespring experience has momentarily imbued me with a powerful confidence that extends to all areas of my life, presenting me with a small window of opportunity that will soon close, I know, once the euphoria of the experience has worn off. But it's enough to help me hook up with this teen-dream queen with an attitude. And I dive through that window like my life depends on it. And it does.

Since I am clueless and broke, I take Barbara to a double bill of obscure art films she couldn't possibly have any interest in seeing (but at $4.50 a ticket, you can't beat it for value), and then to dinner at Delores, a grease pit just across the street from the theater. Even I, in my bachelorhood, am thinking we might be risking salmonella by dining there, but again the price is right, so I'm sold. I figure Barbara is young enough to handle a good stomach pumping at the local ER if necessary. So my future wife (God bless her spirit and strong stomach) and mother of our two children enters my love life via an inexpensive and nondescript little date on the night of January 21, 1980. Just before all hell is about to break loose. But I mean that in a good way.

Keith Olsen is soon to become one of the most sought-after record producers of the '80s. He is already much in demand, having just had great success with Fleetwood Mac's *Rumours* as well as the latest Foreigner album. He has agreed to cut two songs with me. The sessions with Keith are first up and I'm being sandwiched in between his recording tracks for Pat Benatar's new album, *Crimes of Passion*. He's chosen one of my songs but has brought in an outside tune as well called "I've Done Everything for You" that was written by Sammy Hagar. Sammy is, at this point in time, a singer-songwriter with some regional success, and he's been working with Keith as well. Keith Olsen is a great cross-pollinator. If we were girls, we'd all be pregnant. Keith tells me Pat Benatar has passed on recording "I've Done Everything for You" because she thinks it's too macho for her, but he emphatically informs me that it's a hit! It's a good song with a solid chorus, but honestly, at this point he could have brought in "I Am Woman" and I might have gone for it.

When it comes to the song of mine that Keith elects to produce, I'm actually a little perturbed. He picks "Jessie's Girl," a tune I consider a good album cut but not really a single or a standout. Keith, as is his wont, assures me that "Jessie's Girl," too, is a hit—second only to "I've Done Everything for You." I'm not so sure. To add insult to injury, Keith is apparently not a big fan of my guitar playing, the bastard. Although I will play guitar and bass on the other eight tracks of *Working Class Dog*, Keith brings in Pat Benatar's husband Neil Giraldo (of the previously mentioned, repo'd, Linda-Blair-giveth-and-taketh-away four-track tape machine) to play guitar on the two songs he produces. We begin work. A buzz starts to make its way around Sound City as people drift in and out of Studio A and hear parts of the almost-finished tracks. Musicians and studio personnel are asking Barbara if she is "Jessie's Girl." She has no idea what they're talking about.

I produce the rest of the album with studio-employed sound engineer Bill Drescher. We crank up the volume and work our butts off to finish the record. Because we are an "in-house" production, we are squeezed into whatever studio is open when the real paying clients pack up their guitars and drugs and go home. It's a cost-effective way to record, but it means our sessions begin at 2:00 a.m. and end at 9:00 the same morning. Sometimes we get a call telling us there's been a cancellation and we can have the time. I drop everything, fly out the front door with my stinky dog under one arm and my car keys under the other, and make my way at a breakneck forty-five miles per hour (the top speed achievable for a Ford Fiesta back then) to meet Bill at Sound City and jump straight into whatever track is crying for our attention.

It's a tough way to record, but we are more than up to the challenge. This time everything feels different and there is a flow and a vibe to the music and the sessions that I've never felt before. People continue to wander in and out of the studio, hear songs, and tell others about them. The feeling is like magic, Christmas, getting laid for the first time. Lethal Ron is with me through all the sessions and clears the studio from time to time as he lives up to his name. I'm beginning to get a novel idea for the album cover. It involves my ever-present canine soul mate and a rather large shirt and tie.

Being with Barbara gives me a sense of security I've never known before. She's also a major distraction through the recording of the album, and I'm constantly sneaking out of the control room to rendezvous with her in the bathroom, which creates a bit of a stir amongst the natives, especially my manager Joe, who thinks he's paying her to answer the phones, not to work his artist into a sweat in the employee john. We beg to differ. He fires Barbara but keeps me. I keep Barbara and think about firing him. With B behind me I am fearless. Which leads to:

Wish three: The working actor

Out of the blue I get a call from Mike Greenfield, who is theoretically still my acting agent although I haven't heard from the neglectful little bastard in over a year. I thought he might have died. Did he think I had? "Why haven't you called?" I ask him. "You said you'd still respect me in the morning. I've missed you, man." Actually I've missed working. He's been a pretty weird and inattentive agent most of my time with him and I'd heard he'd had a penchant for falling asleep on casting room couches instead of hawking his desperate and needy young clients. I'm surprised and actually a little psyched to hear his voice on the other end of the line. He tells me he hasn't forgotten me and to "suck it" for thinking he had.

He then says there's a soap opera that's casting the part of a new doctor. The casting people remembered me from an audition for another show the previous year (wow) and called Mike because they want to see me for this role. I've never heard of the show: *General Hospital*. The new character's name is Noah Drake and I'm fairly certain the part is not for me. I have a record deal at last. Do I really need this? I say this to Marvin Paige, the *General Hospital* casting director who has called me in. He asks to hear some of my new music, so I play him a couple of the finished tracks. He's not impressed and tells me he thinks my new album will probably get into the lower reaches of the Top 100 chart and then drop out a couple of weeks later. And that is exactly what had happened to my three previous albums.

My Darkness has snuck into this meeting while Marvin and I are chatting and he is *real* glad to hear this assessment of my new record and its potential. "Fuckin'-A, baby," he whispers gleefully into my good ear (yes, even back then I had hearing damage from loud guitar amplifiers). "This guy knows what he's talking about." Self-doubt curls itself around me like a serpent and I agree to read for the part of Noah Drake, M.D. "You won't get this acting gig, either," says Mr. D.

In the adrenaline-filled waiting room for the audition I see another actor up for the same part. He looks more the soap-opera type than I do. He's wearing a wine-colored velvet jacket and has thick, wavy hair. "That's the guy who's going to get the part," I say to myself. I'm actually a little relieved. I go into the reading, run through a scene or two, and then drive home and forget all about it. It's the most anxiety-free audition I've ever had. All I really care about is seeing Barbara again that night . . . plus, I have a record deal, dammit! Whoooo-hoooooo!!!

Marvin Paige calls me the next day. "How do you like being Rick Springfield?" he asks. I reply that it's had its ups and downs so far, why?

"Because you're going to be Noah Drake from now on," he answers.

Against all odds I have landed the part, my first acting role in more than a year.

Keith Olsen has just finished the final mix on "Jessie's Girl" and "I've Done Everything for You," and he is dead-set against the *General Hospital* idea. He tells me he thinks the album is strong and that I don't need the TV stuff. He presciently warns me that doing *General Hospital* will be a double-edged sword I may come to regret. But after all the crap that has gone down so far with my previously recorded work, I am understandably dubious about his enthusiasm for this new album. I take the *GH* gig and the steady income it represents and focus on finishing my first album in four years.

None of us has any idea that the following summer *General Hospital* will become the national obsession, exploding in popularity, drawing eight million viewers a day. Thirty-one million people will tune in for the much-ballyhooed wedding of Luke and Laura. Colleges throughout the country will reschedule classes around this afternoon soap because students aren't showing up on campus during the hour the show airs. Back in their hometowns, mothers are tuning in to life in Port Charles. Along with *their* mothers—and their daughters, too. It becomes a family passion. Oh, and guys like it as well.

The house I'm buying is tied up in a long escrow while the little old lady who sold it to me collects her furniture and her memories from forty years of life lived there. So Joe, feeling bad for firing my hot new girlfriend, lets me crash on the living room floor of a house he's selling in the hills of Encino. I close the door on Maryland Avenue and my life with Diana for the last time, pack up my new dog, my old TV, and a worn suitcase full of bad '70s clothes, climb into my Ford Fiesta (the last $4,000 car ever made), and with the Who's *Quadrophenia* blasting on the stereo, drive away from a life I once believed was my fate. So much has happened so fast that I am spinning. And the real ride hasn't even started yet.

"When you wish upon a star . . ."

Flash forward fourteen months. I'm racing down the darkening Hollywood freeway in my little Fiesta, pursued by not one, not two, but three cars full of shrieking fans who have been waiting at the ABC Television gate for me to finish the day's shoot on *General Hospital* so they can follow me home and find out where I live. They are blasting my music out of all three car stereos and waving, screaming, and taking flash photos as they pass by me and then drop back behind again. I am driving like a frigging maniac, weaving in and out of traffic, missing other cars by inches, getting irately honked at and flipped off as I whip up exit ramps and back onto the freeway, all in an effort to try and shake them before I reach my house. I break out onto the surface streets, spin around a corner at sixty miles per hour, zip up a side street, kill the engine, turn out the lights, and wait in the dark, breathing heavily and hoping I lost them.

Wait . . . *this* is what I wished for?

CHAPTER TWO

MY GOLDEN CHILDHOOD

THE OTHER SIDE OF THE WORLD

The '50s

The world is sunshine-soaked, warm, lazy, and shot through a gossamer filter, at least as I remember it more than fifty years later.

Australia is a majestic, sweeping, raw, bare bones of a country. The single oldest piece of real estate on the planet. The first island to separate from Pangaea, the mother supercontinent, at the beginning of time. It carries within its withered womb, on the Murchison range of Western Australia, at 4 billion years old, the most ancient rocks ever discovered on earth. A truly bizarre and unique assortment of animals, including marsupials (kangaroo and koala bear) and monotremes (platypus and echidna), have carved niches for themselves in its barren earth. Its topography shuttles between parched red desert to lush, rain-soaked tropical bush, all perched on top of nutrient-depleted soil leached of most of its vitality by eons of rain. Its shores have been battered by already ancient seas, and neither earthquake nor volcano has ruptured its primordial body in millions of years. The island continent . . . Gondwanaland.

Moving ahead a bit, Sydney in particular and Australia in general at one point serve as a dumping ground for England's overcrowded prison system. In the late 1700s, the dreaded "transport ships" begin to arrive on Australia's forbidden shores. These are leaky penal-colony vessels, stuffed to the rafters with men and women convicted of petty theft and various other inconsequential crimes. Thanks to the notorious and newly instituted "Bloody Code" of England, anyone convicted of anything from the theft of more than five shillings all the way up to murder was dispatched on the gallows, so truly, these poor fuckers on the boats included men, women, and kids who'd been caught stealing a half a loaf of bread to feed their families. If they don't succumb to the harsh discipline, foul conditions, or rampant disease and manage to survive the six-month journey chained belowdecks, they are immediately clapped into irons as soon as they are herded ashore. And look at the treacherous land they inherited, these wretched, luckless lawbreakers.

This ages-old continent at the end of the earth is full of danger. Hiding in the brush are animals that can and will kill you at the slightest provocation. Of the ten most poisonous snakes in the world, ALL of them are from Australia. Let's see, there are black snakes, brown snakes, the desert Taipan (the number one most venomous serpent on the planet!), tiger snakes, and coral snakes (they're even prepared to kill you in the water).

Spiders: The funnel web, whose venom appears to particularly affect primates (like humans), whereas other mammals—such as cats and dogs—are relatively resistant. How lucky for us. They crawl all over the inside of the little laundry room where I play as a kid. The red-back spider, the white-tail . . . all deadly.

Lizards: Our famous bluetongue. I have one for a pet; actually, I pull him out of his natural habitat and stick him in a chicken-wire cage. I call him Bluey, an Aussie term of endearment, but he still bites me, the ungrateful little shit. Bluey soon succumbs to lack of food (you have to feed these things?!) and the heat of the harsh summer in a wood-and-wire coop.

And then there are the poisonous plants:

Agapanthus orientalis
Agaricus campestris
Aglaonema commutatum

Alocasia macrorhiza
Amanita muscaria
Amanita phalloides
Araujia hortorum

Those are just the A's, and from southeastern Australia only.

Now let's take a walk down to the seaside, which is never far from where most Australians live, it being pretty much a coastal country. Sharks! We used to swim behind shark nets when I was a kid, with plane spotters flying overhead and lifeguards watching for the menacing, shadowy monsters. I never learn to surf because of this upbringing, despite living by the ocean most of my life.

White sharks (very, very famous), tiger sharks, northern river sharks, blues, bulls, and gray nurse sharks. Saltwater crocodiles (always good for a sudden death or two during the holiday season). Box jellyfish, irukandji jellyfish, blue-ringed octopi, scorpion and stone fish, Barrier Reef cone shells.

And lest I forget, the worst of all pests: the Australian blowfly, an invasive introduced species. They won't kill you, but they will drive you totally insane with their constant attention to your mouth and eyes. They are relentless enough to drive grown men to wear dorky little hats with corks dangling from strings attached to the brim to ward off the ceaseless attacks. If the scientist from the sci-fi gem *The Fly* had fused himself with an Aussie blowfly, he would have been unstoppable.

The list goes on. I spend my early childhood swimming and running barefoot amongst these creatures.

And you think you came from a tough neighborhood.

There actually is a Springthorpe (my true family surname) listed in the convict logs for one of the transport ships that brings the poor hapless bastards from England to the ends of the earth in the late 1700s for stealing a loaf of bread. When I hear this as a kid, I think it's pretty damn cool. My father, Norman James Springthorpe, is the youngest son of three Depression-era brothers: John, Jeff, and little Normie. Their younger sister, Shirley, is protected mercilessly and mostly against her will from the local young suitors by her three older brothers until she marries Sid, a nice Aussie boy.

My father, a handsome, barefoot young lad (his family can't even afford to buy him shoes) becomes Dux (valedictorian) of his high school. All three brothers do well in their respective careers, especially considering their tough beginnings growing up during the Great Depression. John, the eldest, rises to the head of the Sydney CIB (Criminal Investigation Bureau), sort of the Aussie version of the FBI. Jeff, the second-born, becomes a very successful architect with a multimillion-dollar home in a private cove overlooking spectacular Sydney Harbor. My dad, Norman, goes on to become a lieutenant colonel in the Australian Army, winning himself an MBE (Member of the British Empire)—the same award the Beatles eventually received, if you want a reference point—for his work in early computer management.

My dad is also a singer, with a rich baritone that wins him competition after competition all over Australia, but he has no real interest in pursuing a music career. He loves the army life and is content to sing for his friends and his church. (I inherit very little of his scholastic abilities, although I do get his love of music.) A few years ago, my mum confided in me that her big dream was to travel to the United States with my father on a singing tour. They say the family gauntlet is thrown down, and it can lie there for generations until someone finally picks it up. I guess I picked it up. (And all the time, as a kid, I thought my old mum hated the fact that I wanted to play music for a living.)

Eileen Louise Evennett, my mum, was born of English parents. She claims that we are actually descended from French aristocracy. (Evennett does sound a bit French, I'll give her that.) Furthermore, she says, we escaped the guillotine by a wing and a prayer and consequently lost all our wealth when our unlucky forbears' ship went down in a screaming gale off the stormy coast of England. As a kid, I much prefer the "convict" backstory. Way cooler.

In any case, her parents have just arrived from the dismal damp of London to the sunny climes of Oz when the aforementioned Great Depression takes hold. Not the best timing, admittedly. Eileen grows up on "stations" (huge Australian cattle ranches in the middle of the bush), where her mum works as a cook and her dad drives and maintains the estate's car. She has a younger sister by seven years named Pat, who is pretty much her only playmate. Her strong spirit is forged of steel, early, by life's fires. When she is fifteen, both her parents die within months of each other from diseases that would be easily curable today. Eileen Louise is left with a baby sister to raise and no one to fend for them. She leaves school, finds a job, and moves into a boardinghouse with Pat in tow. Abuse and neglect are rampant in the orphanages of the day, and she is determined that she and Pat will not end up in one. In what becomes the path she will always choose in the face of ruthless hardships, young Eileen digs down into her soul and finds the strength she needs to do what must be done. She is made of tough stuff, my mother. Thanks to her unbreakable spirit, she and Pat manage to dodge the fate of many of the other unfortunate Depression-era kids, but theirs is a hardscrabble existence and the specter of an orphanage as a very real potential destination looms over her and drives her through her teen years.

Meanwhile, my dad has had his eye on this young, dark-haired, blue-eyed beauty for some time. And on a rainy night in Sydney, umbrella in hand, he catches up to her and elegantly asks, "May I see you home, Miss Evennett?" But at the intersection of their two streets he bids her good night and bails with the parasol, leaving my mum-to-be to make her own way home in the pouring rain. Lucky for me, Norm soon gets better at courting and these two finally get it together romantically, or you'd be holding someone *else's* book right now.

At nineteen years of age, young Eileen is refused permission by the boardinghouse owner to take her little sister out past curfew so they can celebrate Pat's twelfth birthday. She does it anyway. When the girls arrive home at midnight, all their belongings (not much) are sitting out on the curb beyond the very locked front door of their ex-digs. My mum and dad have recently started dating, and fortunately Norm's parents take Eileen in (a bit risqué at the time, but desperate times call for desperate measures). Pat goes to the home of Norm's eldest brother John and his wife Helen. My parents marry on Valentine's Day.

And I, Richard Lewis Springthorpe, am unceremoniously dumped some eight years later onto the outskirts of Sydney, Australia, the most successful penal colony in the world, at roughly 7:00 p.m. on the 23rd of August, 1949, with a pronounced, though temporary, vacu-formed head, thanks to the "plumber's helper" used to pry me loose from my mum, who I guess was reluctant to let me go. (Maybe she had a premonition of some of the crap I would put her through later on after I'd grown a bit.) When a nurse brings in a cup of tea for my mum following her hard work of spitting me out into the universe, my dad, the nicest guy, but very much a 1940s Australian male regardless, takes it from the nurse, thanks her politely, and starts knocking it back. My mum, so the story goes, says firmly, "Norm, that's for me."

My dad stands up. "Oh, yes, Eil, so it is," he reportedly says. He hands the half-drained cup to my mum and then begins cooing over me as though nothing were amiss. Dad has a sense of humor that pretty much allows family matters to roll off his back, while my mum, a product of the British working class, brooks no nonsense. They treat each other with care, and growing up I see they have a warm if somewhat traditional relationship. Their arguments are few and take place in hushed tones.

My mum wants to name me Howard, but my dad sagely points out that Howard could be rhymed with "coward" later on in my school life and decides I should be named Richard instead. ("Dick." "Rick the Prick." "Dickhead." Need I go on? Evidently rhyming was not one of Norm's strongest suits.) After hearing the Howard story later (*Howie Springthorpe*?), I wonder for years, "Does my dad think I'm a coward?"

By turns I either subscribe to that notion or go out of my way to prove it's false, depending on the situation.

I'm brought home from hospital (in Australia we don't add the "the" before "hospital") in a wicker washing basket that my mum buys for double duty: (A) to bring my new ass home and subsequently (B) to load the wet washing in before hanging it out on the clothesline with little wooden pegs. (Jeez, how old *is* this guy? Hey, it *was* Australia in the late, late '40s, and we were a struggling backwater country in the middle of a very pissed-off Asian world, at the end of a brutal war.) My mum still uses this basket today. Not to bring any more babies home, thank Henry, but to load her freshly washed undies into before hanging them out to dry.

Which brings me to my brother, Mike, who is no doubt seething as he reads this part: me seeming so cavalier about our lovely mother's undergarments. Mike (older by three years . . . though you didn't hear that from me) never sees me as a threat to his status as an only child. (I'm convinced he still sees himself as the only "only child" with an actual brother.) To his credit, he holds me in my washing basket/late-'40s car seat all the way home from hospital and thereafter protects me from all types and sizes of school bullies throughout my blessedly short school career.

I don't remember my mother's third pregnancy, but I do remember her going away for a while and returning home seeming much sadder. She'd had a baby girl who died at birth. Nothing much is said in the aftermath of this, but there is a pall over all our lives for a while.

I have a feeling that my sister, had she lived, would have changed my relationship with women dramatically. If I'd grown up loving, living, and fighting with a sister, I might have seen the human side of women much earlier and skipped the whole "madonna/whore complex" completely. Thoughts of my lost sister have never left me; in fact, I think I'm still looking for her spirit.

But "soldiering on" is in our blood. My mum's parents had done it coming out from England the hard way (though, mercifully, the English who came out to Oz by those times were no longer criminals . . . at least, not convicted ones). My mum had done it at fifteen, when both her parents died suddenly and she had to leave school, find a job, and raise a baby sister on her own; my dad and his brothers had done it, forging real careers in the aftermath of the Great Depression. So soldier on we do.

We move constantly, as my dad is an army man and prone to being posted here and there. I have only one memory from my babyhood in Sydney: waking up early one misty morning in my grandma's cozy old clapboard house and hearing the chortling of magpies out in the eucalyptus trees. It is still the most haunting birdcall I've ever heard. The magpie—so much that is Australian to me. Unique, wild, beautiful . . . and meat-eating—snakes, mainly. Our move from Sydney to Bandiana, a tiny army town near Melbourne, is only the first of many painful, tear-stained transplantations. We will live here for three years. I arrive at age three and leave by the time I'm six.

Bandiana is dirt roads, army huts, and miles and miles of parched, brown vegetation. Everywhere, dirt. I don't think I see asphalt until I hit the school playground, literally, when I turn five. Another kid and I wonder about those weird little white logs all over the ground outside our houses. We finally come up with the excellent idea of tasting one; we find it rather salty. I'm horrified when my brother tells me that it's old, sun-bleached dog poo. I love animals, but not *that* much.

The line between animals and humans is still somewhat blurry to me when I offer up my first career choice to my mum. "When I grow up, I want to be a tiger!"

"Uh-huh," she probably says.

Kindergarten is the only time in my life that I actually ever really enjoy school. The first time I board the school bus, I instantly fall in love. It is a rusty, rackety old junk heap on four bald tires that makes the most amazing noises as it wheezes its way to my future alma mater.

With a monstrous steering wheel (at my age it appears to be about four feet across . . . huge!) and the way the driver smacks at it with his meaty hands every time he turns a corner . . . it is aaawwwesssooommme! "Now this is more like it!" I say to myself, and I fall asleep that night with dreams of being the biggest, baddest school bus driver Bandiana has ever seen. Tiger as a career choice vanishes.

It is after kindergarten one day, at the age of five, that I watch (along with two other goggle-eyed boys) as one of our fellow classmates, Vicky-something, takes a poop for us under the old wooden bridge down by the creek. I don't know if she's trying to shock us, just showing off, or sharing the fact that poop is the first original thing we produce as young humans. Anyway, it is an awe-inspiring performance and, thinking back, definitely sexual. At a fairly early age I am vaguely aware that my penis is for more than just peeing out of, and at this point I am already a confirmed pillow humper. My mum (who may kick my ass for telling this) walks into my room just after I've come home from my mind-numbing experience down by the creek with Vicky the poop queen and catches me as I madly give the high hard one to my little pillow, rubbing and grinding furiously. She grabs me by my skinny, five-year-old arm and drags me out to our only telephone (I still see it . . . black, threatening) and says, "If I ever catch you doing that again, I'm going to call the police!"

To be fair, my mum is, herself, a product of Victorian-era English parents with their staggering sense of shame surrounding anything even remotely connected to the human body and its functions, so I don't blame her personally for the psychological scars inflicted by her over-the-top reaction to my harmless little humping. But this incident instills in me a great terror of retribution from—whom? God? The police? Neurotic schoolteachers (more on them later)?—every time I wank off. Needless to say, it doesn't stop me.

My mum may be the product of nineteenth-century Mother England, and perhaps she's not the most demonstratively loving mother, but she does work hard behind the scenes. When I want a pedal car for Christmas, she gets a job for three months to save up the money to buy me the ride of my dreams. A few days before the car is to be unwrapped beneath our Christmas tree, she finds a pattern for a rag Golliwog doll in the local paper and whips it up one evening while I'm asleep. Christmas morning, the car is completely forgotten once I see Gordon the Golliwog, and he is my new best mate and so loved and carted around everywhere that he has to be patched up the next Christmas, and the next, so he can continue to hang with me. I don't know if my old mum was more thrilled that I loved her handmade Golliwog so much or pissed that she worked three months for nothing.

Our first dog, Fella, is a scruffy brown weed of a mutt. He's really more my brother's than mine, but I like him right away, beginning my lifelong love of dogs (if not their poo). It is a traumatic event when Fella bites someone one day, showing momentary signs of rabies, and my dad (who is, honestly, a sweet guy) is forced to take him out back (again, Australia in the '50s) and shoot the little fucker. I see the gun in the kitchen afterward . . . black, threatening . . . not unlike the telephone.

My brother has a rather obvious reaction to having his dog shot to death by his own father. Soon afterward, he wins a little brass toy dog (one that can't bite) at a party. He names it Bonzo and proceeds to tie a string around its neck. He takes Bonzo for walks (drags, really), builds him a swimming pool (muddy little hole in the ground), makes up a bed for him to sleep in (matchbox), and talks to him on a regular basis. I often hear him say to Bonzo, "Everything's going to be okay, little fella, it's going to be okay." I think my parents fail to register how deeply the shooting incident affects both my brother and me.

There is a lot that isn't discussed in my family. We soldier on.

Despite our shot-dead dog.

Speaking of death, my first (and by no means last) brush with it happens in Bandiana. During a game of hide-and-seek in the ruins of the demolished house next door, I squirrel myself away inside the old wood-burning iron stove still sitting in what used to be the kitchen. The door shuts and locks from the outside, and I am stuck in this oven on a 105-degree Aussie summer day while the kids I'm playing with run off to their next adventure. Three hours later my mum, looking for me and wondering why I haven't shown up for lunch, happens to open the old oven door. I fall out, semiconscious, dehydrated, drenched in sweat, and roughly the color of a boiled lobster. She starts to weep with relief until it dawns on her what a dumbshit I am to have locked myself inside an iron stove on a broiling summer day. Then she is pissed.

The first and one of the only times I remember seeing my dad's anger involves a cardboard aircraft carrier my brother and I see advertised on the back of a cereal box and send away for. When it arrives, as a kit, in a thousand pieces you had to put together yourself (we'd both missed that little pertinent bit of info in the ad), our dad spends a long weekend spitting and swearing and gluing it all together. He is very proud when he's finally done and the three-foot-long aircraft carrier is revealed in all its pasteboard glory. Mike and I both look at it, instantly recognize it will never float in the bathtub (cardboard not being the construction material of choice amongst the world's boatmakers), run outside to play, and never bother with it again. My father is so mad that I imagine my brother and me narrowly missing Fella's fate by the grace of our mum's intervention: "Norm, you can't just *shoot* them."

I hear traveling music

That's the sound of my family and me moving again. This time it's to an equally barren army encampment, appropriately but uninspiringly named Broadmeadows. At the age of seven I say good-bye forever to potential lifelong friends, my future career as Bandiana's brilliant school bus driver, and the crappy little clapboard house I love and call home—not to mention Vicky, the erotic poop queen.

We move into the old farmhouse of what was once a dairy farm. Due to the poor quality of Australia's topsoil, the farm idea didn't really work out, so Broadmeadows has been reinvented as a backwater army camp. Our house itself is a beautiful old Victorian that sits perched between the prongs of the *Y* where one railway line divides into two. The rest of the housing camp runs up a small hill and consists of bare wooden barracks-type houses. They are really butt-ugly, hot in the summer and brass-monkey-balls-freezing in the winter. My dad is the senior officer of the little enclave, so our house is comparatively grand, while these more Spartan "homes" are populated by enlisted men and their families.

The township of Broadmeadows is inhabited by hundreds of kids like me. Army brats and the like. But there is a unique contingent—the immigrants. Mostly English and Irish families who have been tricked into populating Australia by our government waving a ten-quid note (about $20) in their faces and saying, "All this can be yours if you come on down to our side of the planet and help us bump up our numbers so we can become a world power one day . . . possibly." They are now stuck in horrible corrugated-tin sheds without plumbing or any form of cooling whatsoever, which in the Aussie summers can be a death sentence.

A big, beautiful, black (not threatening this time; thank the gods of little boys) steam train puffs and boils into the army supply stores by way of our house every Thursday. It is freaking spectacular. I still see its dark iron wheels (taller than I was back then) and the white billows of hissing steam escaping through their spokes. The friendly engineer always waves to me, the little kid on the side of the country road waiting for him to pass by.

"Gee, this place is supercool," thinks my seven-year-old brain, so it's a bit of a surprise when this truly golden part of my childhood begins with a severe whipping. My first day as the new kid on the block, I walk up the little hill with a big smile and an open seven-year-old heart to meet my new best friends—the rest of the kids on the street. They are waiting for me at the top, a group of ten, as I remember it. I'm sure I say something along the lines of "G'day, moy nime's Reechud" (heavy Aussie accent).

My new friends proceed to yank off my T-shirt and give me several sharp whacks across my skinny white back with a brown leather belt.

Welcome to the neighborhood, dickface! This may have something to do with me being the son of the officer on the block, or maybe they just think I need a good thrashing; whatever the case, I take the hint, turn around, and head back to our new digs. (Today they probably would have just shot me in the knees.) I don't mention the incident to my parents; I don't know why. Maybe I think my dad has enough on his hands moving to a new army base, getting over the merciless slaying of our dog, and lugging in the really heavy shit from the moving van.

I soldier on, keeping the ringleader of the "gang" and his pleasant initial greeting very much in my thoughts until six months later, after they've all become my friends. I'm hiding by our side fence one day, waiting for this kid to pedal by on his bike. Unaware that it's "payback time, bitch," he zips by and I take him down and beat him senseless. Proof, I think, that my dad was wrong in his "Howard the Coward" assessment. Okay, the truth is I had the help and encouragement of my biggest, toughest friend, Eric Kelly (from a good Irish family who had the ill luck to think Australia would be kinder to them than their native land). He actually stops the kid's bike for me, *then* I jump out to do the pummeling . . . Dammit, maybe my dad was right.

It is around this time that I come home from school one afternoon and see my dad crying by the fire. I am told that my Nana (Dad's mother, she of the chortling morning magpies) has died, which upsets me, but it hurts me much more to see my strong, manly dad in so much pain. He is crying just like I cry. Silent tears and a few sniffles. I feel weird at first. Seeing this takes him down a peg from Superdad status, but at the same time it is incredibly endearing and makes me see him as more human. I love him even more, and I've never backed down from a good, righteous cry since then.

Or, occasionally, a good, righteous fight, as my dad has had his share of those as well. Whether I get myself damaged from the odd punch-up or just plain sick from one of the myriad viruses running through the state school system, the cure is always the same as far as my mother is concerned: Vicks butterballs. And what is the recipe for this wonder treatment? Take a big glob of Vicks—yes, the Vicks that you rub on your chest. Mix it up with an equal-sized glob of butter, make a one-inch ball out of the concoction, then roll it all in white sugar and insist that I swallow it.

Now, correct me if I'm wrong here, but doesn't it say, really plainly, on any jar of Vicks VapoRub, FOR EXTERNAL USE ONLY. IF SWALLOWED, SEEK MEDICAL HELP? Okay, maybe the warning wasn't quite as plain in the 1950s, but it was clearly indicated for use on the *outside* of the body, yes? Plus butter, plus sugar . . . was this folk remedy thought to be the cure-all for everything from the common cold to a bloody nose? I don't have an answer for that, but I have to say that it always made me feel better. Placebo medication at its finest!

The miles and miles of empty land around our little neighborhood stretch to the horizon in all directions—covered with a very pointy, painfully invasive weed called Scotch thistle. My best friend back then, Billy Groves, looks a lot like Alfred E. Neuman, the bat-eared kid from the *Mad* magazine covers. Of course, I can't really talk—I haven't grown into my own ears yet, and a stiff breeze could get me airborne. Billy and I run around all day long, barefoot, in perceived safety, without a care or thought of injury, abduction, child molestation, or murder. I'm having a fabulous time.

A dog and his boy

For whatever reason—my parents seem to take pity on me or are overcome with guilt; maybe a bit of both—they eventually get me a dog of my own. My very first dog. He is a black-and-white Heinz 57, and I call him Elvis. He is happy and playful and not at all rabid, all of which I take as a sign that my luck is changing vis-à-vis dogs.

I wake up and leave the house at daybreak, before anyone else on the street is stirring. My best friend/dog, Elvis, is always by my side. We run to greet the milkman, who still uses a horse and cart on his rounds through the mists of the early bush mornings. I become his Junior Milk Buddy and help him deliver clinking glass bottles on doorsteps throughout the modest neighborhood. I am given a free half-pint bottle as payment, which I slug back. Then Elvis and I round up all the local dogs for our daily adventure: a run down to the abandoned quarry behind our house while everyone sleeps.

At this young age I am already sold on the idea of the dog. One of God's absolutely greatest inventions and one that needs no more tinkering. The dog is the perfect beast, companion, friend, shoulder to lean on, and scapegoat when too many cookies are missing. And a dog won't hold that against you, either. I am at peace sitting in silence with a dog. Trying to do that with a human being is uncomfortable and a little creepy—"What is this guy really thinking?" You know what a dog is thinking: "This is so great. You're great. Could you pet me or rub my ear or . . . okay, there ya go. You're so great. This is just great. Really, really great."

And the whole welcome-home thing? "Wow, you're BACK!!!"—y'know? They are the best. And they are fuzzy and I have always loved the smell of a dog's paws. There are people I've met who agree wholeheartedly on this matter. It's a kind of Fritos corn chips, grassy, unwashed, animal stink kind of thing that's always the same from dog to dog. Unlike people, who have a variety of mostly noxious aromas.

So Elvis, with the good stinky feet, and I gather up the neighborhood canines for a wild-boy romp through the smoky Australian bush as the day breaks. Every morning and all summer long. Truly, there must be twenty different neighborhood mutts who anxiously await my arrival each morning, tails wagging, ready to go. The fast-rising heat of the new morning, the dry, stringy-bark gum trees full of kookaburras looking for breakfast, the forever view of the bright blue sky, and the knowledge that it's just me and all these slavering hounds: I feel connected to my life, the earth, and my existence in a way that I have very rarely known since.

Though I am literally the Pied Piper of the canine world, there is one chihuahua that I can never get to join us. He's a timid little freak, shaky and bug-eyed, but I'm determined to bring him into the fold. The fact that he belongs to the hottest girl on the block (Josephine, my first real crush) doesn't have much to do with it, I tell myself. Toward the end of summer vacation I finally win him over (though I'm not so lucky with Josephine), and he joins us all on our mighty quest to the great red quarry every morning where I am sold on the idea that dogs do indeed rule.

Since Oz is in the Southern Hemisphere, Christmas falls in the middle of the summer. One year I get a pogo stick for Christmas. It becomes my pseudo-bike (which I think we couldn't afford then). I hold onto the wooden picket fence in front of our house and hop up and down the dirt road 'til I fall off. Then I get up and do it again. And again. And I get really good on that thing. All day long as Elvis runs beside me, barking like a maniac. The idea of that little kid hopping around a tiny Aussie country town on his pogo stick versus the guy I see in the mirror today is one of the biggest mind-fucks of my life. I used to wonder where that kid went, but I eventually realized that he's still in here.

It's 1985. I'm standing on a stage at the Nürburgring Speedway in Germany at an outdoor music festival in front of a crowd of 250,000. I've never seen so many people all looking in the same direction at once. It's mind-numbing. A sea of faces, stretching to the horizon. The energy from the crowd is so powerful that I actually feel physically lighter. It almost lifts me off the stage. I play and sing and leap around and feel like I'm flying, and I realize that this is where that little kid went. Onstage. It's the only time I feel that connection I had when I was running with dogs in the morning sun to the quarry and back. It feels so long ago.

First stab at fame

Let's be honest: No performer ever lacks the innate and insatiable desire to be noticed. So it's no surprise that early on I come up with this little scheme: I will grab the nation's headlines as the eight-year-old kid who is . . . GorillaMan.

I take one of my mum's old sheets (construction materials being somewhat hard to come by) and make a little shirt and mask for my alter ego. Really just two pieces of the sheet tied around my chest and face, and in pencil—pencil, mind you—I write "GorillaMan" on the chest. I find a stick, attach a small stone to it with string, and stand outside our house for a couple of nights in a row with my cheesy homemade mask and costume, swaying from side to side, waving the stick/stone combo and making grunting noises any time a car passes by (and they're few and far between, let me tell you, when you live way out where we do).

I wake up every morning and check the newspaper my dad has discarded. Damn. No mention of my nighttime alter ego nor of the fear this frightening figure must instill in the passing motorists. I sometimes wonder if GorillaMan morphed into Rick Springfield eventually. Probably, huh?

Pop tunes

Around this time, my brother Mike brings home the first pop record I have ever seen, a 78 rpm copy of Paul Anka's "Diana." Even though it's state-of-the-art for the times, it looks like an ancient and fragile relic to me, that 78. Huge, heavy, magical, and still with the word "Edison" printed on the label. I'm sure that my small obsession later, writing songs with female names in the title ("Kristina," "Allyson," "In Veronica's Head," "What's Victoria's Secret?") stems from that first encounter with

"Diana." My brother proceeds to play the fucking thing fifty times a day for the next three weeks until we all want to shoot ourselves—or him.

The first pop song I remember hearing on the radio is "Dream Lover" by Bobby Darin. I hear it on the bus on the way to school one morning and can't get it out of my head. It's cool and catchy and nothing like the music my parents play around the house. I don't know them by name yet, but those four glorious chords—D, B minor, G, and A—are the same four chords I will use twenty years later to write my own first hit song of the '80s, "Jessie's Girl."

School

It's still okay at this point. I'm now attending Faulkner State School a few miles from our Victorian farmhouse. At Faulkner State, many of my immigrant classmates are fairly poor kids. Some of them ask me for my apple core and sandwich crusts after I finish eating lunch each day. I don't think anything of that, but my friends and I give them a lot of shit just because they're different. "Pommie bastards," they are known to us boys of the Great Southern Land, "Pom" and "Pommie" being derogatory terms reserved specifically for the British by the Aussies. The derivation is obscure, but the most popular theory is that the reference is to the red "pom-pom" atop the hats of British sailors who supervised the transfer of prisoners to the Colonies. Another is that "Pom" was an acronym for "Prisoner of Millbank" after the area of London where prisoners were held prior to their transportation. The best one, and the one I subscribe to as a kid because it's so damn funny, is that it comes from the French word for "apple" (*pomme*) because the unsuspecting English skin turns bright red, like an apple, under the fierce Australian sun. (I guess it eludes me that I am actually a half-Pommie bastard myself.)

Teacher's pet

Miss Hamilton is my fourth-grade teacher and I know I'm her favorite. Everyone in the class does, too. One day she asks me if I'll stay behind and help her with something after class. After all the other kids have gone, she leads me into her "teacher's room" at the front of the class and pulls out a thick brown leather belt. "Uh-oh," I think, panicking. "Am I in for another whipping?" At this point in history, teachers clobber us kids on a regular basis, for the slightest infraction, without fear of lawsuits or any retaliation whatsoever. But Miss Hamilton hands the belt to me. She tells me it's a new one she just bought and wants to know how it feels before she whales on any of the kids in her class. Would I please hit her with it? *Wait, what?!* She repeats her request.

So I do. She says harder, so I do. I must be there for ten minutes whacking her into a lather and beginning to feel a wee bit uncomfortable in the process. I eventually tell her I can't miss my bus and bail. I'm not sure what she does after that—probably best I don't know.

Clag

Glue that is very Australian and always a part of every new school year's purchases, along with books and pencils. It is a thick, stinky, grayish-white gel, in a glass bottle with a wood-and-bristle brush, that doesn't glue anything but paper to paper. Who makes glue that doesn't glue anything? *Spit* holds paper to paper. And what a catchy name, Clag.

I was about thirteen when I surprised myself by actually producing some real "manly" semen after a furious little wank. Once the wonderful shivers had subsided I remember thinking to myself, "Wow, this looks just like Clag!" And speaking of Clag . . .

Girls

On the monkey bars in the playground, the girls at school tuck their dresses into the bottom of their underwear, so when they hang upside down us boys can't see their panties. But the whole implication of this act, and the fact that we can see the panty line, just fuels our innocent white-hot passions further. Charlotte has twin braids hanging down her back and apple-red cheeks. My friends dare me to kiss her behind the bike shed, so I do.

Television

We are the first family in our neighborhood to get a television set. Considering our dad is the commanding officer of the area, it seems only fitting. I've never seen a television before. Our previous evening entertainments have been listening to the radio (wow, I feel old) and gathering around the player piano (no one in our family could actually play an instrument yet) and singing my parents' favorite songs like "Hot Diggity Dog," "The Surrey with the Fringe on Top," and "Abba-dabba-dabba-dabba-dabba-dabba-dabba Said the Monkey to the Chimp." Swear to God—that's a real song.

So it's big news when we get the first TV within a hundred miles. Our dad plugs it in, and my brother and I race into the living room and park ourselves about three inches from the screen. What is *this?* It looks like a bunch of fuzzy black and white dots! This is TV?! Our dad suggests we move back about ten feet. We do and suddenly a football game comes into focus. It is unreal, like something from a futuristic movie, in glorious black-and-white. The whole neighborhood comes down to our place to watch whatever is on our set some evenings. It becomes a communal thing, like having our own drive-in movie theater.

Cricket

The sport, not the insect. It's like baseball on Valium. I never liked the game, and when I get hit hard in the breastbone with a solid red leather cricket ball during a school match, I find a fairly acceptable reason to bail on the sport forever. My dad, on the other hand, loves cricket and watches it on the telly 'til the day he dies.

American programs

I love the show *Leave It to Beaver*, but it leaves its scars. My mum thinks I look like "The Beaver." Thank all that's decent in the world I don't live in the United States at this point. She takes a photo of me and enters me into a local "Beaver look-alike" contest. I'm pretty mortified, even at that age, and to add insult to injury, I don't even win.

Then there's *The Mickey Mouse Club*. My parents see it as wholesome family entertainment. The host, Jimmie, looks like a human Howdy Doody, and a bunch of sweet, talented youngsters sing and dance like old vaudevillian adults. All I see is Annette and Cheryl—girls seemingly my own age with supernaturally large adolescent breasts pushing up though their tight Mouseketeer sweaters. None of the girls I know even *have* breasts yet. Walt Disney is no fool. Still, I have a local girl, the aforementioned Josephine, nearer and far more tangible to me, if less blessed in the chest department.

Davy Crockett is Americana at its finest to a boy like me living out in the Colonies. My mum manages to make me a "coonskin" hat just like Davy's for Christmas from an old fur coat she has. I don't even know what a raccoon is. Could one kill you? I'm not sure. Probably, if it's anything like the animals I'm familiar with.

Another older woman

A big dark blot on my idyllic life at the farmhouse occurs one afternoon when I wind up at the house of the twelve-year-old girl next door. I'm only eight at the time, so I have very little idea what's really going on, but we wind up under her parents' bed with her underwear round her knees and her hands tugging at my jeans, which are being held up by a prodigious, though probably quite tiny, erection. So far, so good. Then her parents come home. It is a dark, guilt-ridden day at the Springthorpe house when my parents are indignantly informed of their son's deviant behavior with the neighbor's innocent daughter. What? I feel very shamed by the reaction of the adults concerned.

Later that night my dad tries to reassure me. He says something along the lines of, "It's okay, don't worry, son. And by the way . . . good on ya!" (an Aussie expression meaning "way to go"). Still, the incident leaves another scar related to sex—thank you, Victorian England and all your tweaked, ex-convict, deviant descendants.

Adventures with animals

Another dog fiasco: yes, another mauling of a stranger by one of our beloved canines. Not Elvis, thank Jesus. He continues to be the light of my life. The offender this time is the family Dalmatian, Freckles—she is sent packing. My parents decide that we should get something with fewer teeth. Living in the country as we do allows for a gentler, grazing-type, less rabies-prone creature. I opt for a lamb and get one a few months later. Stormy (because his wool is kind of a dirty gray color) runs up to me bleating his little greeting when I come home from school every day, after Elvis has had his way with me. He keeps the dried brown vegetation we laughingly call a "lawn" neatly clipped with his tiny choppers, and his poop is so small, even if you step in it you don't notice. He is very cool.

Unfortunately, as he grows, Stormy becomes more and more dependent on us humans. After my parents come home late and are forced to keep all the house lights off and change for bed surreptitiously for the hundredth time—because Stormy will start bleating for food or company as soon as he sees the slightest movement inside the house—they decide he has to go.

I can't believe it. Don't they know what people do to sheep? They eat them, for Chrissakes! I am not about to have Stormy served up to some trucker one morning with his eggs . . . wait, that's pork. Still, you get my drift. No one is going to eat my close personal friend. I cry and moan and plead, but my parents do not waver. In the end I have to accept their decision. One morning I get up and my woolly friend is gone. Stormy has left the building. My mum assures me that Dad has taken him to a farm where they've promised not to eat him. I soldier on.

But you begin to see why I have animal issues.

Though I'm horrified when my pet sheep is taken from me, I have no compunction about lopping off the heads of the chickens we keep in a corner of our yard. We eat one every now and then for Sunday dinner. Merrily chopping off their heads is the start of a bloodlust that will later lead to full-scale mock-guillotine executions in my weird, certifiably insane adolescence. No real victims, mind you, but I will greatly enjoy pretending that my least favorite people are lined up in the stocks, ready for a healthy decapitation.

We ace the chicken and then Dad lets its headless body flap around the yard until it flops over, gives a final kick or two, and is done. I then drop the body into a vat of boiling water in the funnel-web-spider-infested laundry room to help remove the feathers. (That God-awful smell will suddenly come back to me twenty-five years later at a big chicken dinner and consequently turn me off eating chicken for life.)

Life in the bush

I go to the "icebox" for food. Not the refrigerator . . . the "icebox." It isn't even plugged into the wall. My mum washes all our clothes in something we call the "copper kettle." It is a huge vat filled with boiling water in which she mixes the laundry and a little soap around with a big wooden pole. She wrings the excess water from the soggy mass with the power of her own two hands, tosses the clothes into my old baby seat, and hangs them out in the hot sun to dry. By the way, those strong hands of my mum's can deliver a hearty whack to the ass too. Mostly to me, my brother generally being less deserving of a thumping. We mow our dry, barren lawn with a rusty hand-pushed mower and beat at the flames of summer bushfires that lap at our wooden fence with old burlap bags.

Thinking back on these days, it's a wonder I didn't strap on a six-gun, saddle up my hoss, and mosey on down to the general store to get me some hardtack. What century were we living in, anyway?

Elvis and I frolic just as we are supposed to do. All through the long years from eight to ten he is my beloved dog. And they do seem long—in a good way, the way time stretches endlessly when you're a kid. Holidays seem to last forever and school semesters even longer. My enthusiasm for school is slowly diminishing. Yet every day Elvis meets me at the gate, sleeps with me, eats with me, and never, ever bites anyone. A perfect dog for a perfect place and time. I tell you, it's a Norman Rockwell moment. I am so happy.

CHAPTER THREE

GIRLS, GUITARS, AND GLORY

LONDON

1960–1963

That pure happiness doesn't last long. It never does. Elvis has just reached manhood—well, doghood—when Dad comes home one night, all excited. Besides being a smart and charming man, my father is also very good at whatever he does. He has been charged with a major assignment: spearheading the introduction of computers into the Australian Army. He announces that—now that we are all securely settled in our home with fast friends and a warm, fuzzy feeling of belonging—we are moving to England! And although it will be a great adventure for us to see the world, sadly, the animals will not be sharing our joy or our journey.

Are you kidding me? Leave Elvis behind and go to friggin' England . . . where all the Pommie bastards are from? Leave my friends, my dog, my world . . . Miss Hamilton?

What the hell!

Other unpleasant surprises lie in store. We all get our vaccinations and they hurt like a bastard. Yellow fever, typhoid, cholera, hoof-and-mouth, every disease I've ever heard of plus a few more. My arm aches for weeks and I start to get really scared.

Exactly where are we going that I need this much viral protection? I have no real sense where England is in relation to the holy ground of Oz. I do know that I have given plenty of shit to some English kids at school. Man, will those deeds ever come home to roost soon. It's waiting for me, just down the pike in the land of ice and snow. Talk about instant karma.

I continue to plead and beg on Elvis's and my own behalf. I campaign desperately for weeks. "Please let him come with us . . . please! I'll walk him whenever you say. I'll even pick up his poo, and you know how I feel about that. Well, maybe you don't, but I will anyway." My parents don't budge. Eventually I have to, again, take it in the shorts. Defeated, I make a deal with one of my friends, Colin, to take Elvis for the rest of his life.

On the final day, I insist on taking Elvis to Colin's house myself. No one is home there so I have to walk my boy down the long driveway, tie him to a post by the back gate, kiss him for the final time, and walk away from him forever. He howls mournfully because he knows. Looking back, I don't know how I did it. The truth is, I deserted my best pal.

He's long dead now and I often wonder what kind of life he had after I went on to my new future in a foreign land. Did he miss me? Did he adapt to his new life? Was his spirit as broken as mine was? What happened to the pal I loved and was made to forsake? Deserting him leaves a lifelong hole in my heart that I still try to fill every time I see a dog—on the street, at an airport, at a Starbucks—it doesn't matter where. Wherever I am, I get down on my knees to make myself his/her new best friend in a vain effort to heal the "Elvis wound" to my ten-year-old soul.

At the time, I feel sure this move is due to my bad luck with dogs. If I hadn't gotten Elvis, we'd probably all still be living in the little farmhouse at Broadmeadows in the middle of nowhere.

The one saving grace is that we're traveling to our new home by steamship, first class. The Australian Army may be sending us to hell in a handbasket, but they are certainly doing it in style. We board the SS *Orsova* at the main pier in Melbourne on the appointed day. The ship is built more along the design lines of the *Queen Mary* and the *Andrea Doria*

(thankfully, I don't grasp the concept that ships can still sink) than of the floating hotels of today. Streamers fly, all the people wave, and friends shout out their last good-byes as we slowly pull away. It's like a bloody movie. I think of Elvis one last time and then I'm on my way to jolly old England and some serious retribution from the Pommie bastards.

My first morning at sea, I get up early and run down to the first-class dining hall, where I'm informed that all this food is *free!* Not that I've had to pay for much of anything up to this point in my life, but, come on . . . FREE? That's the magic word, isn't it? I grab two plates and proceed to fill them with a messy assortment of eggs, bacon, sausages, toast, mugs of hot chocolate, and anything else that looks vaguely edible. I scarf it all down and am returning to the buffet for a second *free* monstrous helping when I start to feel quite a little unwell. In fact, I sense that my whole breakfast may be quickly backing up.

One of the stewards notices the color change in my face and asks, "You all right, lad?" I am light-years from "all right." I fly up the stairs, race along the gangways, and burst into our cabin just in time to yak up the whole breakfast, plus dinner and lunch from the day before, all over my sleeping brother and his bunk. He is not pleased. For three days I don't move from my own (much cleaner) bunk. I moan and hurl continuously, stopping only when I have purged my stomach of what must be everything I've ever eaten—all the way back to the crusty old dog poo from when I was three. And when I am done . . . I have my sea legs! I have never been seasick since. I may have scared my body into never throwing up again for fear I might hurl internal organs.

For the next six weeks we sail leisurely from Melbourne to London on the high seas. I see the most amazing sights. We stop at ports I've never even heard of, in countries that are incredibly obscure to me, like India, Egypt, and Italy. Obviously geography is not a particularly strong subject for me in school. Where have all these countries been hiding? And do they all revolve around Australia like the planets around the sun, as most of us Aussies believe? So I learn geography the only way it should be learned . . . up close and on the ground.

It is a journey of firsts in my young life: the first dark-skinned human beings I've ever seen. The first blind, legless beggar. First kids on the streets begging for cigarettes. My first limo, oxen, whale, dead person, camel, Egyptian Coca-Cola, dolphin, erupting volcano, hot Italian girl, turban, rupee, desert, pre-Christian city, servant, flying fish, Seventh Wonder of the World, and rickshaw. I am completely turned on by the world I am now seeing. Sailing through the Suez Canal before it becomes a political hotspot. Driving in an old bus through the dry Arab countryside before the possibility that we could all be blown to hell by terrorists. Visiting Ceylon in all its "raped by the British" glory before it was renamed Sri Lanka. Visiting India when there is still clean fresh water for everyone. Walking through Naples late at night and not, as we would be now, taking our lives in our hands.

At our Naples port of call my mum, being a history freak, insists on a side trip to Pompeii. This venerable Roman city, along with most of its hapless residents who worked and lived at the foot of Vesuvius, an active volcano, was buried under boiling pumice and ash when Vesuvius exploded in 79 A.D. We wander through its cobbled streets and long-deserted houses, markets, and amphitheaters all afternoon. It is a beautiful place, and I start to acquire my mum's love of history, though I probably don't realize it at the time.

A collective giggle goes up and there are a few assorted jokes from the men in our small tour group when we are brought to the door of Pompeii's famous Roman-style brothel. The guide mentions that there are certain "wall paintings" inside and that the younger children might want to be left out in the freezing rain while the rest of the lucky miscreants get to go in and check them out. Obviously the ancient Romans were way cooler about this stuff than we are today.

"You'll have to wait out here, Richard," says my mum and strolls inside with the rest of the group, including my brother! My mind works feverishly, trying to imagine what can possibly be inside that is so rude and forbidden that I am denied access. The guide mentioned "wall paintings." Is there a depiction of a half-naked girl under her parents' bed? Possibly an erotic poop queen or two? I have no idea, but my prepubescent libido reels with the possibilities. When I finally see the famous "wall paintings" many years later, I find the crude depictions of various sexual positions more comical and cartoonish than erotic. I realize that even at ten years old my mind was working to create a better pornography—and succeeding quite well.

The big port of call for me is Cairo, Egypt. Ancient Egypt, actually. Although I take it in stride, it is a mind-numbing juxtaposition for me, one moment, to be pogoing down a dirt road in the Aussie bush and the next, walking into a room in the Cairo Museum that's filled with the gleaming golden walls of the Egyptian pharaoh Tutankhamen's burial chambers. My mum may have felt much the same, one minute sweeping the floors of our little farmhouse, the next getting off a camel beside the great pyramid of Khufu and stepping right into a pile of camel crap because she'd under-tipped her native guide. There's a great photo of her, in her new sun hat, stomping angrily away from the camel and its smirking owner.

If I had liked school better, I may have spared the world a few hit songs and gone on to become an eminent Egyptologist. It blew my mind that much. I have read everything on the Middle Kingdom, and the discovery of Tutankhamen's burial chambers in particular, and I still go to any nearby museum featuring an exhibit of the treasures from that tomb. It's weird, but every time I've gone to an exhibit of Tutankhamen's belongings, something strange and almost supernatural has happened. But that's a whole other subject and book. All right, yes, I believe I have some sort of past-life link to that time and place, okay?

Thank God for all those painful vaccinations, because in true RS form I get off the ship in the squalid East African city of Djibouti and promptly step on a piece of grimy old wood that pierces my sandaled foot. My mum freaks out for a few minutes, but honestly, given the hideous crew cut and gaudy matching Hawaiian shirts she's inflicted on my brother and me for the trip, I find her reaction a little over the top. I get a slight fever, but I never throw up. Other than the time I'm busted for climbing up an outside "crew only" ladder to visit the dogs in cages by the base of the funnel of the ship (if I'd fallen, I'd have hit the water seventy-five feet below and been lost forever), everything goes swimmingly on the rest of our trip to the UK.

We arrive at Southampton in December of 1959 and are booked into the Howard Hotel in central London. I secretly hope this isn't a bad omen for me, given the whole "Howard the Coward" thing. London is the most astounding city I have ever seen. How could all those dopey Pommie bastards I'd known in school have come from such an amazing place? There is age to this city, serious age and history—even at ten years old I get that. And so much energy! The lights, the bustling crowds of Christmas shoppers, the red double-decker buses, the smell of diesel fumes, hawkers on frosty street corners selling really supercool tin toy airplanes that turn somersaults every few feet—"Mum. Can I have one?"

"We'll see. Maybe for Christmas."

"Mum, it *is* Christmas!"

"We'll see."

The action is nonstop. It is HUGE! Where the hell could a kid pogo?

Our days at the Howard Hotel begin with piping hot chocolate served from a polished silver pot. We see live West End shows like *My Fair Lady.* Buskers on the streets play and sing and look for tips, white-gloved hotel doormen usher us into the street and look for tips, Cockney taxi drivers look for tips, toffee-nosed waiters hand my dad a bill and look for tips on top of the outrageous price for eggs and sausages. It seems like all of London is after what little money we have.

The city holds all kinds of great and grisly attractions for a ten-year-old boy. London is still plagued by thick fogs back then, and I am mesmerized. I am just getting into the whole boy-loves-monsters thing, and the heavy fogs are so "Jekyll and Hyde" that I just know Jack the Ripper must be waiting around some bleak corner to tear us all a new one. It is creepy cool.

We visit the Tower of London and view its very nasty and much-used chopping block where the heads of two of Henry VIII's wives were separated from their lovely, non-male-heir-producing, allegedly adulterous young bodies. A collection of old agony-inducing implements is on display, laid out on shelves and in glass cases like so many "Grandma's tchotchkes" that you just can't bring yourself to throw away. The Iron Maiden, the Boot, the Pear of Anguish (don't ask—it was one of their freakier inventions), racks, whips, spikes, pots for boiling oil—all of it leaves a deep impression and stokes the fires of my unsettled young imagination. The British are so damn good at torturing that I'm in awe—and a little worried regarding what this says about the people I am now amongst. I will soon be trying to befriend the descendants of the crazy bastards who invented these staggeringly painful torture implements, at whatever new school I must shortly attend.

The prospect of school is very much on my mind throughout our three-week stay at the Howard the Coward Hotel. My mother keeps dropping lines like, "As soon as we get settled in our new home, we must get the boys into school . . ." as though we're actually missing something wonderful. I know that my long days of freedom are almost over and that I must face my worst nightmare—going to a new school—again. And on top of it all, this time it's *me* who will be the stranger in a strange land. The very prospect of having to go through all this is beginning to freak my little head out. The increasing dread spoils my fun in London, like the dark prospect of Monday morning that hangs over every Sunday afternoon.

My brother takes it a step further, entering what we will later refer to as "the black spot stage." He starts looking under the bed and searching the closets immediately upon entering our hotel room each day and asking the strangest questions. "Mum, should I ask English teddy boys [local toughs] if I have to wash my hands after handling dirty English coins?" Mike sees black spots on his hands and does a lot of obsessive washing of his various body parts. (Seems like the beginnings of OCD to me now.) I tell you, we are stressed out. But we never talk about how freaked we all are. That just isn't part of "soldiering on."

My dad has a giant responsibility squarely on his shoulders. He must comprehend and assimilate a brand-new work platform—computers, in all their complex and bewildering infancy—and eventually take all this knowledge back to the Australian Army. My mum, though she never says so at the time, worries about us going into yet another school, as well as her own issues about running a new home in a new country. My brother and I are out of our minds with the anxiety of it all, not to mention having puberty on the horizon.

And just when it seems my anxiety cup is filled to overflowing, I am in the hotel bathtub one night when my brother pushes me into the water heater, a primitive, gas-fired, broiling, all-metal contraption placed conveniently over the tub at ass height, if you're ten. I end up in hospital (no "the" in the UK, either) with third-degree burns on my later much to-be-filmed ass. I admit we were goofing off, but I would have accepted a simple "Richard, stop horsing around," rather than suffer the indignity of having a young English female nurse pull my pants down to my ankles to examine my severely scorched butt cheeks in the local emergency room. The next day I have a fever, I ache, and I can't sit down. It is on this day of misery that I am told I am starting my new school the very next morning.

Whoopee!

Our new home lies about twenty minutes by train from London in the county of Surrey, in the town of Woking (pronounced "*Whoa*-king"—should have been a clue). To be more specific, the township of Horsell. Or to be even more specific, "Horsell, *near* Woking," as our mailing address reads. This basically means, "Horsell is a piece-of-crap, insignificant little clump of houses that you could miss if you blinked, but to help you find it, should you ever really need to, then it's somewhere near the bigger, more important town of WOKING." The only really notable thing about Woking is that H. G. Wells chose its sandpits, where I will soon ride my bike, as the landing place for the Martians in his classic sci-fi tale *The War of the Worlds*.

The English have such a unique approach to their home addresses. Every house in our neighborhood has a name! The one we're renting is a small (my dad would say "bloody tiny"), whitewashed, tile-roofed, leadlight-windowed little number called Randene. The house names are usually a melding of the husband's and wife's first names. Our home's owners are Randon and Maurene (I kid you not). My dad jokes that Randene is a way better choice than the other possibility, Mauron.

In January of 1960, the Springthorpes move into Randene. My brother and I share an upstairs bedroom facing the street. There are enough rooms in our new house for us each to have our own, but we've always shared a room and will continue to do so until I leave home at seventeen, such is our need for companionship in our ever-changing landscape. Mike and I are the only constants in each other's lives, and it is an unspoken given that we will always be there for each other. Certainly at that age, I depend more on him than he does on me.

I set off for Goldsworth Primary School/House of Horrors, with a terminal case of nerves, not to mention being a bit sore in the singed-bum area. The school is located in an old, dark brick, scary-looking assortment of World War I–era buildings that now brings to mind the insane asylum from the film *The Elephant Man*. The other kids in my fifth-grade class are so far ahead of me in both maturity and scholastic ability that I feel completely out of my depth. It takes only one day of school for me to begin to understand the true nature of the shit I am in: I'm an Australian country lad from the '50s dropped off twenty miles outside one of the most cosmopolitan cities in the world. I feel utterly bereft and alone. For the first time, my brother is not there to protect me. He has moved on to face high school and his own demons, leaving me to fend for myself, the inconsiderate prick.

My mum walks herself up to the schoolyard on one of my first days and peeks in to see how I'm managing with my seared nether region and my new classmates. I hear her telling my dad later that night that she had seen me standing alone in the corner of the yard at lunchtime with my head down and my shoulders slumped. She says I looked pathetic.

Oh, great—now I'm a *pathetic* coward! I already know that the first kid who tries to befriend me will be the school dork. That's just the way it goes. The new kid is always that thin ray of hope for them. And predictably, the school dweeb with no friends already has designs on me. I guess I should be grateful for any olive branch of friendship, but in the competitive, punishing environment of the playground, if you're seen with the school dork too many times, then you are, by association, a dork yourself. And I cannot afford to be typecast as a dork. Not here in the land of the Pommie bastards.

Out of my feeling of isolation and the need to belong to something, I've started joining a bunch of kids' mail-order clubs. I still have all the badges and pins they sent me to let me know how truly and deeply they cared. THE BIGGLES AIR POLICE. THE DOLPHIN CLUB. And unfortunately something called Harold Hare's Pets Club. The H.H.P.C. sends me a membership pin with a cute golden bunny adorning it and the words HAROLD HARE'S PETS CLUB in bold block letters. I make the unfortunate miscalculation of wearing this particular little number to my third day at Goldsworth Primary Insane Asylum for the Precocious and Mean-Spirited Little Pommie Bastards, thinking they'll agree with me that it's cool and therefore instantly envy me and possibly win me their friendship.

It has the reverse effect. I'm roundly derided for being a "baby" and shoved and punched around the schoolyard by a bunch of them until the asphalt and I meet for the first, but most certainly not the last, time. Over the next few weeks I'm called "Australian pig," "convict," and "little baby" by the meaner faction. I don't mind the first two, but really, the "baby" thing is too much. So I push back. I get into a couple more fights that are quickly broken up by vitriolic teachers who I'm sure would much prefer to watch us beat each other to a bloody pulp.

One thing that changing schools so frequently teaches me is to stay in the game, because eventually things can turn around. I've experienced this many times already, as I will many more times in the future. These experiences will serve me well twelve years later, sustaining me through all the bleak and lonely times of my first years in the United States.

Lesson One: The circumstances will change if you stand your ground

And stand my ground I do. I do not back down nor do I kowtow to the bullies. The school I'm currently being tortured at is looking for a new goalkeeper for their abysmal soccer team. I volunteer even though I've never played a day of soccer in my life and still believe that Aussie-rules football is the true game of the gods. I try out for and win the position of goalkeeper by throwing myself onto the asphalt, ripping bloody gashes in my knees in the process, and deflecting the ball away from the chalk-drawn goal, the way I'd seen it done on TV. Slowly, gradually, I begin making friends through playground games and sports. After the first interschool soccer game, I proudly tell my mum that I stopped the other team from scoring eight goals. "How many goals you did you let in?" she asks. "Eight. They beat us eight to nothing," I say without a hint of irony.

Regardless of this small "victory," I am still stressed and start to engage in some very odd behavior at home whenever I get into trouble or am denied my way. As I said, our second-story bedroom window faces the street. And this is a very conservative, very English, very proper neighborhood. I take it into my ten-year-old head that when I am thwarted at home, usually by my mother, my most productive course of action is to race upstairs, throw open the bedroom windows, and scream at the top of my lungs into the chilly English night, "Help, help! They're killin' me! Please, someone call the police. God, help me!"

The first time I do this I see, with great satisfaction, the bedroom or living room lights of every house on the street switch on one by one. It is so excellent. And I know my parents are cringing in shame in the kitchen. "That'll show 'em!" I think. But it doesn't. And the next time I'm threatened with punishment, I run upstairs, throw open the windows and . . . well, you know the rest. This time only fifteen houses do the "lights-on-what-in-God's-name-is-happening?" thing, instead of the whole street. The next time, only five houses, then one. And finally the neighbors must all say to themselves, "Oh it's just those crazy fucking Australians again. When are they leaving, anyway?" So I stop.

Lesson Two: Lesson one notwithstanding, if it isn't working, change your approach

So I do. I stop screaming bloody murder out of my upstairs bedroom window into the cultured English evening and start to figure out what

I can do to make my stay in this cold-as-a-nun's-tit country bearable. Instead of resisting my new life, I choose to accept it—even embrace it. Gradually, I begin to appreciate the magic in this beautiful town of Horsell, near Woking. Before I even realize it's happened, I am a part of it. The smell of woodsmoke in the English autumn, riding my new bike with my new friends (*yay, I have some!*) around the vast, leafy Horsell common and through H. G. Wells's Martian-landing sandpits, listening to a kid tell me how he knows my parents have "done it" because that's how I was born (I'm grossed out; this thought hadn't occurred to me yet). Soccer, trips to London and the English countryside. Seeing the 150th bloody centuries-old church . . . truly, my mum is obsessed.

The cold, frosty English winter nights. My first Christmas in our new town, and the first time I've ever seen snow, waking up one morning to see snowflakes drifting past my bedroom window. Mike and I build the world's fugliest snowman in our backyard, a tall, skinny, lumpy pillar of snow, with a head, a scarf, and a hat. We roll in the snow, throw it at each other, and change clothes at least ten times that day. The only thing missing from this perfect scene is a dog. A year after our move, I'm in love with the place, finally feel at home, and never, ever want to leave.

I graduate to secondary school, moving over the brick wall and next door from the primary school/psycho ward I've been attending. The older secondary kids subject me to the usual harassment. There are scary stories of initiation rites where they rub black shoe polish into the hairless ball sacks of the wretched newcomers. A color that will take months to dissipate. You certainly couldn't scrub it off. Fortunately, the worst that happens to me is getting "bounced" (grabbed by the arms and legs and tossed into the air a few times), because I have a tough older brother who all the students are afraid of and know will kick their asses. Ha ha. God bless Mike.

It is December 16, 1961, and the school is having its annual Christmas show, which consists of marginally talented students performing while their parents watch and swoon. Tonight is the first night I will ever touch a guitar and kiss a girl on the mouth. I'm backstage, just hanging out and hoping to kiss Heather, an older girl my friends have bet me I'll be too chicken to lip-lock with. I've never noticed this girl before—she is cute but way, way, way older. My friends and I are all eleven and she's sixteen!! Almost married, for crying out loud, isn't she? Still, I'm waiting for the right moment.

One of the older boys has a guitar that he's on the program to play. I ask, as every other kid is doing, if I can hold it. He hands this stunning instrument to me—a Höfner semi-acoustic. The mighty world-changing American Fender and Gibson guitars haven't yet made it to Europe at this point; English kids are stuck with Höfners (made in Germany; Paul McCartney did pretty well with one of these), Hagstrom (Swedish), and Eko (Italian). I pluck the first two bass strings, E and A, and goddammit if it doesn't sound like the theme song to one of my favorite TV Westerns at the time, *Cheyenne*. Good Christ, I can play the guitar!!!

If that isn't momentous enough, I then meet Heather in the dark playground outside the school hall, where she proceeds to lean down (she towers over me) and plant one on my lips. I have never been kissed on the lips before. Certainly not by a much older woman who's "got it all goin' on." The English girls in my class, with names like Jill Braithwaite-Smythe and Gwendolyn Ainscock, are way more mature than the girls I've known back in Australia. They are into kissing and darkly hinting at the possibility of more. . . . Honestly, where do all these predatory, sexually aggressive girls go when, years later, I finally get up the nerve to try and actually have sex? I'll tell you where they go . . . they vanish from the playing field like mallards fleeing a shotgun blast.

As the parents are doing inside the hall, I swoon like a giddy young girl after this kiss. Technically speaking, I'm not really all that far from being a girl. My balls haven't dropped and there isn't even a wisp of pubic hair on my scrawny little body. But baby hormones start racing through that scrawny body and I fall instantly, madly, cinematically in love with Heather. It's pitiful, actually. I've worked all winter long on a paper route in the freezing snow and the cutting wind to save up enough money to buy halfway decent Christmas presents for my family, and after the kiss I drop that plan like a flaming dog turd. Yes, I'm already scheming about the cheap crap I'll give my family instead so I can buy my new love something wonderful and expensive—a sign of our deep and passionate bond.

I settle for a little piano music box/jewelry keeper thingee. It has a purple velvet lining and looks very sophisticated and suave . . . *I* think. I'm certain that this music box will one day become a treasured heirloom that will be passed on to our children and down through the generations along with the impossibly romantic tale of how their father first wooed their mother with this simple yet elegant treasure.

I creep up to the back door of her semi-detached, thousand-of-'em-in-a-row house one night before Christmas and leave the carefully wrapped music box/jewelry keeper thingee, plus a staggeringly romantic and, may I say, very grown-up-sounding love letter, for her discovery the following morning. That night, in my bed, I have visions of her running to me, tears in her eyes, picking me up (I am a pretty small kid) and swinging me around and around as the violins swell. In truth, I never hear from her again. For all I know, she threw my precious gift in the trash. "Randy little bastard," she probably thought.

I kept a small red diary for exactly one year in my childhood, and it happened to be this year, 1961. I can now actually look up what I was doing the day my future wife was born, which was December 22, 1961. And what was I doing on the day the future mother of my children was having her own struggle down the birth canal? Delivering that goofy music box/jewelry keeper thingee to the "other woman." And I know for a fact that I got up that morning at exactly a quarter past eight, because it says so in my diary. I went to bed at a quarter past nine that night, if that's of any interest to anybody. In fact, *every* friggin' entry begins and ends with what time I get up and go to bed. Why I thought my reveilles and bedtimes were so compelling is beyond me.

Hahahahaha. I just read the entry for December 20, 1961, and I quote: "I love Heather Flint but I'm not sure she likes me." Well, at least we know her surname now and can punish her accordingly for breaking my tender young heart. She's probably a grandmother by now.

From this point on, my twin obsessions are established and fueled: music and girls. The two have always been inextricably entwined for me, much as I hoped to be with them. And my fast-approaching pubescence is stoking them both.

My New Year's resolution for 1962, as written in my red diary, is: "Not to eat *any* sweets. To brush my teeth every time I do eat sweets." I am already giving myself an out, which doesn't say much for either my self-control or my sense of self-honesty. Speaking of being honest with myself, whenever someone asks me about acting versus music, which came first (and they do this a *lot*), I always answer music, of course. But I now realize that the truth is I started with acting, at age eleven. *Scuttleboom's Treasure*, you remember it? Neither does anyone else.

Miss Inman, our fetching English teacher, is rumored to be partial to the tender young flesh of us schoolboys, or so all the older boys smirk and whisper. She gets me alone after school one day and I panic, thinking, "Uh-oh, not another deviant request for a whipping or God knows what else." All she wants to do is talk me into playing the lead role in the school play—Captain Scuttleboom, he of the famous treasure. The idea of doing anything public like "acting" scares me to death—I'd be happier if she had, in fact, pulled out a velvet cat-o'-nine-tails and begged me to lash her quivering buttocks while Mr. Hales, our red-faced, bug-eyed, heart-attack-waiting-to-happen of a math teacher, watched and whacked off.

But no, I am lumbered with the part of the pirate captain. On the night of our first and only performance, in the same school hall where I had touched my first guitar and fallen in love with what's-her-name, I jump up on a box to rally my sea-mates and fall ass-over-teakettle in front of all the parents. I struggle to right myself and carry on with as much dignity as I can muster amidst the howls of laughter. It makes an impact on me that I have survived my first encounter with the guitar and the older woman but made myself a laughingstock in the acting department. No wonder I don't touch acting again for another fifteen years. Screw that, I think, and—realizing that girls are still out of reach—I take a second look at the guitar.

Enter the very first Fiesta-red Fender Stratocaster guitar ever to see the light of a soggy, sodium, English dawn, circa 1961. The band's name is the Shadows, and they are led by a Buddy Holly look-alike Englishman named Hank B. Marvin. They're an instrumental band that most Americans would consider a surf band, but, truly, they are way beyond that to us kids living in Europe in the early '60s. Hank is the inspiration for all those young boys in England picking up their first guitars and looking for guidance. Jeff Beck, Ritchie Blackmore, Eric Clapton, Brian May. Hank is IT!

So, at age eleven, I zero in on that red Fender Strat, pictured in all its teen-dream glory on the cover of the second record I ever buy, *The Shadows to the Fore*. Music is my way out of life's noise and confusion. That red guitar is exactly what I need. The bad news is that there's only one of them in all of England at the time and Hank B. Marvin owns it. If I'd wanted to acquire one back then, it would have cost my dad a year's worth of paychecks, had we even been able to contact a U.S. dealer in what was then an impossibly huge world. And the Americans! Well, they have brighter teeth, prettier women, stronger men, better cars, and cleaner kitchens, and they have the world under their collective thumb. We didn't even dare.

I do what I've always done when I can't get something I want: I make one for myself. This is true of the Roman gladiator's outfit I beg and beg for (but which has yet to make an appearance at a birthday or Christmas) and eventually construct out of cardboard (the building material of the gods). I cut and glue/tape together a helmet, breastplate, and shin guards, all covered in silver foil. This is also my plan for the REDFENDERSTRAT, as the guitar becomes known in my mind.

Cardboard again, which to my young mind is possibly not *the* preeminent building material for an electric guitar. Anyway, it's all I have available to me at the time. I draw, paint, and cut out a full-scale, really sucky version of the guitar, tape a piece of bamboo to the neck to support it, throw a line of cotton thread around it as a strap, and proceed to pantomime all the Shadows records I own (three), in the reflection of the small living room window at Randene. I manage to rope some of the kids who used to beat me up into playing the other members of the band. They use inverted tennis rackets. I am the only one who plays the REDFENDERSTRAT. Check me out!! I am swingin' cool!

At this point, Europe is gung-ho for instrumental bands like the Shadows and crooners like Cliff Richard and Frank Ifield (a good Aussie boy), but a new noise is being born up north a ways. I have a vague memory of a kid at school, in late 1961, telling us all about a really "smashing" ('60s Englishese for "outstanding") rock-and-roll band he's seen at the next-door town of Guildford the night before. He didn't like their name, though: the Beatles.

Along with every other eleven-year-old boy in England at the time I fall in love with Hayley Mills. She is an English child actress and the youngest daughter of British film star John Mills. I've just seen *The Parent Trap* at our local theater, and her spunky attitude and pouting mouth win me over instantly. I write away to the Official Hayley Mills Fan Club, at an address I've managed to get somehow, and ask for an autographed photo, which dutifully comes back signed "To Richard from Hayley." I put it by my bed and kiss it good night every single night. I still have it and I can see the smooch marks I left, as a besotted eleven-year-old, all over her face.

So, encouraged by this first photo, I send away for another, possibly more revealing one. It arrives a few weeks later and I am ecstatic, until I compare the new signature to the original one and see that the handwriting is completely different. I know that flunkies have signed them, not my fantasy-inducing Hayley. I go from ecstatic to crushed in a heartbeat. So to all those folks for whom I later had someone else sign a photo or an album cover: forgive me. Blame Hayley Mills.

My dad works hard. He is away a lot and is always studying, studying, and studying. He is pretty sressed out about all the work he's involved in, so when summer vacation, circa 1962, rolls around, he's looking forward to a quiet, relaxing few weeks at Randene, "the smallest bloody house in the county of Surrey," as he calls it. My mum has other plans.

She, conversely, has been *cooped up* in the smallest bloody house in the county of Surrey throughout the long school months while Dad has been traveling, and she's now looking to get "away." Hence her idea of a summer vacation: a camping trip around Europe. My dad is dead-set against it. So off to Europe we go. And by the end of the trip, we've all had such a blast that our vacation becomes known as "Dad's brilliant idea to take his family to Europe over the holidays."

Again, we are dragged by our mother to more amazing, staggeringly beautiful, centuries-old churches and abbeys, palaces and castles, built by the blood and sweat of our wretched forefathers. We see so many landmarks that I get to the point where if I see one more I really am going to OD. And then one morning in a little burg in France called Amiens, we're taking a town walk before we pack up the tent and head to Belgium when, in the window of a toy shop, I see it: the perfect, kid-sized Roman gladiator's outfit, rendered in plastic and Saran-wrapped to a cardboard shield. It looks exactly like I have always pictured it in my child-mind.

Of course the shop is closed. And of course we have to leave Amiens at 8:00 a.m. and the damn shop doesn't open until 10:00 a.m., and of course we can't wait, we have a schedule to keep. Of course I kick and scream and of course we leave at 8:00 on the frigging dot and of course I soldier on, sod it.

I am a headstrong little dude in my early youth, even though I never seem to get my way. Or maybe *because* I never do. When we finally arrive at the campsite outside Brussels, the capital of Belgium, I am still fuming about my gladiator outfit that some French kid is probably wearing at this very moment, poncing about like he's Marcus friggin' Aurelius. We pull into the campsite and unload our dark-blue canvas tent and a thousand million tent pegs. I immediately bail to go scouting for the bathrooms or anything else that will get me out of the atrocious task of erecting the tent. I find a charming swimming pool on the far side of the campground, with tin cans and dead animals floating in the nearly black water, and although the weather is a little on the rainy, chilly, and foggy side, I am going for a fucking swim.

"Absolutely *not*," my mother says. "It looks as if it hasn't been cleaned in years." "No, son, you'll get sick," my dad says, backing her up. "Bye!" I yell and run off in my shorts before either of them can grab me by a lily-white arm or leg. I thought I'd thrown up a lot on the ship coming over here, but after a fifteen-minute dip in the Black Lagoon of Belgium, I am already hurling as I stumble my way back to our campsite. My mother is furious, as she's the one who has to carry each bucket of my tossed cookies through the foggy night, past tents full of snoring travelers, to the bathroom I had so conveniently located earlier (all right, a point for me).

Apart from that episode and the rough, canvas, three-feet-in-diameter folding bath we are forced to use to cold-water wash our shivering bodies whenever Mum catches a whiff of boy stinkiness, the trip is spectacular. I know why I love to travel now. It's because I've never really stopped and I've seen the most amazing things. I've been moving almost from the moment I was born.

We carve a swath through Germany, Luxembourg, France, Belgium, Spain, Switzerland, and Austria, stopping only when we reach the Eastern Bloc. We also go to Scotland, where we camp by Loch Ness and my brother goes fishing and actually hooks the famous Loch Ness monster. I can't believe all the centuries of fuss over a three-inch fish. Mike is thrilled. We go to Wales—not really part of Europe. Not part of anywhere, really. I experience it as a kind of Alice-in-Llanfairpwllgwyngyllgogerychwyrndrobwillllantysiliogogogoch type of place. (That's the name of a Welsh town. Honest to God.) Did I pass through a looking glass to get here? It seems otherworldly. I find Edmund the Eel (cast on the rocks by some careless angler) and bring him home curled up in an old corn tin. We live together (my only English pet) for six months and then he buys the farm. Chokes on a pebble or something. My luck with pets is holding steady. He was really hard to cuddle with anyway. Wouldn't lie still, squirming and slippery. Making the bed all wet.

And everywhere there are music, guitars, and girls. Though I have not a whole heck of a lot to do with them yet, I am very aware of their omnipresence all the same.

The seasons begin to roll by faster, in all their English grace; I am forging friendships that could last lifetimes; I feel alive and hip and at the center of the modern world . . . and I know the end is coming. The feeling is all too familiar. It's like a Sunday night when I lie in bed, struggling to stay awake because I know when I wake up it will be Monday morning and time for school again. As it always does, Monday comes.

I know our time in England is getting short: Even before we arrived here we knew that we'd be sent back to Australia once my father had learned what he came here to learn. I begin to brace myself, like so many eighteenth-century kids did before me, for the dreaded transport ship. I start assembling an odd assortment of toy figures that I imaginatively name "The Gang," possibly to take the place of my real-life friends when it is time to hit the open seas and head back to Oz. I don't really know. My new facsimile pals begin with a pair of red plastic lips I find on the street one day. I instantly recognize the beginnings of a new friend—a ventriloquist's dummy, which I will construct and name Pierre! I look around for suitable building materials. Again, cardboard leaps out at me as the construction material of choice. An old shirt box for his torso, a smaller box as his head. I attach a spring-and-pulley-type gizmo so I can open and close his mouth. I sew some clothes on him, draw a face, and voilà: Pierre, my new best friend. I have a small bear as well, named Cheyenne, who I also make a suit of clothes for.

I entertain myself for hours with all the crappy stuff I make. I think this is part of the reason I'm such a toy freak today: because I never had any *real* toys as a kid. As an adult, I have a better collection of toys than either of my sons ever had. And they aren't allowed to touch 'em, either. Especially my supercool-neato *Star Wars* toys, of which I have some of the rarest in the world and . . . Hey, did your eyes start to glaze over just then? They did, man. I saw your eyes begin to roll back in your head. Let me tell you, there are people out there who love this nerdy toy stuff. Like that guy in the movie *The 40-Year-Old Virgin*. Some of the figures I have are worth thousands of dollars and I . . . You just checked out again! Goddammit! Doesn't anybody find this shit interesting? All I'm going to say is . . . Boba Fett. Okay? The *only* Italian-carded version in the universe. And I own it . . . All right, that's it. I saw that look. I'm moving on.

It's mid-1962 and after two and a half "smashing" years, the time to leave my sweet England draws near. More tears, more begging, and vows of "I'm never doing this to my kids when I grow up." I'm almost thirteen, desperate not to leave my really cool friends and sure that I want to live in Horsell for the rest of my life. No matter that visiting strangers have to be told that Horsell is near Woking, or they'll miss it. As a parting gift for a "job well done" in England, our mum inflicts another brace of unlovely Hawaiian-style shirts on my brother and me, made out of what looks like curtain material, and an additional round of atrocious crew cuts. In almost every photo from the trip home, we are wearing these extremely hideous garments. We catch the train to Southampton, not unlike all those unlucky travelers who headed for the *Titanic*, so many years before, and three of my best friends, who were probably some of my nemeses when I first arrived in England, are standing on the side of the railway tracks, crying and waving, as we separate for all time.

Another alternative future blown to hell.

CHAPTER FOUR

THE UGLIEST KID IN THE WORLD

AUSTRALIA

1962–1965

I'm quite the seasoned world traveler by now, so our voyage home on the *Wilhelm Rhys* (a liner out of Holland) in June 1962 isn't all gosh-golly-wow. It is pretty spectacular just the same. Apart from almost rolling over in a heavy storm as we cross the Bay of Biscayne, the trip back to Australia is pretty much like the trip over—minus the first three days of me tossing up my breakfast, of course. This time violent rocking and rolling doesn't faze me a bit.

The ship isn't very crowded up in the swanky first-class section, so I'm stuck with a fat little Dutch kid who can't speak any English and a bizarre older girl who keeps hinting that we should go somewhere our parents can't see us. I get her drift, but she also scares me, so I resist. Her name is Anne and she gets the strangest look in her eyes sometimes. I think I see that same look years later in photos of Charlie Manson. Hey, wait a second, maybe I didn't *completely* get her drift after all. Together we cross the vast Atlantic, Indian, and Pacific oceans.

On the day of our arrival at the Port of Melbourne, Australia, I dress my twelve-year-old self in my coolest clothes for our homecoming. I put on my Cuban-heeled boots, the same style the Beatles will soon make famous. I fought tooth and nail to get them—my mum thinks they're too "thuggish-looking" and that people might mistake my skinny butt for a hooligan who wants to eat their children. I look in the mirror at the guileless *Leave It to Beaver* freckled face staring back at me and beg to differ. To the boots I add my only pair of big-boy pants (long trousers) and a supercool purple mohair sweater that my old mum has knitted for me. I comb my longish hair and check my look. Yeah, totally swinging, pal!

I run up the gangway to the top deck and stand with my parents and brother on our auspicious homecoming to Australia. I look out to see my homeland and am shocked. What is this? The whole pier is lined with fucking losers! All of the guys have buzzed '50s haircuts, white golf shirts, baggy gray flannel pants, and flat, square, brown shoes, and the girls are all dressed like my *mum*. It will change soon, but in 1962 Australia is woefully behind the times. To me, highly impressionable and desperate to be cool, it seems like I've taken a big leap backward.

From the moment I step ashore I begin suffering from cultural memory loss. As far as I'm concerned, I am now a Pommie bastard, and if these Aussies have a problem with that, they can kiss my pasty white English ass. Every move so far, despite my initial misgivings, has seemed like a move to somewhere better, but this time I feel like I've been sent back to the farm after I've seen Paree (as the old song goes).

One of the first things we do as a family is attend an Aussie-rules football game, the fastest ball game in the world—a mixture of the wild-ass pummeling of ice hockey, the finesse of soccer, and a bit of the thuggish rugby mentality thrown in for good measure. I buy a three-foot-long wooden souvenir stick with a walnut stuck on the top, painted in my team's colors. I wave it around wildly and unwittingly whack some guy behind me in the head. He tells me I'd better quit it or he'll knock my head right off my scrawny little shoulders. The good news is my brother and my dad are right there beside me, and after a few angry words are exchanged and our neighbor doesn't take the hint, they beat the crap out of him and his friend. It's a righteous fight and I am mightily impressed. My dad can cry *and* clean someone's clock.

We settle into a hideous bright-pink house with black trim on Frederick Street into the Melbourne suburb of Ormond. My brother and I are enrolled in McKinnon High. How many times have I done this now? The process has lost any and all of the excitement and new-beginning promise it might once have held for me. My least favorite part of the prep is buying the school uniform, which all Aussie and English kids had to wear in those days. It always seems that I'm wearing the jacket of a club I know I'll never truly belong to, although I try to get into the whole "school spirit" thing. The unreadable, arcane Latin motto on the pocket of everyone's blazer translates to sayings like "Work First, Then Play," "Forever My Best," and "Pummel the Shit Out of the New Kid."

By this time I am completely burnt out on the whole process. I so know the drill. The class nut job no one wants to hang with is always the first to make any overtures, of course. This is followed by the usual baiting and testing of the new guy by the class cool clique. But this time, the girls are casting sidelong looks and making snide comments, too! The teachers are cruel and psychotic. The only positive aspect is that these kids all think, much to my secret satisfaction, that I am English. McKinnon marks the beginning of the end for school and me, and also my first real introduction to a most unwanted and uninvited guest: a Darkness inside me that I just can't seem to shake. This new voice in my head tells me softly and consistently: *You are no good.*

There are a couple of bright spots while we live in the appallingly pink house. As soon as we're settled, however briefly, we get a dog. Cleo is a tiny black/brown mutt we all shower with affection after three long years of pet deprivation. Unless you count Edmund the Eel, which to be perfectly honest, we don't, Cleo (my mum always chooses names from another century) will be the only animal, thus far, to live out her allotted life span in our keeping. My dad is a loon with nicknames and comes up with some doozies for Cleo. Clee, Cleenzie, Tombalina-Jackson 459, Tombee. It goes on. I inherit this trait, unfortunately, later giving my own dogs (and even my sons) thousands of free-associated nicknames. It is obviously genetic.

I am about to turn thirteen and my mother asks me if I still want the guitar I'd previously asked for as a birthday present. I tell her that I've changed my mind and would prefer this really cool-looking robot I've just seen at a local toy store. "Oh . . ." says Mum. She's as transparent as a politician's pre-election promises. I realize she's already bought me the damn guitar, so I say, "No, hang on. Maybe I want the guitar," and in my mind, this totally awesome robot waves bye-bye as he heads to France to hang with the kid who's still wearing my fucking gladiator outfit. So a guitar it is!

Well, of course, it's a Woolworth's special that cost five quid—about $15—and is completely unplayable. I immediately take a saw and cut it in half lengthwise, paint it bright red (where am I going with this?), chop off its head and nail on a Fender-style one of my own manufacture, add some papier-mâché, then put it all back together with Tarzan's Grip glue. My first REDFENDERSTRAT! Just like Hank B. Marvin's. I'm elated—until I try to play the thing and realize I have completely trashed it in the process. So I tie a string to it, put it around my neck, and lip-synch Shadows records, just as I did in back in England with my cardboard guitar. The bloody steel strings had hurt my fingers anyway. Fuck 'em.

Oh no, I hear traveling music again. Yes, folks, we're on our way once more. This time to a town called Syndal. *Syndal?* Did they make that up? It isn't even a real word. I've just turned fourteen, and our moves are happening more frequently now. There's almost no time to make real friends and consequently have soul-destroying farewells, but this endless relocation troubles me more and more. I suggest to my parents that we should just buy a gypsy caravan so our stuff can stay pretty much packed up all the time. I recently read that moving is right up there in stress level and freak-out factor with public speaking and being on a crashing airplane. No wonder my anxiety bucket is approaching capacity.

We move to 13 Subiaco Court (really, are they running out of real words for streets now too?), Syndal (near Melbourne), Victoria, Australia. I peer nervously out of our new cream-brick abode on Subiaco Court. Every house in Australia at this point is either cream brick, red brick, or clapboard painted pink or some other heinous color. It is a devastating anonymity for a young, hip "English" lad still fresh from London, the most with-it place on earth in the '60s.

I look for welcoming neighborhood gangs with leather straps. Nope. A big kid who doesn't know I have an older brother. Nope. Anne, the scary chick from the ship (Charlie Manson's sister). Nope. It's looking pretty safe out there. Birds singing, sun shining, breeze blowing, laughing kids in the street playing cricket (world's worst game). Yep, I think I'm good.

My first friend in Syndal is a neighbor, Rob Newton. Rob is a twisted young private-schooled lad my own age, whom I'd actually met once in England and had assumed was English. In fact, his dad is a transplant Aussie Army officer just like mine. Rob has a heavy British accent and dislikes Australia immensely and for the same reasons that are making it so hard for me to fit in. We both feel like we climbed aboard a time machine headed in the wrong direction. At this point the world sees Australia as a backwater burg of indeterminate geographic location, full of hapless rubes. Rob and I, as young, hip, wannabe Europeans, want none of this. We know there's something bigger out there in the brave new world. We've seen it! Close up. We bond quickly over our shared disdain for our location and our situation. He plays the guitar, too, which interests me.

Then somebody shoots John F. Kennedy, the president of the United States, in the head. To all of us outside of America, it seems that suddenly the land of perfect people has a big dark secret it's been hiding. Not just that they managed to get their president killed, although that *is* incredibly disturbing, but that the good guys don't necessarily always win, like we've always believed they would. I start to feel that maybe all the school bullies and beatings are just the tip of the iceberg. The world is actually a bad, scary, and dangerous place to be. The constant underpinning of anxiety that I've lived with for years deepens into a grimmer, low-level depression. The fact that teenage hormones are kicking in and wreaking havoc on a cellular level no doubt has something to do with my gradually ever-darkening mood.

I become preoccupied with torture, dismemberment, and death. Rob and I share a growing urge to torture and ritually execute all the idiots in our lives—at least in effigy. I start building working guillotines in the backyard—one is actually twelve feet high—much to my old mum's dismay. Now, every time we have a bad argument she runs out, grabs an axe, and chops these guillotines down. I guess it's her version of hanging out the window and screaming, "Help, they're killin' me!" I finally get wise and construct a portable, five-foot-tall version that lives in my bedroom alongside a small gallows with a spring trapdoor for the "long drop." At fourteen, Rob and I spend hours "executing" all the jerks we know, including schoolteachers, bullies, and shopkeepers who've caught us shoplifting from their stores. It's all good, clean, dark fun. We have connected on a very bizarre level and encourage each other's alienation and unhappiness. I'm surprised, later, that I never see him staring out of the local newspaper in a mug shot, having been arrested for eating the people next door. I suspect that in the years since, he's looked for *my* mug shot.

Another new school, this one my last, though I don't realize it going in. Ashwood High is the same game all over again. The dork, the bullying, the girls smiling or sneering depending on their coterie affiliation. It's so drearily and stressfully familiar. And as usual, lots of insane, sadistic teachers who hate children and have disgusting bronchial habits plus a desire to punish younger people for their own lives' shortcomings. I've been the new kid a few too many times. For the first time, there doesn't seem to be any upside. Just more alienation and despondency.

The only bright spot in my unhappy existence is that I'm falling in love again, and this time I'm pretty sure she isn't going to break my heart. She is sexy-hot and curvy, has a long beautiful neck and a rather small, pretty head with three tuning pegs sticking out of either side. Yes, the guitar is back in my life, this time to stay. With my parents' help, I buy myself an acoustic with an electric pickup. (Hey hey hey!) If I had a guitar amplifier, which I most certainly do not, I could plug it in and play really loud, which I most certainly cannot because of the added financial strain. I now begin to choose friends based strictly on whether they can (a) play the guitar and (b) teach me anything new. I'll take the train for an hour and a half to go to some spotty, weirdo kid's house just so he can teach me the latest George Harrison solo.

Speaking of which, some smart Aussie promoter, early on, books an unknown band from the north of England, and when they hit it big he has them already signed up to perform way down here at the bottom of the world. So like many of their sorry countrymen and women aboard the convict ships of the 1800s, the Beatles have to drag their now-very-famous asses to the ends of the earth. I go to this show with my brother because we still haven't formed any strong friendships in this new place yet.

I'm just another teenager in the audience when the Beatles take the stage in Melbourne, 1964. Everyone starts screaming when they appear and, so help me, completely against my will and much to my own chagrin, my mouth opens up and out comes this high-pitched girly scream that doesn't stop until the band has left the stage a short thirty minutes later.

Maybe it's just my age, or the adjustment to high school, but I'm not really connecting with the kids at this new place. The guy at Ashwood High who gives me the most grief is a handsome blond kid named John Kennedy (no relation to the recently departed president of the United States). One day I'm at my locker with this future juvenile delinquent standing over my shoulder, giving me shit, when he notices a photo of the Shadows featuring the great Hank B. Marvin, taped to the inside of my locker door. This is how cool being a kid is: *everything* changes in an instant. "You like the Shads?" he asks incredulously. And we become best friends for life, just like that. The power of music at age fourteen.

This friendship becomes a saving force at this point. (I keep in touch with John to this day—the song "Me and Johnny" is about our early relationship—and neither of us has really changed much. Okay, maybe we're a little older.)

The British Invasion is in full swing and music is changing so fast and furiously that it's mind-warping. Every day I hear new and more amazing songs on the radio. John and I hang out at school and at each other's houses on the weekends. All we do is talk about music, play our guitars, and write hopelessly banal songs. It's all we want to do. Out of our mutual inferiority complexes, we also start a rather destructive habit: we spend a lot of time staring at our changing faces and bodies in the bathroom mirror and belittling and berating ourselves to each other for our perceived faults and staggeringly misshapen appearance. His nose is too big, mine is too fat. His ears are too small, mine are the breadth of Batman's cape. His chest is concave, mine is too. Neither of us has any real pubic hair and we are sure girls are utterly repelled by the sight of us. We are cut from the same cloth, John and I—probably why we've stayed such good friends. We start "rehearsing" with the idea of putting a band together and begin to look for a drummer. Back then, no one wants to play bass guitar. That position is left to the worst guitar player in the group, and neither of us wants to be lumbered with that. We also start smoking (Kools) and drinking (cherry brandy) but still remain, much against our wishes, luckless virgins.

John and I find our drummer and we name the band the Icy Blues. We also find a gullible kid whose first name is Breckstin (you can't be a rock star with a name like Breckstin). His parents are obviously feeling guilty about saddling their kid with a name like that, so they've bought him a really expensive guitar amplifier that John and I plug *our* guitars into and then unplug him because he sucks. We actually get our first gig playing at a school friend's birthday party. We are paid three Australian pounds (about $15) and are completely blown away that we have actually made money doing something we would gladly have done for free. This is the most money I have ever made, including what I earned from mowing neighbors' lawns and running a paper route. It's a very revealing moment for little Ricky, who, as a boy in Broadmeadows, carried "cash" (newspaper cut to size) around in a sack because he liked the feel of "having money." But more important, we get attention from girls—and the open invitation for the odd (still chaste) date now and then.

Invitations from girls are big news, because the teenage dating ritual back then is set in stone and never varies. Certainly not for me, anyway. I don't know if it was true for all guys, but every encounter with a girl invariably ends the same way when I am in my early teens. I go to a local party, hook up with a girl from my school, go off into a dark corner, and start kissing. My hand, beginning under her dress at the knee, s-l-o-w-l-y creeps its eager little way up, up, up as though, if I go slowly enough, she won't notice. When I get to mid-thigh—*thwack!* her hand comes down on top of mine and I hear the dreaded words, "I can't." I swear, I try it twenty times a night with the same girl and every time I think, "Yes, yes, this is it. *This* time . . ." Then, like a cat toying with a half-dead mouse, she lets me get just so far and . . . *thwack!*

I start to think the problem may be familiarity, so I take a different tack. At the next party I spy a girl I don't know. I ask her if she wants to dance and soon enough we are in a dark corner. I start with the slowly creeping hand—only this time she doesn't stop me. I am flabbergasted. Hang on, this is *not* how it's supposed to go! Doesn't she know the rules, for God's sake? I reach the top of her stocking (very sexy, the top of the stocking in the days before pantyhose) and I have no idea what to do next. I am mortified. The hunter, balking at the moment of the kill. I stay there all evening while my clueless fingers toy with the lower edges of her underwear but dare to go no further. The next day at school I consult the "mature" kid in our class—you know, the one who starts shaving before anyone else does, and who, kids say, has "done it" lots of times—to get some advice. He laughs at me. He knows the girl and says she is a "go-er" (Aussie slang for a girl who puts out). Damn it! Had I blown my best shot at losing my virginity?

I grow into a *fifteen*-year-old virgin that year. What is God saving me for? Why can't I, as all the other kids in my school swear they have done, get lucky? My hormones are breathing down the back of my neck, and to add injury to insult, John is suddenly transferred from Ashwood to a private school because his dad doesn't like the influences at the public one. Our relationship suffers a serious blow. As I've invested all my time in him and no one else, I'm left with no real friends at school. This also spells the doom of the second-best cover band in Syndal, the mighty Icy Blues, just as I feel we are on the cusp of megastardom.

Other than my guitar, the love of my life at this point (though she has no idea) is a girl named Tania Hunt. She looks like a young Elizabeth Taylor, with violet eyes and thick, dark hair (actually, not unlike early photos of my old mum I've seen . . . wow, that's *weird*). I love her and I am terrified of her. I worship her from a safe distance. All the kids in my tenth-grade class know I am insane for this girl, and when she breaks up with her boyfriend at a weekend party that I'm attending, these same bastards from school chase me up the dark street, pick me up, drag me kicking and yelling back to the party house, bodily throw me into a bedroom where she is alone crying, and slam the door shut.

Tania sits, moist-eyed and beautiful, on edge of the bed; it is the most romantic and yet humiliating thing that's ever happened to me in my young life. "Hi," I say from the floor, sweating and breathing heavily and trying to ignore the fact that I'm obviously socially inept. "You're shy?" she asks. And I am in like Flynn. Another valuable lesson learned. Girls also like the shy, lost guy—a role I will play to much success when I eventually hit my twenties and actually start having sex with anyone who looks at me twice.

But at fifteen, I'm content to go by her house at 2:00 a.m., sneak her out her bedroom window, and find an unlocked parked car so we can steam up the windows with some harmless kissing and rubbing. I then walk three and a half miles back to my home at four in the morning, nursing the most staggeringly painful brace of aching balls in the history of teenage love, curl up with my guitar, and dream of glory. I'm sure I and my painful testicles have a doctor's visit in our future until a kid at school clues me in to "Mr. Blue Balls of the Unrequited Boner."

Still crazy in love with her three months later, I leave her—for the lame reason that I'm afraid she'll eventually leave *me*. I wonder where I got the idea that all my relationships *have* to end painfully? Couldn't be the incessant friggin' traveling since the day I was born, could it? Huh? D'ya think? With John and Tania both gone from my life (for now, anyway), there is only my fellow executioner Rob remaining, and in no time at all, even *he* takes a powder. Gone. Army brat too, y'know. And I'm basically left alone, save for a few not-so-close friends at school.

After the forced breakup of the late, great Icy Blues, I start looking for bands that might need a young, insecure guitarist. I find one in a bunch of older guys who call themselves Moppa Blues and focus on the more obscure songs of Little Walter, Lightnin' Hopkins, Muddy Waters, and other black American blues artists I've never heard of. I change my allegiance from pop to blues in a heartbeat and immerse myself in the Moppa Blues guys' formidable record collections.

By the age of sixteen, I'm running with a very different crowd. Although music has brought us together, we are a very disparate group. The singer, Snowy, is a twenty-three-year-old ex-convict who has a nasty growl of a voice. Dennis, the twenty-five-year-old bass player, seems eloquent and arty to me, and he's deep into the history of the music we are trying earnestly to reproduce with varying degrees of success. The drummer, Jim, is an old schoolmate of my brother's. The roadies and hangers-on are made up of fellow ex-cons the singer has met in prison. Needless to say, these are not people I would normally have hung with, and I'm in over my head. The fact is, I am fast becoming an insecure, self-conscious, teenaged mess.

I'm also doing really poorly at school. I no longer care about anything my sadistic teachers are trying to teach me. I have trouble retaining the information, and my grades slide from dreadful to abysmal. The social gauntlet of school has become so agonizing, and my insecurities are growing so fast, that I literally cannot force myself out the door each morning to attend Ashwood High, and I've pretty much given up trying. Our home receives regular calls from the principal, Mr. Potter, asking why "Richard" has been absent for the past few weeks.

Unrecognized for what it really is, my new lifelong companion—depression—starts to really dig his sharp and shiny hooks into me. Looking back, I think what gave birth to it was a unique and potent combination of being rootless for so long with no real place to hang my little peaked cap; having just lost my most important human connection, my best friend John, to the academic life of private school; hormonal teenage angst; and most definitely something already in my genetic coding. Also the damn dog thing. And girls. I have no name for what's happening, but I'm starting to feel not at all well in my own skin. My Darkness is glad to be home.

Most mornings my mother and I run the same drama starting at 7:00 a.m. She wakes me for school again, I tell her I'm not going again, she freaks out again, we yell and argue back and forth again. Eventually she has to leave for work, and I roll over and go back to sleep feeling bad about myself but relieved that I can stay safely at home for one more day. My dad, always the peacemaker, calls later in the morning to see how I'm doing. I start the day with a shower and a healthy (though still guilt-ridden) wank and pull out one of the horror novels I've stolen from the downtown bookstores I frequent. I read for a few hours, play guitar, and then read some more. My parents have correctly guessed that I am stealing all of these books. I have no spending money at all, yet I come home periodically from the city with fourteen new books under my arm. I think now, though, we're all pretty glad that I wasn't breaking into the neighbors' houses to steal their TV sets so I could hock them to support an amphetamine or coke habit.

This schedule leaves plenty of time in the afternoons to stare at my face in the bathroom mirror and begin the dark journey of really disliking what I'm seeing, which causes me, in my woeful state, to literally bang my head against the wall in frustration 'til it aches and throbs. I eventually find my way into my room. I take refuge in music—specifically writing songs, all of them some variation on the theme of "She doesn't want me," "Why doesn't she want me?" "What the hell's wrong with me anyway?" Playing my guitar and spending time with our dog Cleo are the only moments that bring any peace to my soul.

Meanwhile, all the other kids appear to be happily in the high school flow—going out to clubs at night, eating lunch with their circle of friends, dating, breaking up, and getting back together in the eternal ballet of adolescence—while I remain perpetually on the outside; ugly, distant, and untouchable. With John gone I have no close male friends and feel sure that none of the girls will ever give me a chance. I increasingly come to see myself as an outsider. I hate my large-pore-dotted red nose, the zits, the hairdo that has a mind of its own, my shamefully underdeveloped (for my age) sexual organs, and the acute discomfort I feel in my own body, which, much to my dismay, still has not a wisp of hair on it. I am overwhelmed with self-loathing. I know, absolutely, that deep down inside I am not enough. I will never be enough.

My mum finds some of the drawings I've been making of people being tortured and getting their heads chopped off like so many backyard chickens, complete with blood splattering the pages. She takes them to a psychiatrist one of her friends has recommended, to see what he thinks of her now quite depressed young son. He is sufficiently concerned to ask to see me in person. I visit him for a couple of sessions, then stop going. It seems pointless; our "therapy" is going nowhere. He keeps asking me to draw myself in relation to sex. (What sex? I haven't had any yet!) I figure he's just graduated from shrink school. It is pretty pedestrian stuff he's handing me, and even in my tormented state I know it.

In my economics, history, and math exams, I write long poems explaining why I'm unable to answer any of the questions. "Dear Mr. Emery, please do not despair because you see no answers written anywhere." Very shortly afterward, Mr. Potter again calls our house, this time to inform my parents that "Richard needn't come back to school next year, thank you very much." And this is a public school! Where they take *anyone*! Though I couldn't care less about school, I feel like I've failed to successfully navigate one of life's major milestones; my parents are devastated, wondering what will become of their black sheep of a son. Everyone else—neighbors, friends, parents of friends—is looking at me like I've just bitten the head off their pet parakeet and stuck it on the end of my dick.

A week or so after the headmaster's call, and on a particularly bleak afternoon—my mum has stormed out once again—I'm sitting on the floor in the hallway with a deck of playing cards in my hand. I flip them over one by one. Every time a red card (hearts or diamonds) comes up, I smash it into my ugly red nose in anger and frustration. When I'm done, my nose is bleeding profusely, my eyes are watering, and my head is throbbing. I literally feel I can no longer fight the crap that's going on inside me. It's as though the decision literally descends on me. My parents are both at work, my brother is away somewhere, and it's another bad day in which I have accomplished nothing and can only see more of the same ahead. I hit a wall. The Darkness finds his way in. And in a violent blossoming of my first brutal bout with depression, I run outside to our backyard shed, hate-filled, broken, and determined to finally do something to strike back at all that is hurting me. I cannot stand another minute of suffering and uncertainty; I just want the pain to end.

I am quite adept at making hangman's nooses by this time, due to my execution obsession, so I hastily fashion one out of rope, throw it over a ceiling beam and tie it off, stand on a small chair, slip the noose over my head, and kick the chair away without a moment's hesitation. The image of the pogoing kid comes to me in a sudden flash; it seems another lifetime ago. I hang suspended for fifteen or twenty seconds and am just sliding into unconsciousness when the knot tying the rope to the beam somehow unravels. I'm slammed hard to the concrete floor, rather the worse for wear. I lie there bruised, sore, and disoriented as a fiery red-purple rope burn blossoms across my throat. Eventually I get up, groggy, and return to the house, more stunned than anything else, but the anger and frustration have definitely taken a backseat for the moment.

My failed hanging attempt gives me a measure of relief. I have the strange sense that maybe I've been saved for something. I know how to tie knots; I am amazed, not to mention relieved, that I am still alive. I've felt different from others for years, but now I feel different in a new way: I have gone down into the abyss and survived. It's perfectly clear that school isn't going to work out for me. From this point on, music will become my salvation and save me from most serious, self-inflicted harm. I start resolutely directing myself toward music. I choose my path for the love of it, but I'm also driven by my feelings of inadequacy and doubt. I'm desperate to prove to myself (and all those girls at school I hunger after) that I can become much more than what I am now—the ugliest kid in the world.

CHAPTER FIVE

NOT YOUR REGULATION USO TOUR

VIETNAM

1968

I don't tell anyone about my near-miss in the shed. I hide the angry violet rope burn on my neck from my parents until it heals. (I'm sure they wonder about the dark woolen turtleneck their son is wearing when it's 150 degrees outside.) I'm still somewhat lost, and my misery is far from over, but I do see a window beginning to open in my life: music.

I start going to as many concerts as I can. The performers are all British. Among the first ones I see is, believe it or not, Dusty Springfield. A friend of the family who is in radio, takes my program to a party, and Dusty's is the first real autograph I ever get (not counting the soul-destroying Hayley Mills deception, of course). I see the Who one night and bump into a young, black-haired Pete Townshend the next morning while I'm making the rounds of Melbourne's few guitar stores. That's how small and interwoven the music scene in Australia was back then.

And as an impressionable sixteen-year-old, I'm not exactly hanging with the best crowd, still spending most of my time with the ex-convict and his friends in the Moppa Blues. I see John occasionally on weekends. His move to private school is obviously not helping his JD tendencies very much. The two of us steal an expensive guitar from a music store in town and sell it to a kid at John's new private school. With the money, we buy a car from a dealer who sells us a junker because he knows we're underage. I hop a curb and almost drive it into a neighbor's living room the first time I get behind the wheel. I almost kill us both the few times I drive it (my driving skills haven't improved much since then, either), and John parks the badly dinged-up vehicle on a side street near his house. Someone steals it from us two weeks later, and we can't report it to the cops because we aren't supposed to have it in the first place. Kind of like being a drug dealer when someone steals your stash.

Most nights, I sneak out of our house after everyone's asleep and meet up with my bandmates in Moppa Blues, now called Group X. They pick me up in their Holden FJ (*the* quintessential Aussie tough-guy car) on a street corner. We stay out all night, drinking and eating cheeseburgers from Greek hamburger joints (the only ones still open at this time of the morning) and occasionally holding up convenience stores. Incredibly, I remain blissfully unaware of this part of the routine for a while, until we pull up outside a liquor store late one night and all the other band members get out and tell me to stay in the idling car. The next thing I know, I hear a shot and a scream. They all tumble back into their seats, laughing hysterically and screaming "GO, GO, GO!!!!!" I find out that they've just robbed the store and as a parting gift, Snowy (the singer) has fired his starting pistol at the clerk to scare her. Thank God all the cops are sleeping back then, or my next move would've been to Juvie or worse.

The write-up in the paper about the robbery is my *first press!* I proudly keep the local newspaper article in my bedside drawer for months, along with a second one headlined THE THINGS SOME PEOPLE WILL DO. The story is about a car full of "hoodlums" (that would be us) who climb up a city streetlight on Christmas night, cut down a six-foot inflatable Santa that the city has erected with funds for underprivileged kids, stuff it into their car, and race away. The cops give chase. Fortunately, we get away. I am so desperate to "belong" that I'm willing to achieve it on any terms—even these larcenous ones. Sure, my band may be leading me toward a fairly lengthy prison term, but I get none of the head games I have to endure at school. It seems like a pretty fair trade-off to me. Being older "men," my bandmates don't have all the familiar hang-ups the kids at school do. I'm temporarily lifted out of my black moods. And they do turn me on to some amazing music.

But even I can see that this isn't the path to "girls, guitars, and glory." In fact, I'm beginning to think I may soon wind up sharing a cell with Snowy. I think he gets arrested again, because before I know it we have a new vocalist and the band name changes yet again, this time to the Daniel Jones Ensemble. We're now playing Hendrix and Cream songs and getting more regular and better gigs—with hotter girls in attendance. I'm actually playing a real Fender Strat, although it belongs to Danny, the new singer.

Praise Jesus, in the early hours of my seventeenth year, I finally get laid. The DJE is playing a beach gig over Christmas in the Aussie town of Mallacutta, and we're living on the beach in tents, as befits our low-rung status. Another Heather enters the frame. (What is it with the name Heather, Christmas, and my formative experiences with girls?) She sees us play at the local club, and that's all the foreplay we need. We have sex on the dark beach; I think it lasts all of three minutes. I remember thinking, "Wow, I'm no longer a virgin—but that wasn't as much fun as wanking." Though there *is* less guilt. Needless to say, my bandmates are merciless in the shit they give me onstage the next night. *Of course* I told them! That's the first thing you do as a young male!

Pete Watson is an Aussie rock star of the '60s. The first time I see him he's wearing a searingly hideous electric-blue suit, playing bass in a band named the Phantoms, and opening for the Beatles during their one and only Australian tour. By the time he next emerges, Pete's apparently learned quite a lot from his tour with the Fab Four. Having shed the aforementioned repellent electric-blue suit, he is now in a successful Melbourne band called MPD Ltd. which is enjoying a string of hit singles on the local charts. While I'm enduring the torment that is high school, MPD Ltd. decides to head for England and a shot at worldwide fame. Like so many bands before and after them—until the Bee Gees' big breakthrough—they come back home with their collective tails between their legs, telling everyone who'll listen how tough the English music scene is.

Pete is now playing regularly at dance halls and clubs around the country, headlining a popular show band called Pete Watson's Rockhouse. The "show band" is an Australian anomaly: a weird amalgamation of cabaret, rock and roll, and vaudeville. Pete has chosen '50's-style rock as his band's theme. Dressed in gaudy, matching '50s-style shirts (hang on, maybe Peter didn't learn that much after all), his Rockhouse covers Chuck Berry and Big Bopper songs with a mix of purposely goofy Elvis and Buddy Holly impersonations thrown in for good measure.

Pete has been a fixture in the Australian pop scene for a number of years by this point. So it comes as quite a shock one afternoon while I'm playing guitar in my bedroom at 13 Subiaco Court, Syndal, and my mum interrupts me long enough to say that Pete Watson is in our living room, waiting to see me.

"Really? *The* Pete Watson? Here?"

"Yes," she says, in answer to all three questions.

I have, at this point, to my great horror, been talked into repeating the eleventh grade that I so badly blew the year before, by my mum's pragmatic advice: "Richard, you need a trade behind you." She means I need to learn to be an electrician or pick up some vocation I can count on when the music thing blows up in my face. "You can't make a living playing the guitar, son," she adds, as so many worried mums have done before. School starts up again in a month, and I'm wavering. Suddenly here, in our suburban living room, fidgeting with his brand-new wedding ring, sits my salvation.

Pete says that he's seen me playing at a local bar and asks if I'd be interested in joining his band, which is working regularly and actually getting pretty good money. To their everlasting credit, when I ask my parents what they think I should do, both say, "What do *you* want to do?" It's an easy choice. Pete Watson has himself a new guitar player, and school, that giant monkey on my back, can kiss my hairless ball sack and take a permanent hike. The only downside is that when I tell the Daniel Jones Ensemble and their accompanying bunch of misfits of my impending departure, they threaten to break both my legs. And they really mean it.

After a tension-filled gig the next week with the DJE, I'm sitting in the band's van trying to figure out how I could play the guitar from a wheelchair when the van door is suddenly yanked open and in steps the toughest guy of them all, another ex-con/roadie named Hamish. He slams the door shut (but honestly, you have to do that or it won't close) and sits there wordlessly looking out into the darkness for a few minutes. "Shit, this is it," I think as I anxiously study his heavily pockmarked face and thick, calloused hands. Hamish takes a deep breath and, still looking out the window, says to me, "You go do what you need to do. I'll take care of these guys. Good luck, mate." I could kiss him. I don't, but I could. I thank him and have never forgotten him.

Once I'm completely free of school and making a little money doing what I love, the dark cloud vanishes from inside my head. All thoughts of bloody guillotine victims and teenage suicide dissipate—for the time being, anyway. Pete Watson's Rockhouse has a Canadian drummer named Joe whose accent sounds American to us, so we are supercool. Pete introduces me to his band as "Rick Springfield."

"It's not Spring*field*, it's Spring*thorpe*," I correct him.

"No one will ever understand 'Springthorpe,'" replies Pete rather callously. And he's actually quite right. All my life people have mistaken my brilliantly enunciated "Springthorpe" for "Springfield." Were they all trying to tell me something? So Pete isn't the first to call me "Springfield," but he is the first to make it official.

"From now on, you're Rick Springfield," says Pete. And I am. In true Australian fashion, they soon familiarize it to "Ricky," a name I still have to live with when I go home and visit the old crowd in Oz.

I share the innate neediness factor of all performers, and the public attention makes me feel good. I'm starting to get laid at a fairly prodigious rate. All this attention from girls in particular makes me feel even better about myself. It is a very "young" thing, this giddiness over the sudden availability of the opposite sex, but it's understandable considering how, up until this point, that very same "opposite sex" has avoided me the way a leper avoids arm wrestling. For now it's all heady and new.

The band plays mostly '50s rock and roll, and while I'm not thrilled when he does it, Pete sometimes dresses up to look like Elvis, the first bad Elvis impersonator I will ever see. The first recording I make is with this band. Unfortunately it is a fruity novelty song called "Itty-Bitty Hippopotamus." I start to get fed up with the campy side of Pete's band, and I think he sees the writing on the wall for the future of a '50s show band as well. He transforms us into a cabaret act, playing songs like "Please Release Me" and "It's Not Unusual" and books us into the Whiskey A Go Go. This is definitely not the hip teen jungle that the one in Los Angeles is. This Whiskey is a nightclub by the ocean in St. Kilda, a district of Melbourne, that serves as a pickup joint for hookers. It has a huge open dance floor to give brawling, drunken sailors room to swing a decent punch. Again, not your optimum gig. Plus Pete brings in his old bandmate Danny to play drums, so we lose the coolness factor of our (almost) American drummer.

At seventeen I'm still by far the youngest member in the band, and I get ruthless treatment from the rest of them, especially when they see me with a girl. They say the most embarrassing shit, and there are many times I want to crawl into a hole, but I learn a lot about being a young road dog from them. The first time one of the club's weekly visiting girl singers gives me a blow job, I fall in love. (Not again!) The whole band is only too happy to bust my balls by telling me she's given them all head as well and not to get too cocky (so to speak) about it. I am crushed. Again, the violins were playing, I had the ring picked out, I'd made a down payment on the cottage by the sea and was just about to mail out the invitations. Well, not quite, but I tell myself I have to stop falling for every girl who smiles at me.

I'm riding a Vespa motor scooter at this point and have already been in several wrecks, but I've managed to limp away from them all. Unlike the cars everyone else in the band is driving, my little Vespa doesn't have much of a backseat for mating purposes. But I do manage to use it as a sort of "duck blind" so I can have sex *behind* it with girls I meet at the club, hiding my naked butt discreetly from the busy street as it pumps up and down at two o'clock in the morning after a gig.

I'm just about ready to go find another, more rocking band when Pete walks in one night and says that we are dropping the cabaret thing. It's time to learn some Doors, Hendrix, Cream, and Dylan covers, because we've just been booked to play Vietnam. The year is 1968—not at all a good time to be traveling that far east. But traveling is now in my blood, and Pete says they will pay us really well. Plus, we will fly through Singapore, a very desirable destination for the young musician, inexpensive-hooker-wise. Regrettably, he doesn't mention the war, and I, being a very selective reader (I read books, not newspapers), don't think to ask. So in October of 1968, still seventeen years old, I cluelessly head off to join our U.S. allies at the front.

We land at the Saigon airport and step out into a bleak, sweltering, soot-soaked Vietnamese afternoon. It looks like a bloody John Wayne movie. I see soldiers with helmets, flak jackets, and M16s everywhere. Hueys, the main troop-carrying helicopter in Vietnam, pump thick, black, toxic exhaust into the sky. We are based out of desolate French villas (with a rat population that's bigger and smarter than the human one) in the two main cities of Saigon and Da Nang. Wait . . . I gave up the Whiskey a Go Go and humping in the sanctuary of my Vespa's shadow for *this?*

I truly think we all believed, based on films we'd seen of the Korean War, that this would all be a very safe, Bob-Hope-USO-fully-protected-

and-sanctioned-by-the-U-S-of-A-type tour. It most definitely is not. We've been hired, I find out much later, by a private American promoter who rounds up gullible bands like us from Australia, the closest Occidental country to Vietnam, and has them play for troops in the rougher, slightly more dangerous parts of the war zone, where the USO will not go. But I *am* playing music and I'm pretty happy about that!

It takes us three days in Saigon, a broken city full of Vespas (whoo-hoo!), bicycles, straw "coolie" hats, sandbagged entrances to half-burned-out villas, and really, really skinny cats, before we all get stoned on the local shit. It is my first time ever doing any type of drug, and the first joint offered me for a dollar, by an eight-year-old kid on the street, is an opium-soaked Thai stick. I smoke it. Apart from my three-day bout on the SS *Orsova* and my quick laps in the Black Lagoon of Belgium, this is the most I have ever barfed in my life. Then we discover the hookers. How else, in a war-torn country like this, can these sweet girls make money? I think. And so I make it my business to be sure they earn a good wage. Or, at least, any money that I have, which isn't much. The promise of big bucks has been vastly overstated by our fearless leader Pete and has evaporated into the exhaust-choked air like a chicken fart.

Paul, the band's bass player, is my main accomplice as we seek out whatever action there is to be had. Two weeks into our tour of duty, Paul and I haven't eaten in four days. We've spent all our money on weed and girls. So we actually stalk one of the skinny Saigon kitties with a half-formed plan of cooking the poor little fur-bag. I will never look down my nose again at airline crash victims who dine on their fellow travelers in order to survive. We (and the cat) are rescued by a Filipino band that happens to be staying at our villa. They take pity on us and put some cold leftover rice outside their door so Paul and I can eat and the cat can go on to have many, many, many more kittens in this Godforsaken hellhole.

Once my stomach is reasonably full, I turn my attention back to the beautiful local girls, many of whom are an exotic mix of Vietnamese and French. And then God stops smiling and ships us out.

I thought things were bad in Saigon, but once we start getting dropped off (by Huey helicopter) at firebases in the plains and jungles of South Vietnam, we have a new respect and a healthy yearning for the relative peace of the big city. The firebases generally resemble a really lethal camping ground: some central wooden structures surrounded by a grouping of army-green tents, surrounded by barbed-wire fences, surrounded by coils of razor wire, surrounded by rows of Claymore antipersonnel mines. Once again, not your optimum gig.

We sleep, unguarded most of the time, on narrow, inflexible army cots covered with the ever-present layer of red dust. The only thing worse than being awakened in the middle of the night by mortars and rockets lobbed over the fence by the Viet Cong hiding under cover of the thick tropical vegetation is having them land *around* us when we're playing a gig. We usually perform on the back of a flatbed truck, elevated and highly visible to any enemy snipers or attacking forces.

If the show is in one of the slapped-together wooden officers' clubs, our only warning of an attack is the sight of fifty guys diving under their tables for cover. We're then hustled out to a small sandbagged bunker to wait for the *thump-thump* of the explosions and the automatic gunfire to cease and hope there won't be any actual hand-to-hand combat that might involve, possibly, us.

We can never get clean. It is a constant battle with the wind, heat, dust, oily smoke, and grimy living quarters, so I stop bothering to shower . . . for about three weeks. I earn the name Pig Pen, and I deserve it.

Sometimes we play in the afternoons, outside, atop a quickly erected wooden stage or on the back of a truck for a group of GIs sitting around in the dirt, dressed for combat, carrying fully loaded M16s, grenades, and other ordnance. After the show, they head off into the surrounding fields or jungle to begin their daily patrols. We then load our amps and drums into the officers' quarters, which are sometimes blissfully air-conditioned, and do a set for the NCOs in the evening. We either sleep on chairs and couches in the officers' mess or go join the grunts in the filthy, roasting tents.

They're all good guys, the GIs, and they take us in and make us feel welcome. Every one of them has a great stereo system (courtesy of the PX, the army supply store) and copious amounts of grade A hash and weed. We all get stoned and listen to Hendrix. Eventually they pull out the photos of the girl back home, the car, and the family. Every one of them seems desperately lonely and eager for a connection to the outside world . . . and it appears we are that connection.

We get to know and like one group of navy guys (based near Marble Mountain, outside of the city of Da Nang) so well that we come back on a day off to do a free show for them. We agree to stay overnight and hang with them during whatever enemy action they might face. As soon as the sun dives for cover, my bandmates are positioned in foxholes, with an M16-armed guard, around the perimeter of the encampment. I choose the radio shack and the mortar site on top of the only small hill. Not outstanding decisions by any of us, certainly. Of course we are attacked that night. It starts at about 10:00 p.m. and it's like a laser-light show as we watch the fluorescent-green tracer bullets arcing out into the dark, ominous countryside. I watch as a Huey helicopter in the distance is brought down by enemy fire. It explodes in the trees and burns all night. It's so surreal that at any moment I expect to hear the director yell, "Cut! Print!"

Around midnight, movement is detected close to where I'm hyperventilating next to the radio operators. It is confirmed that there are no "friendlies" in the vicinity of the hillside, so they line up the mortar tube and I throw the mortars down the big-bore barrel. There's a loud *whump* as each mortar takes flight, then a shower of lethal red-hot sparks and blistering metal as it lands and erupts in the brush. A radio call comes in requesting a change of trajectory, so I drop more mortars down the tube and watch them detonate, alarmingly close to us. We stay up all night. How could we sleep?

The next morning we have breakfast with everyone whooping and hollering about the excitement of the previous night like it was some harmless football game where we kicked ass. One of the men we hung with the night before asks me if I want to scare the hell out of my fellow bandmates. After all the crap they've given me? Yes, I think so! He gives me what he calls a "dummy" hand grenade and says I can pull the pin and throw it at my friends. It won't explode but it will scare the crap out of them. Okay! So I have great fun all morning pulling the grenade's pin in front of an unsuspecting band member, dropping the grenade, and running. Whoever is on the receiving end of the joke laughs in relief and then pounds my arm into immobility with his fist. It's all fun and games until someone loses a testicle.

We climb into the back of the "deuce and a half" (the workhorse army truck that brings us and our gear through the jungle and along dirt roads to the bases when it isn't far enough to chopper us in) and head back to the main city of Da Nang, waving good-bye to the company. My bandmates are sitting around me while I reset the grenade's pin and pull it once again, as I have done ten times back at the camp. Instantly the top of the grenade becomes white-hot. I drop it onto the floor of the truck with a cry of pain. Pete, who has been watching me with growing anger and apprehension at my cavalier attitude toward a potential weapon of death, scoops up the grenade from the truck-bed floor and hurls it into the already life-threatening countryside.

There is a loud concussion. Sparks and smoke erupt from where the thing lands, and we all dive for cover as shrapnel whips overhead. We lie there, bouncing along the dirt road, in stunned silence. That is, until Pete lets loose with a string of profanities that, had they not been directed at me, would have impressed me immensely. I think "useless dick-fuck" was definitely in there. I say not a word in my own defense, because I realize how close I've just come to killing us all. I figure of my nine lives, I now have eight left—seven if you count my failed suicide attempt. And I learn another lesson: Have respect for things that can kill you.

The Filipino house manager, who helps us unload the amps from the truck when we get back to our villa in Da Nang, has already lost three fingers on his right hand and three from his left in a (gulp) grenade accident. I somehow manage to slam one of his digit-challenged hands in the truck loading-gate, and he ends up, eventually, losing two more fingers. I am shamed by my negligence and can only repeat "I'm sorry, I'm so sorry," over and over, as he wraps his bloody hand and takes himself off to the local doctor. I'm trying to process what just happened with the poor guy as well as the near-death experience in the truck when a bunch of the guys from Marble Mountain come running into our villa yelling, laughing, and screaming. They tell me that one of the mortars I'd fired the night before had found a target. It killed a Viet Cong soldier. Everyone is jumping around and slapping me on the back. I feel sick. Thinking of it now, I still do. All in all, not a real good day for anyone.

I am not fearless. In fact, I'm constantly thinking, "I could actually get myself killed over here." But even after the close call with the grenade, I take chances I shouldn't. My bandmates and I climb inside M48 Patton tanks as they fire their cannons at the horizon. I join the crew of a Cobra gunship on a mission and scream with adrenaline as they fire their Miniguns (100 rounds per second) and launch their rockets into the jungle below. I blast the bush with automatic weapons and grenade launchers every chance I get. Shoot 50-caliber machine guns that take my breath away and pummel my chest with shock wave after shock wave.

Every Vietnamese person we see on every street of every town is supposedly the VC, the enemy, once the sun goes down. Still, one night in some small town, I end up with a local girl from the local bar. We walk to her little room through the dark streets, something I know better than to do. After we have sex a couple of times (well, I *am* eighteen) she pulls out a basin of water and carefully washes my entire body. I feel almost holy. I tell her I really had fun, thanks a lot, and now I'd better find my way back to camp, the band is probably worried.

She switches personas in an instant and says to me ominously in broken English, "If you leave, I do number ten to you." In the pidgin dialect employed between the soldiers and the locals, "number one" means "the very best" and "number ten" means "the very worst." I have visions of her ripping an AK-47, the VC weapon of choice, out from under her bed and drilling my now-satiated testicles with hot lead. I accept her kind invitation to spend the night and curl up beside this crazy-ass woman in a strange bed in a strange town in a strange part of the world hundreds of miles from anywhere I know as home. I hightail it out of there the next morning as soon as the sun comes up.

The bigger army bases we sometimes stay at also give me my first taste of American-style food. Thanksgiving is a holiday we don't celebrate in Australia for obvious reasons (no Indians, no Pilgrims), so I've never seen a turkey before. Although only parts of the poor little guy are served up to me, he is impressive. I can't get over the monstrous size of the drumstick. It's like a chicken on steroids. I carry the Fred Flintstone–sized drumstick around to all the band members, and we're all laughing hysterically like so many rubes. And the refrigerated chocolate-milk machine that dispenses ice-cold beverages at the pull of a lever? My dad had told me stories of his platoon meeting up with the U.S. Army in New Guinea during the Second World War, and about how amazed he was that the Americans had managed to get steaks and whiskey and even ice cream sent out to them in the suffocating heat of those isolated islands above Australia.

We get shot at quite a bit, mostly by the enemy, but one night the driver of our truck, with us riding in the open back, drives through a checkpoint in Da Nang. He says later that he didn't see it; also that it was only an ARVN (South Vietnamese Army) checkpoint and didn't really count. Well, which was it? The ARVN guard who hails us to stop shouts once, and then we all watch as he aims his weapon at our retreating vehicle. We all dive to the floor in a pile and bang on the driver's back window as M16 bullets whiz over our heads and spark off the sides of the truck. Our parents might understand us taking a bullet from the enemy, but not from our own side, for Chrissakes!

We *do* get free dental work, though, so it isn't all bullets and bombs. The band is in an army field dentist's tent outside Phu Bai getting some fillings and extractions when we hear some muffled thumps and the dentist says, "That's incoming, gentlemen." Meaning, the base is being hit with VC mortars. We all bolt outside and into the closest sandbag bunker to wait out the attack. There are the usual explosions, screamed orders, and return fire from machine guns and tanks. After the all-clear siren sounds, we head back inside to resume our dental hygiene and find Paul, our bass player, high as a kite under sedation, still sitting in the dentist's chair, completely unaware that we'd abandoned him and left him a stoned sitting duck. We don't tell him when he wakes up, either. He'd only be upset.

The months, the towns, and the "tour" grind onward. Cam Ranh Bay to the south, coastal Nha Trang, once a beautiful vacation spot, Pleiku, Vung Tau, Dong Hoi. Stoned, bored, and scared shitless a lot of the time, Paul and I start writing very trippy songs, inspired, I'm sure, by the copious amounts of cheap pot we are smoking. To supplement our meager incomes, the two of us take to selling cigarettes on the black market. Then we even sell the clothes off our backs and gifts we'd been given by the GIs.

We find ourselves stationed in Quang Tri, two miles or so from the DMZ (demilitarized zone, the border between the warring factions of North and South Vietnam), during Tet, the Chinese New Year. The previous Tet had been the time of the big VC offensive in which the enemy had run en masse into every city and town in the south (even Saigon) and killed and died by the thousands. And we have the extraordinary luck of being two miles from North Vietnam for *this* Tet. I think we're in enough danger until we get the call saying that the army wants us to fly over the border to play for a platoon on patrol in *North* Vietnam. They tell us that they will have Hueys all ready and running to take us out of there if any shit hits the fan, which I imagine it most certainly will once we get the guitar amps and PA cranked up nice and loud.

Thank God we've all had enough adventure by this point, and Pete declines. As darkness falls and U.S. flares burst open in the Chinese New Year night sky, illuminating dangerous little figures trying to cross the no-man's-land between our encampment and their bush, with mortars going out and coming in and tracer bullets crisscrossing through the inky firmament, I truly wish I was safe at home in my bed with Cleo the family dog cuddled up at my side. I have had enough. I think to myself, "I'm going to close my eyes, tap my heels together three times, and whisper 'There's no place like home,' and when I open my eyes again, I WANT TO BE BACK IN KANSAS. Or anyplace but here." After almost six months, plus a Christmas and a New Year misspent in Vietnam, we finally arrive back in the good old United States of Oz.

Photos of me from that time show a thin, haunted-looking young man. On the ride home from the airport my mum tells me that I seem jittery. I can't imagine why—doesn't everyone duck for cover at loud traffic noises? I move back into my parents' house for a few months to recover. The drug thing is no big deal to kick, and I never think about trying to score any once I get back home. Or hookers, for that matter. I do continue to write songs and play guitar in my upstairs bedroom, but there's a curious and familiar darkness returning to settle over me.

Regrettably, I've left my only electric guitar in Vietnam with the lying son-of-a-bitch promoter, who has sworn on his life to send it to me in Oz the first chance he gets. Maybe he gets shot or drives over a mine or something, because it never shows. I loved that guitar, an Australian-built Maton, and I still feel melancholy when I see an old photo of myself playing it. Did it end up hanging in some Vietnamese pawnshop, or in the young hands of a future member of the People's Republic of China?

Adding insult to injury, we soon find out that Pete, our fearless leader, has contracted a fatal lung disease in Vietnam and has been given only a year to live. I run to the doctor, as we all do, and have a chest X-ray. It turns out that Pete is the only member of the band who has been stricken. I think about our days off, in the field, when we'd often split up to hang out with different groups of GIs we'd befriended, and I wonder where Pete went on those days off that the rest of us did not go. A year and six months later, the guy who delivered me from the horrors of a terminal scholastic career, saved me from a shrapnel-riddled death, named me "Rick Springfield," and introduced me to the musician's life, is dead at the age of twenty-six. No good deed goes unpunished.

CHAPTER SIX

BACK THROUGH THE LOOKING GLASS

LIVING IN OZ

1969

The Beatles' *White Album* (*The Beatles*) will always remind me of those few surrealistic months I spent at home after my Vietnam experience, decompressing and trying to process the previous year's chaotic events. Because the music I am drawn to is so healing, as I think it is for everyone, I play the new album nonstop. The Darkness has fully descended upon me again now that I am on my own and have time to think and reflect, but the music helps to keep a light shining through the gloom. "Dear Prudence" is a song I particularly love, and I teach myself the finger-picking guitar part note for note. Which is quite helpful when my old Vietnam bandmates, Paul (my cat-stalking accomplice) and Danny (our non-Canadian drummer) come calling, looking for a guitar player now that Pete is terminally ill and we are officially disbanded. They've hooked up with the biggest music promoter/band manager in Brisbane (that's in Queensland . . . it's up north of Sydney . . . never mind, it doesn't matter). His name is Ivan Damen, and he's looking for a hot new band.

Post-Vietnam, I've been trying to figure out what to do next. Paul and Danny say they already have a guitar player in mind, but if I can play "Dear Prudence," then I'm in and he's out. I am incensed that they are asking me to audition, but I'm also practical enough to know a potential good thing when I hear it. I whip out a version of "Dear Prudence" for the judgmental bastards and get the gig, and soon we're in a smoky, held-together-with-pieces-of-tape, crap heap of a station wagon that's stuffed to the ceiling with suitcases and guitars, headed toward Brisbane, almost a thousand miles away. I'm also headed toward my nineteenth birthday.

We arrive in Brisbane and find an apartment just north of Surfer's Paradise on one of the longest, most perfect beaches I've ever seen—and there are a lot of outstanding beaches in Australia. Surfer's Paradise looks like Miami now, with giant skyscrapers and casinos on the waterfront, but back then it's a sleepy little surf town of single-story shacks. We hire a keyboard player I'll call Jay. I'm never really sure of his actual surname, because we keep changing it later on, every time we do any interviews. Jay Daytime, Jay Fury, Jay Cheesecloth, Jay Farmer . . .

The "Farmer" name comes from the rather disturbing fact that Jay, who once worked on a sheep farm, confides to us that he's actually had sex with a sheep! He was forced to do it, he tells us, by the rough-and-tumble group of unhinged hired hands that usually make up the crew of a lonely sheep ranch out in the middle of nowhere, with no access to any female company and nothing else to do but drink liberal amounts of beer. Being Aussies, Paul, Danny, and I have all heard of this type of fairly deviant behavior before, but we've never actually met anyone who's done it, let alone freely admitted to it! My unasked question, of course, is, "I understand they *forced* you to do it, as an initiation into the group or whatever, but looking at the ugly ass end of a sheep, what possessed you to get sexually aroused enough that you could actually, well, consummate the act?" I later share an apartment with Jay, and I'm careful not to wear any of my woollier sweaters around him, just in case he gets ideas.

Four young, single musicians, living in one apartment on the beach, with time on their hands . . . and who should live upstairs but a young Scottish lass with a husband away at work in the field for months on end? I'm not exactly sure what "in the field" means, but the important thing to us is that he's not around. So the first night in our new bachelor pad, we invite her down to have dinner with us . . . okay, honestly, to make us dinner. It soon becomes painfully obvious that we *all* have designs on her. And she bravely receives the message. Tipsy from wine, she whispers to me in her husky native brogue, "I can't possibly take you all on tonight." But I have to hand it to her: she does. And does it well, with a passion and an appetite that keeps us all coming back for more through the next few weeks. I start to feel that it's more about the well-cooked free meals than the sex. What is it with young men, that they can't get the cooking thing together? Christ almighty, are we completely useless?

We drive into Brisbane to meet Ivan Damen, our new manager. He's an affable older guy who looks a little *mafioso* around the gills and who calls everyone "Father," although to him we're really "his boys"—and he vows to make us stars. We need a name for our new band, and some idiot suggests Wickedy Wak. "Yes!" we all shout in unison, and a band with that unlovely name is still going strong in the pubs and showrooms of Brisbane forty years later, although the membership has changed considerably. Ivan and the four of us have some pretty high hopes for our future even though we haven't played a single note together as a band at this point, but that's the magic of the '60s for you.

Speaking of the magic of the '60s: I don't mean to give the impression that it's all about sex, but at the age of nineteen, it *is* all about sex. I'm fortunate enough to be alive and sexually active during the only fifty-three years in modern human history when you couldn't die from fucking: between the discovery of penicillin and the onset of AIDS. In Vietnam we all managed to sidestep the "black clap" (which in itself was a miracle), an STD that was very prevalent and widely believed to be incurable. So I am completely bummed when I walk into a men's room in Brisbane one afternoon and start peeing razor blades. The pain sends me to my knees on the bathroom floor. Successfully navigating the sexual minefield that was Vietnam only to get "the clap" back home in Australia is like learning to skydive, then tripping over a rock on the way back to the car and breaking your fucking neck.

Despite my mum's threats of turning me over to the police at age five if she ever caught me humping my little pillow again, and the residual sexual hang-ups that this may have caused, she has raised a sexually accountable young man and a responsible lad. At the time I'm seeing a couple of girls, so I have to figure out which one has given it to me and who I've then passed it on to. The giver is obvious: the "party" girl I bang one night under the stairs of the apartment building, because I don't want the rest of the band to know I'm seeing her. She freely admits it, "Yeah, sure. I gave you the clap." The unfortunate receiver is a beautiful dark star named Barbara, a college girl and an absolute sweetheart. I feel like such a scumbucket when I tell her. She shrugs it off and gets her shot, and we continue to see each other now and then—when we're feeling the urge—for the six months that I live in Brisbane. But at that moment, while I'm trying to pass a very painful piss in a public bathroom, I'm cursing womenfolk in general.

The appallingly named Wickedy Wak eventually begins playing shows at Ivan's own dance hall, Cloudland, as well as assorted pubs around Brisbane. We are still just a cover band, playing everything from Tommy Roe to the Who to the latest Beatles single, but we also perform the occasional show-band number complete with our macho, sheep-serenading keyboard player dressed in drag and the rest of us in whatever silly outfits the song requires. We make sincere spectacles of ourselves singing old Ray Stevens numbers like "Ahab the Arab" and "Guitarzan." It seems that Pete Watson's show-band mentality is still alive and well in those of us who have gone on. Sadly, up to this point, the only people who regularly come to see us play are the few girls we're dating, plus the eager Scottish lass upstairs. I have more guitars stolen, too, so it's not only the Vietnamese who have designs on my beloved instruments.

Our "big break" arrives when we appear on a local live music TV show called *Club 7* where we dutifully get the girls screaming. The national music press starts to take a little notice. To be honest here: the "national music press" at this point consists of one music paper called

Go-Set, and it is to this "press" that I am referring. Australia is still, and will remain for many more years, a king-sized "small town." The whole Australian music industry could fit into a studio apartment in West Hollywood and still have enough room to swing a large-sized cat. Still, it is the first noncriminal press I've ever had, and my photo appearing in the magazine does not necessitate a trip to the local lockup in handcuffs. Things are indeed looking up.

The writer of our first "national" magazine piece is a woman who will become a crusader of sorts for me and is second only to Pete on the list of benevolent guides who help me find my way. Her name was (and still is) Michelle O'Driscoll. Michelle is a hip, cutting-edge freelance writer who, though only a few years my senior, has a tendency to mother me. Although she is obviously kind of giddy about and around me, I believe her to be of indeterminate sexual orientation, so the 600-pound gorilla in the room that is the question "Should we or shouldn't we have sex?" is, thankfully, not an issue and we can actually get some shit accomplished. (P.S.: I was wrong; she was straight.) She writes glowing articles about me, some of which actually get published—none of which are true—and she maneuvers behind the scenes to get me to the forefront of the band.

After she's been to a few of our shows, it is Michelle who first whispers the words in my ear, "You should go solo." Up to that point and for some years to come, I consider myself a member of a band, a guitar player, and maybe a songwriter. But it is Michelle who puts this "go it alone" worm in my ear, for better or for worse. She is my first experience of a "true believer." True believers will prove to be the grist in the mill that is my career and my life.

Of course, having *left* Melbourne to form the band in Brisbane, our big goal now is to go *back* to Melbourne, so we can "make it" nationally, Melbourne being the center, at the time, of all things Australian swinging and cool. Ivan books us a showcase at Bertie's, one of the hippest clubs on the Melbourne music scene, and we actually pull it off and impress people. So much so that the big local hit songwriter at the time, a guy named Johnny Young, gets us in a room afterward and plays us his newest creation, a ditty called "Billy's Bikey Boys." He says that he wants us to record it and that Molly Meldrum, another big name in the Australian music biz, will produce the record. Molly is a man but is openly gay, hence the "Molly" tag. He's still doing good things in the Aussie music world and is, even now, a good friend. But back then, a more outrageous queen you could not meet. Of course, he loves us—me, I think, in particular.

I will never be more excited about a recording session than I am for this very first one. Everything is happening so fast. John and Molly both want me to sing lead vocal on the song, and I'm euphoric. Paul, the bass player—and the other singer in Wickedy Wak—is not nearly as euphoric as I am about this decision. In fact, he's so pissed that he won't even play on the session, so we bring in a bass-playing ringer named Beeb Birtles. Beeb is in a popular teen band called Zoot, a poofy-looking bunch of pretty-boys who dress in pink and are adored by the girls. Beeb will later go on to become one of the founding members of Little River Band, so you should always be careful about which musician you call a pansy. I will be seeing Beeb again soon, although I don't know it at the time. The session is arranged and it all feels like magic.

We record the song, it sounds like a "hit," everyone loves it, the record company prints up some promotional copies, there is talk of a national tour, and the industry buzz is good. I am on cloud nine, ready for my first taste of fame, when Paul, the disgruntled bass player, pulls the plug and says he's quitting. The band breaks up and it all turns to shit. Luckily, I'm already home in Melbourne, and since I'm pretty much wearing all the clothes I own and I don't have any immediate prospects, I simply move back into my parents' house.

I learn another valuable lesson. It involves counting certain unborn poultry before they're fully incubated.

There are a lot of new Aussie teen bands springing up in the wake of the British Invasion of the '60s. One is the aforementioned, poofy-looking

Zoot, and another is the (not quite as poofy-looking) Valentines. Zoot dresses in pink and the Valentines dress in red. I think the idea is to make them appear as poofy rivals. Both the Valentines and Zoot are after yours truly as their new guitar player now that I am single again.

I met and liked the guys in Zoot when Beeb played on the not-long-for-this-world "Billy's Bikey Boys" single, and the Valentines have two really substantial singers. The second singer, the one who stands in the back pretty much all the time, clapping his hands and doing most of the background harmonies, is a young, skinny, friendly bloke named Bon Scott who will turn everyone's head ten years later as the lead screamer of one of our best exports, AC/DC. I finally settle on Zoot because they are only a three-piece with a singer, so I don't have to contend with another guitar player. A little conceited of me, but I'm beginning to feel my oats. Besides, my new guru Michelle thinks this is the better move.

I also buy myself my very first American guitar, a Gibson SG. I still have this guitar. It is a touchstone of sorts, and I use it in the studio to this day. (It's on this same guitar that I will, years later, pluck out the tentative opening lines of "Jessie's Girl" for the very first time.) Some old habits die hard, however, and the first thing I do is paint this beautiful instrument. I do not saw it in half, thankfully. But I cover the magnificent cherrywood finish with a couple of coats of very pink paint.

I thought the unattractively named Wickedy Wak had a pretty good handle on the girl market, but joining Zoot takes it to a whole new level. They are cute *and* famous . . . how can you beat that? Although my new band and I have a lot of common musical interests like the Who and Led Zeppelin, Zoot—already with a couple of bubblegum hits under their pink belts—seems locked into the teen thing.

We rehearse for a couple of minutes and then jump straight into the biggest national tour of Aussie artists Australia has ever seen. Called Operation Starlift, it features *all* of the top Aussie bands and singers (I told you the scene was small). I'm scrambling just to keep up, musically speaking. We fly, en masse, all over the country and bring our special brand of music and hedonism to the towns of Oz. Back then there is a general feeling among the public that a foreign band (American or British) is naturally better and more interesting than the homegrown variety. We get far less respect and, more important, far less money. Way less. As a band with two hit singles, Zoot is only making $80 for a half-hour set. That's not $80 each; it's $80 between the four of us. Five if you count the ever-present bloodsucking manager (sorry, Jeff). So there's a kind of "us-against-the-world" feeling among the musicians from Oz. And over the short course of this tour, a lot of us who aren't already friends become so. Especially while sharing drinks and girls, which is done most nights.

I've written some songs with the band in mind, and we start recording them for our one and only album. This marks the first time any song that I've written has actually been recorded. It encourages me to focus more on songwriting, and I think at this point my guitar playing takes a serious backseat. I don the pink outfit for a few weeks and then state the obvious: that we have to leave it behind. We'll never be taken seriously wearing pink. It is a pretty bold step for the new kid, but I'm used to being the new kid and have learned to cut to the chase.

The band, all talented players, agree, and I come up with the "brilliant" idea of having a photo taken of us all naked, with our twenty-year-old asses to the camera, looking over our shoulders as if to say, "kiss this." My original idea is to give the photo a heavily overexposed, hard-to-see-the-detail, burned quality, but the national magazine (the aforementioned influential *Go-Set*) prints it in full and living color. My old mum almost has a coronary when she sees it. "What on earth were you thinking, Richard?" She isn't completely against the nakedness per se, but she's always been of the opinion that you have to leave a little bit to the imagination. "A bit of lace is much more interesting than seeing the whole doohickey," she actually says.

"It's okay, Mum, it's one photo, in one printing of one music magazine. No one will ever see it again." Two weeks later we play at the most popular gay club in Sydney, and the whole backdrop for the stage is a gigantic blowup of the naked photo. Each of our butts is at least two feet across. And it is alarming to see them that big. This type of photo never,

ever disappears, and I have had to see and sign my bright idea many times over since that day. But I have no right to complain because—by popular demand—I included it in the photo insert of this book.

After the Sydney show, a young girl wearing an Asian-style dress comes up with a copy of the photo for me to autograph. I ask her name and in a deep, resonant voice, he says, "Roger." I'm a little thrown by this but not as much as I am soon after when the predator (meaning me) becomes the prey (me, again).

Zoot is taking whatever steady work we can get, and one of these not-so-stellar gigs is opening for the Beatles film *Magical Mystery Tour* as it winds its way through the theaters of the Australian countryside. The pay isn't great, and we sleep consecutive nights in (a) an old abandoned bank's basement vault (no lie); (b) a motel (all of us in one room) crawling with fleas and various other biting things (some of them probably life-threatening, considering this is Australia); (c) a fan's parents' house—one of us has to "give it up" to the fan for the privilege of a good night's sleep—and (d) our van on top of all the amplifiers. But we are playing music for the people, and that is all we want to do.

The guy who owns the rights to the *Magical Mystery Tour* film in Oz is a nice enough fellow and he loves us, so when the tour is over he invites me to his home to check out other Beatles stuff he owns. I am pretty naïve (still am), and when I arrive at his house one afternoon, he shoves a drink in my hand and takes me upstairs. "Cool," I say as we climb the stairs, "I can't wait to see what you've got."

What I think I'll be seeing and what he's intending to show me are two vastly different things. Up in his bedroom he pushes me into a corner and starts kissing me and unbuttoning my shirt. It is so totally unexpected that I don't know what to do and I freeze. I don't want to appear unhip or uptight (it is the '60s, after all), plus I *really* want to see the Beatles stuff. But after a couple of seconds, I get my head together, push him away, exit the bedroom, and catch the next bus back home. Yep, still no car—in fact, I haven't even bothered to learn to drive yet.

After that experience I begin to rethink my approach to girls/women.

This guy made me feel like—well, quite frankly, some sex object. Another possible lesson. By all means have sex, but don't be a Neanderthal about it. It doesn't slow me down, but I think I'm a little kinder to the next succubus I meet.

I sometimes have sex with several different girls in a night. At a party in a bedroom with one, then in the van outside with another, and again, a knee-trembler with a third by the back door of her parents' house as we drop her off for the night. Having as much sex as I am now, the STDs are coming faster and furiouser. I might as well walk into "The Clinic" backward, with my jeans lowered. The first time I get an antibiotic shot in my ass cheek for the clap, I pass out right there in the doctor's office. I wake up with my pants around my ankles and the nurse holding a long silver syringe, not really smiling but, well, yes, smiling. And we should have bought stock in the company that made A-200—the "crabs" cure of the day.

Although we (the band) are all screwing our brains out as often as any citizen of the Colonies, we still have to prove our masculinity to some of the male members of the audience, mainly because (a) the girls love us, (b) we are relatively famous, and (c) we used to wear pink and they can't get over it!! This last one is hard to argue against, honestly, and I often find myself siding with the guys who want to kick our asses. And kick them they try. We get so harassed and are goaded into so many fights after gigs that we begin to load the equipment into the van with microphone stands—a long, solid piece of metal can be a good deterrent—in our hands. And yes, even though we are a "name" band, we have to set up and break down our own gear. A bit of a buzz-kill when you're trying to be all starlike and special.

One night, a gang of these beer-swilling numb-nuts actually makes it into our dressing room (by virtue of the useless venue security) and start swinging. Girls are screaming, blood is flying, and I crack one of them in the head so hard with a bottle that I would have caused brain damage if he'd only had a brain to begin with. Beeb ends up in the local emergency room getting stitches in a gash over one eye, and the rest of us are treated for assorted bruises and cuts. I don't see any of the guys who launched the attack in there, so I assume we got the worst of it.

A lot of the time there's no security at all at the gigs we play, and fights break out in the crowd while we're performing. We can see the skirmish work its way through the audience until one of the rowdies gets knocked out or throws up. If it starts heading our way, we all move a little closer to our mic stands or unhook our guitars, which, when gripped by the end of the neck, turn into formidable defensive weapons. We wind up bashing a few drunken heads with our beloved guitars from time to time.

I am sick of the shit we're getting from the blues-rock crowd. We can play rings around most of the bands the in-crowd thinks are cool, so I look for a way to lift us up. The songs I've written thus far, the gigs we've played, and the press we've gotten haven't done that. So I work on a heavy, guitar-based interpretation of the Beatles' "Eleanor Rigby." It's a version I think Hendrix might play. I take it to the band, thinking they'll blow it off as too long and too weird, but they love it. At this point, records on the radio are all short and velvety-smooth with no rough edges. We go into the studio and cut the song "live" with my guitar feeding back and squealing and all kinds of noise, ambience, and uncontrolled junk on the track. It is actually, now that I to listen it, quite proto-punk.

Our friends, other artists, radio people, and even our bloodsucking manager (sorry again, Jeff) think the song is rubbish and suggest we go in and cut a gentler song about the "new generation" and how the times are a-changing. We like what we've done and ask for it to be released anyway. It goes to Number 1 and is the biggest hit we will ever have. I still get token residuals from the sale of that record. I learn another lesson: Don't listen to all the people who say they know the path you should be taking. They are most likely full of shit.

Then one morning while taking a shower and giving my hair its monthly wash (eeuuww!), I feel a lump on my skull. "Oh, God, no," I think. "Oh, God, yes," my fingertips say as they feel around the small nodule on the right side of my head. I am sure this is it. I've got brain cancer. It's over before it's even begun. I drag my sorry ass to the local doctor who looks at it and says things like "Hmmm" and "Well . . ." but not much else. "I think we better get this X-rayed," he concedes finally. Back in those days there is no such thing as immediate test results. For any type of analysis you have to bloody well wait 'til they are damn ready to give them to you. I leave the doctor's office absolutely certain I have only months to live. My old friend depression, my Darkness, comes winging his way back into my life in a heartbeat, like he's been sitting off to the side somewhere waiting for my eventual arrival back on earth. He says to me, "Looks like it could be cancer, Boyo."

Because of the complex nature of depression, it still manages to weave itself in and out of my existence. Sometimes the Darkness slips in at discernible moments—like this one, when I'm faced with my mortality and possibly my untimely demise. At other times my Darkness descends seemingly out of nowhere, without any real triggering event. No one really knows what to call my moods at this point. Even me. I think maybe it's just part of being an "arty" kid. Weren't all my favorite writers, artists, and musicians in the same leaky boat I now find myself in? Poe, Hemingway, van Gogh, Wilde, Beethoven . . . I get to write and play music, and the trade-off is that every now and then I feel the urge to off myself. Maybe it's a fair trade. I can accept that. It's give-and-take.

We're flying to Adelaide the next week to open for the '60s British band the Hollies, and the rest of the band is ecstatic. We've all loved them since we were little tykes. But people keep asking me what's wrong. I'm unusually quiet, and dark circles are starting to form under my eyes. I can't eat and what little meat I have on my bones is melting away fast. I'm not sleeping, either. We hear the Hollies being interviewed on the radio, and the DJ plays our version of "Eleanor Rigby" to see what they think. They hate it. "That's crap!" they say publicly and in unison. The guys in Zoot are crushed. I feel like it's just one more log on my funeral pyre and don't care either way.

About three hours before we're to go onstage and open for the bad-mouthing, judgmental fucking Hollies, my dear old mum calls from

Melbourne to tell me my test results from the X-rays have come in. "It is a bone tumor," she begins ominously—my heart sinks—"but it's nothing to worry about," she adds brightly. "The doctor says just to keep an eye on it and make sure it doesn't get any bigger." "Mum, couldn't you have said that last bit first?" I think but don't say. I'm all clear!! I am good. I literally fly onto the stage that night, where we proceed to play the worst show we've ever played. I break four out of the six strings on my guitar, trip ass-over-Scuttleboom during "Eleanor Rigby"—our big song—and have the best time of my life!

Not long after that I turn twenty-one during my tour of duty with Zoot, and what a birthday it is. In the middle of the night, on our way back from a gig, our van breaks down and we're trapped in the smelly thing, under the pouring rain, miles from anywhere, deep in the Australian bush. That's what I love about being in a band: we're all in it together, for better or for worse. Kind of like a really good, open marriage. We crack a warm beer and toast my twenty-one years on this earth, with nary a sign of a malignant brain tumor. It is not the worst place I could be at that point in my life. It's almost poignant, for crying out loud. And it is fucking awesome to be alive!

CHAPTER SEVEN

FAME AND FAMINE

IN HOSPITAL

1970–1972

When I turn twenty-one, my dad is fifty-one. Now, in retrospect, he seems like a youngster to me. For a while I've been vaguely aware that he spends some days at home, when he is "sick." I'm too busy with my life to really grasp what is happening. My mum takes care of it. I later find out that for fifteen years he's had a "bad stomach" and has been convinced that it's stomach cancer. But he would never go to a doctor to check it out, because he might find that he's correct. So he occasionally has miserable days when he can't even get out of bed.

I'm home alone with him on the morning when he collapses in the bathroom. I hear a thump and pry open the bathroom door to see him lying unconscious on the carpeted floor. My dad is a very masculine, virile, in-charge kind of guy, so seeing him fallen, naked and helpless like this scares me. I get him up and into his bed, then call the doctor and my mother. An ambulance arrives and takes him to hospital with my mum riding shotgun, and I wave from the front door thinking it will all be fine. He'll be home soon.

We all go in to see him that night and he's sitting up in the bed, smiling and looking quite dashing with his disheveled gray hair and hospital jammies. We are told it's just an ulcer and that if he'd only gone to see a doctor earlier it could have been taken care of a long time ago;

he wouldn't have had to suffer all those years of pain. There is some urgency to the situation now, because the ulcer has attached itself to the major artery of his stomach, but they're watching it, they say, and will get him into surgery as soon as a slot opens up on the schedule. I've never seen my dad in this type of debilitated condition before—he has an IV in his arm. Despite his ever-present humor, he seems fragile somehow—and it freaks me out a little. At his bedside that night, I feel woozy and pass out for the second time in my life. As the nurses are bringing me back around, I hear him joking.

"Must be all that hair on his head made him top-heavy." We laugh in relief, kiss him—my dad is never one to stop kissing his boys, no matter how old they are—and head home feeling relieved that he's in good hands. We're all sleeping soundly when the phone rings at 3 a.m. Mum picks up the receiver and a man's voice on the other end asks if he can speak to the eldest male in the family. We know something is very wrong.

"What? What is it? What's wrong?" my old mum pleads, but the disembodied voice on the other end of the line is an old-world Aussie male, doing things by the book, and he won't tell a mere woman anything. He needs to speak to a "man." If I knew who he was today I would rip his black heart out and feed it to him.

My brother Mike gets on the phone and we hear him say, "Yes . . . yes . . . all right. We'll be right there." By his stoic face we know things are not good. For my mum, the years peel away. Old memories rush, like bubbles from a drowning diver, to the surface. Time freezes, and in the background, our mum whimpers like a puppy—she is a fifteen-year-old girl hearing again the news that her parents are dead—and she is alone.

My brother hangs up the phone, turns, and delivers the news we already know. "Dad died," he manages. "They got his heart going again, but the doctor doesn't know if he'll survive."

Mike is told that the ulcer on Dad's artery had burst and blood had literally poured out of him, stopping his heart. A visiting doctor, who just happened to be in the ward at the time, saw all the blood and rushed to his bedside to give him CPR. Our man had been dead for fifteen minutes before they finally got his heart going again. They've taken him into surgery. They doubt that he'll survive, and if he does, he will most certainly have massive brain damage.

We all go into survival mode. Everything shuts down, save that which we need to do to get to hospital. I don't even remember the ride, in the dead of night, to be with him, our father. We sit huddled together in a small, dim waiting room for the news that will change our lives forever. Just the three of us. Like it has always been, in a new house or in a new land. It feels like he might just be away working, as usual. Hours pass.

Finally at daybreak a doctor comes out to tell us that they've managed to save our father's life, but we shouldn't get our hopes up, as the amount of brain damage is severe. The doctor seems a trifle inconvenienced. Is he upset that he couldn't have done more for our wretched little family or that he'd blown that putt on the ninth hole this morning? It's hard to tell. He certainly doesn't say much else to us. So we wait to see what is left of our good man.

We walk into the hospital ward. Dad is sitting up in bed in the hard morning light, a tracheotomy tube sticking through a hole in his throat. His face is slack, hair combed all wrong. His eyes are unfocused, like a baby's. No movement grabs his attention.

"Hi, Norm, it's us, love." My mum's voice catches in her throat. She is a strong woman but this is too much.

He doesn't respond in any way to our feeble attempts to bring him back. "You look good, Dad." "Are you hungry?" Even the nurses chime in. "He's quite the ladies' man with that silver hair of his." Nothing.

The word "vegetable" enters my head. I hate the sound of it, but it goes round and round like an echo, and the more I try to push it out, the louder it gets. Twelve hours ago he was joking with us about my fainting spell at the foot of his bed. Now, we don't know where he's gone, but he sure isn't here with us. We stay all day and there's no change. Does he even know he's alive anymore? At last, completely spent, we head home and pull sleeping bags into the living room. No one wants to sleep alone tonight. I wake up at 2 a.m. and hear my mum sobbing softly, helplessly. It's real. It's actually real.

What the hell do we do?

Dad stays in hospital for a couple of weeks until he's strong enough to come home. No improvement, though. We sit him in his chair in the living room. He looks like a big dad-mannequin. Where did Norman James Springthorpe go?

The first reaction we ever get from him is a few weeks later, after the new Zoot album is released. Mum shows it to him, and believe it or not, his eyes suddenly light up when he sees it. A bone-white, crooked, and shaky finger lifts slowly from his lap and points to my image on the front of the album jacket. We all yell and cheer like we've won the freaking lottery. He is in there still! We just have to help him find his way back out, through all the blown fuses and broken wiring.

And so we take turns sitting with him and helping him rediscover himself. He's like a little kid who knows he should be doing better and can't figure out why he's not. He begins to remember our names, but he doesn't know who anyone else in his world is. I sit with him in the afternoons out in the backyard, as he writes down the names of his best friend, the friend's wife, and their daughter, trying to figure out who is who in his splintered life. The words come out of his pen in a thin, trembling script, completely unlike his old handwriting. The conversation goes like this:

"George is my friend and he's married to Mich, and . . ." he says uncertainly, consulting his fluttering notes.

"No, Dad, George is married to Nan."

"Right, right. George is married to Mich . . ."

"No, no—Mich is their daughter. *Nan* is married to George."

"I'm . . . so . . . stupid," and he hits his sweet, scrambled head with both clenched fists. "What's . . . happened . . . to . . . me?" He knows that something has. We tell him his heart stopped for a short while and that his mind has gotten a little forgetful, but that we're with him and will help him through it. My mum is with him the day he remembers his own mother has died.

"My mum's dead?" he asks incredulously, and his voice is like that of a little boy. Fifteen years have passed since his mother's death, but he cries and cries, reliving it again, because, God knows, going through it all once wasn't enough!

I ask him, a long time later, if he recalls anything from the fifteen or so minutes during the time his heart had lain silent and unmoving in his breast. He says that he didn't know if it was a dream or not, but he remembers walking through a garden with beautiful flowers everywhere and people were smiling, working the earth. He asked them where he was and why they were smiling, but no one answered him. They just continued to smile, tending to their plants. Years later, my aunt Helen has a similar uncanny view of life on the other side. John, my father's older brother, died early, leaving his wife Helen alone. Twenty years later when it's her turn to go, she says suddenly, pointing to the foot of her bed, "Oh look. There's Johnny," and passes quietly into the next world.

Dad slowly comes back to the mental level of, roughly, a five-year-old. The thing he hates most is not being able to drive the car. One day, frustrated but determined, he climbs into the family auto when no one is looking and proceeds to drive the thing forward, through the back of the garage. He doesn't try it again. We hurt for him. My parents' old friends come to visit, and a lot of them can't handle seeing my dad the way he is now. Most never call again.

My mother still has to deal with the blatant and heavily fucked-up male chauvinism of the era, whenever assorted loonies call to do business. They want to speak to the "man of the house," and when she informs them that he has health issues and they should deal with her, they all give her so much high-handed, misogynistic crap that, again, if I had a gun . . .

But I do have a band, and it's to that band that I escape when things get too bleak at home. Zoot plays all summer along the beaches of Melbourne, around the same time the mighty Australian blue-ringed octopus is killing hundreds of happy, carefree beachgoers in the tidal pools of our dangerous continent, sometimes not fifty feet from our stage. But it's as if the band itself has collectively stepped on one of those charming but toxic little cephalopods, because Zoot is not much longer for this world.

The reason you've never heard of Zoot (well, most of you anyway) is because we break up just as we are about to make it in the big world, circa 1970. It's an idiosyncrasy I've experienced before (thank you, Wickedy Wak). EMI in America has heard our version of "Eleanor Rigby" and wants to sign us and bring us over to the States. We are beside ourselves with excitement and can't believe our good fortune.

America has always been *the* go-to country for worldwide fame, as far as I'm concerned. I've seen too many Aussie bands slinking back in defeat from the UK and so far, *no one* has tried the USA. I've *lived* in England, and I know that they're all just normal folks over there (with the possible exception of Hayley Mills)—but America! Well jeez, we're all pretty sure they're a different breed altogether, maybe not even *human*. I know what I'm talking about—trust me. Ever since I was a kid I've watched their movies and TV shows. Was John Wayne human? Clark Gable? Clint Eastwood? JFK? Annette Funicello, Elvis? The guys who landed on the moon, for Chrissakes? I don't think so. I've always felt that the *unknown* is more accessible to me than the *known*. And anyway, America is so big! I'm absolutely sure there's a parking space with my name on it somewhere in America. And we're going as a band, so I'll have friends with me.

Unfortunately, our parasitic Aussie record company, as you might imagine, refuses to release us to follow this dream. This is my first inkling that maybe the record business doesn't give a flying fuck whether I, personally, make it or not. Okay, we think, we'll break up, re-form under another name, and then head over to the States. So we do just that. We break up. And that's it. We never do re-form.

Beeb goes on to Little River Band, Darryl (the lead singer) pursues a TV career, and Rick (the drummer) joins another band and starts taking better-quality drugs. Michelle is pushing hard now for me to go for the solo thing, but I'm not sure what I should do. And then a chance knock at my front door one morning, when Mum has taken Dad for a drive and my brother is out, offers up a small gem.

At the door is a young insurance salesman who wants to sell *someone* some life insurance. He quickly realizes I'm not his mark, and after inviting himself in, proceeds to regale me with the philosophy revealed in a book he's just read: Napoleon (they still call people "Napoleon"?) Hill's *Think and Grow Rich*. Written during the Great Depression, it is the foundation of all those positive thinking books (*The Power of Positive Thinking, Psycho-Cybernetics, The Secret*, etc.) that will come after.

It is a revelation to me. You can actually move yourself forward in life by the power of belief and resolve? It's lost on me at this point that the very first book advocating this stuff was also a best seller . . . the Bible. But God and I aren't really on speaking terms at the moment after what he did to my dad.

I slowly back away from my father's rehab in order to pursue my own life and career. It is a decision that I now understand, but that doesn't lessen the pain I feel over what was still ahead for our little family. In his own quiet and damaged way, my dad becomes my rock and my champion through the long and sometimes empty years ahead.

But right now I'm devouring *Think and Grow Rich* like a hippie does pot brownies. I start making lists and slogans and daydreaming/visualizing what I want and where I want to be. What I want is, and has always been, to follow a musician's path. And where I want to be now, is—America! Ever since I stopped pretending I was English, I've had my eyes on the prize that is the States. I still think of England as the place I want to live, but I will find fame and fortune in America . . . I think. I have my own dream now, and Michelle has herself a solo *artiste*. It's 1971, and I am going to the U.S. of almighty A.

Robie Porter was a teen sensation in Australia for a short while in the early '60s, first as a musician playing rock-and-roll songs on an electric Hawaiian guitar (not an easy task), and then later as a singer. I'd bought his records as a kid and so I know who he is when he shows up at Zoot's final gig, approaches me, and offers to help me get a record deal in the United States. He says he's hooked up with Steve Binder in Los Angeles. Steve was the director of the T.A.M.I. (Teenage Awards Music International) show—a concert in Santa Monica, California, that featured the very nervous young Rolling Stones following one of their idols, James Brown—and the previously mentioned Elvis-comeback TV special. Robie is scouting for talent in Oz for the new production company that he and Steve now operate together. He wants to know if I have any songs. *If I have any songs?!* I send him a demo tape with more than fifty tunes. "Speak to the Sky" is the one he picks out as a hit single.

I still have the original lyrics I wrote to "Speak to the Sky." The song is inspired by the change in my family's lives after my father came back from hospital. It's a song of young, naïve hope and is written on the back of one of Dad's spidery scribbled notes as he was trying to find his way back home and figure out where his good mind went.

Speak to the sky whenever things go wrong,
And you'll know you're not talking to the air . . .

I write on one side of the thin sheet of paper.

Take a number from one to tend [sic] *number . . .*
If you have a number then double it from one to ten then take . . .

my dad has written on the other side. Both of us reaching out for help.

We record the song, and I'll be damned if Robie Porter isn't right. "Speak to the Sky" is my first solo hit. It becomes a Top 5 single on the Australian charts.

If I were to compare my success in Australia so far to an ice cream sundae, I would say I had achieved ice cream, bananas, and nuts; and now the success of "Speak to the Sky" in Australia has placed a big, fat cherry on top. Elton John presents me with an Australian Pop Poll Award for most popular guitar player—not *best*, mind you, most *popular*, dammit—of 1971. It is my first encounter with Elton.

Now I really want a shot at the bigger world. Australia remains a pretty small place, musically speaking: there's still just the one music magazine and the one music TV show to do now and then. Since every Australian musician is still going to England for a shot at the larger world stage, I have chosen America for mine. I mean, jeez, it's been a good steady climb this far without too much crap, so how hard could America *be*? I mean, *really*. C'mon.

Michelle feels vindicated by my solo hit, and although I'm feeling good about it, I'm also doing what I believe I should be doing: focusing on getting to the States. I am now (thanks to the chance meeting with the insurance guy) completely obsessed with getting to America. I know what I want. I write to the Canadian consulate after the U.S. consulate turns me down as a possible immigrant and future sizeable taxpayer (thanks for the vote of confidence, motherfuckers), and I am fully prepared to sneak across the border like the illegal alien I'll be if I can't do it on the up and up. I want it so bad I even see clouds in the sky shaped like the map of America.

It's a sign, a sign, I tell ya!

I don't bother forming a new band or touring with this newfound solo success, but I do start writing songs every chance I get. I also start to acquaint myself with the psyche of what appears to be one half of my new management team, the Porter of Binder/Porter. I sign a bunch of documents without even looking at them, one of which relates to the ownership of the publishing rights to all my songs. I ignorantly sign 100 percent of these over to Binder/Porter Management, thank you very much. Who the fuck needs 'em?

Robie and I start going through my vast catalogue of unrecorded songs. We're looking for ten good ones just in case a U.S. record deal materializes in the near future. I'm thinking, "Come on, they're signing everyone over there. What's one more friggin' little Aussie?"

But things are complicated. For one, I'm in love. Allison is the young wife of Zoot's record producer and she is a very successful singer herself, with a sweet country voice. She is also my first full-on relationship. That's a euphemism for hot-sex-and-love-and-wanting-to-spend-my-life-with-her-plus-meeting-her-mum. All while she's still married. But at twenty-one I'm pretty unaware of the extent of the carnage I'm creating and what I'm doing to the guy on the other side of it all, her husband Howard. In lieu of going on tour myself with my own hit song, I become her guitar player so I can tour with her instead. Michelle gives me a lot of "What the hell do you think you're doing?" but at that age a young man tends to think with his dick a lot more than with the other, larger, more reasonable brain.

Allison teaches me everything I want to know, including the fact that girls get off too. What? Girls enjoy fucking? That is *awesome*! She is an insatiable and loving tutor and I am her eager apprentice. Of *course* I fall in love with her. And of course, we're just thinking of breaking the news of our relationship to everyone when the call comes that Steve and Robie have landed me a record deal with Capitol Records in the States and I'm going to London to record an album of my songs that they plan to release worldwide. I'm supposed to leave for Los Angeles in a month. Of course.

Am I being tested? How much do I want it?

Well, I want it a lot. A real lot. Enough to leave my sick dad and the girl who is now the love of my life. The last two weeks before I head to the USA, I continue to ignore my own career and play guitar for Allison on her homecoming tour of New Zealand. We fuck our way through that place. Before the show, after the show, on the bus, in restaurants, everywhere and everyplace we can. I think we know that this is *it* for us. She drives me to the Auckland International Airport on the morning of our final day.

I board the giant white Pan Am 747 in Auckland on the last day I will ever see this young, passionate girl. I kiss her good-bye and although we write to each other for a while of undying love, the letters eventually slow and then stop. She goes to prison many years later after a drug bust. I write a song for her ("Allyson") on my third album, *Living in Oz*, but the song is more about the guilt I feel over our illicit affair than about what an amazing and awakening relationship it was for me.

The 747 is aimed straight at Los Angeles. I have waited for this moment for so long and have seen it so many times in my head that I feel prepped. I appear quite calm as I board the huge plane. There's no turning back. I'm both elated and terrified. And who is this in the seat next to me? It's my old friend the Darkness. He's coming along, too. Oh, *goody*. Well, I'm too damn jacked up to be worried about his presence right now. But he does direct my gaze out the window to the slight figure with long auburn hair blowing in the ever-present New Zealand breeze, waving good-bye from the gate . . . Allison. He also reminds me that my dad is missing me, too. And points out that our dog Cleo isn't getting any younger and might not be around much longer, as well as the distinct possibility that I could fall flat on my face in the U.S. and have to crawl back home in the not-too-distant future. I turn to him and tell him to go take a flying fuck. Now is not the time.

We are launched into the sky. That night, in a strange hotel in Hawaii, alone and missing absolutely everyone, I write tearful letters and wonder if I've just made the worst mistake of my life.

CHAPTER EIGHT

ILLEGAL (HOLLYWOOD SEX-RAT) ALIEN

LONDON/NEW YORK/HOLLYWOOD

1972–1975

Rising early—tired, jet-lagged, and full of misgivings—I walk out into the bright Hawaiian morning sun. I am instantly transformed. It all looks bigger than life. Like an Elvis movie in Cinerama and Technicolor. Rich, secure, and at the center of the world. Ahead of me is a sign that says PEARL HARBOR. And that would be *the* Pearl Harbor. Not some phrase in a book or a line from a John Wayne film, but *the* fucking Pearl Harbor. Honestly, no one born in the U.S. can ever truly understand the impact of the greatest PR machine on the face of the planet—the American Movie—and the effect it has had on us foreign kids raised on them. I stand there staring, feeling disoriented and slightly surreal. It's all so familiar, but now it's in 3-D—a living, breathing kaleidoscope of smells, noises, and energy.

Hey, I don't feel so bad. I board the plane (it looks like the same Pan Am jet I took from New Zealand) and snap photos like a rube tourist as it taxis and takes off, butterflies in the pit of my stomach. I look to my right. There is no sign of Mr. Darkness, and I feel on the brink of something new and incredible. The in-flight movie comes on right away (wow, these Yanks have everything) and we are asked to close the shades on our windows. Twenty minutes into the flight, the film switches off and an ominous voice says, "Please keep your seat belts fastened, we are returning to Honolulu." We make a low pass once over the airfield and I see a red-and-white cluster of fire engines and ambulances lining both sides of one of the runways. Apparently we've just been circling the airport for the last twenty minutes. People are starting to panic.

The same disembodied intercom voice speaks again. "We are experiencing a problem with landing gear deployment and are making an emergency landing. Please remain seated." WTF? "Has this all been for nothing?" I think to myself. I look over and suddenly the Darkness is there and he seems to agree with me that, yes, quite possibly it has, and we are all about to be incinerated beyond recognition in a wave of boiling jet fuel. But we land safely and there are no charred bodies on the six o'clock news and my dream can go on. I do like Hawaii and decide right then and there that I will live here someday, but I'm anxious to see the mainland, and eventually I arrive in Los Angeles on a thick, warm, smoggy late afternoon.

Robie Porter has lived in LA for several years now. He picks me up at Los Angeles International (Oh my God) Airport in his giant Cadillac Coupe de Ville. I am duly impressed. He steers with one finger as we drive down Hollywood Boulevard. I don't know about power steering yet, and I think to myself "Wow, does America make everybody so strong that you can drive with *one finger*?!" I've never seen power windows before, either, and I play with the one on the passenger side, up and down, up and down, up and down, 'til Robie finally yells at me to knock it off.

We arrive at Steve Binder's house and, man, it's in *Beverly Hills*! Could this day get any better? Steve is a warm, affable guy, full of confidence and funny stories (all about very famous people, of course—Sammy Davis, Jr., some bigwig record executives I've never heard of, and of course, Elvis), and I feel like this is my entrée into the big leagues.

Steve tells me that he's heard my demos and really likes them and my voice. He says he saw a photo of me and thought, "Wow, and he looks like *this*?" I'm unsure of what he's getting at. Is that a good or a bad thing? By the way he's carrying on, he leads me to believe that it's a positive. I'm beginning to get a glimpse of the value put on appearance here in America. By now I have some quiet confidence that I am indeed not the ugliest kid in the world, by way of certain female attention and words whispered during sweaty, heated moments, and although I have had my own depression-related issues with feeling ugly and undesirable, how you look isn't that big of a deal where I come from. In Oz at this time there is no great premium placed on a guy being handsome. In fact, you're likely to get the shit kicked out of you if you're good-looking. The way Steve is talking, being attractive appears to be a crucial prerequisite in the U.S. for everything from superstardom to soap carving.

I like Steve. He has had his own successes in the TV-directing world, and I feel that perhaps I'm in good hands. I am fairly naïve about how things work in America and assume these guys are smart enough to steer my career in the right direction. Although I don't understand it at the time, *their* idea of "the right direction" and *my* idea of "the right direction" are 180 degrees in opposition to each other. Welcome to the world of divergent interests, Rickyboy. And in 1972, despite the record companies' money, success, excess, great game plans of action, and brilliant if heavily stoned minds, the success of any given act is still pretty much a giant crapshoot.

I'm told that Binder/Porter have lined up a photo session with *16 Magazine*, the biggest weekly in the country. I've never heard of it, but figure it must be some trendy U.S. music magazine. I'm to take the red-eye to New York (New York? Jesus wow) and meet Gloria Stavers, the head honcho herself at the *16 Magazine* offices. Unbeknownst to me, Gloria has had great results sexualizing Jim Morrison of the Doors for the young girl readers of *16*, and has also gotten into fights with Donny Osmond's mother for trying to do the same thing with little Donny.

I get on that plane to New York and I do not sleep a wink.

When I land early in the morning, a limousine is waiting to take me into the city. Never having ridden in a limo before, I jump in the front passenger seat next to the driver, leaving the vast expanse of seating area in the back vacant. It's cramped up front and not really what I expected from the stories I'd heard about limos. The driver gives me an odd sidelong look, shakes his head, and proceeds to take me into New York City. The place is gigantic, sits right on the edge of the water, and looks like the biggest and most realistic movie backdrop I have ever seen. Golly gee whiz!

I check into the Warwick Hotel and walk myself to the *16* offices. It's now about twenty-four hours since I've slept, and I'm running on pure adrenaline. I'm also convinced—based on the stories I've heard of how violent the city is—that I will be mugged at some point before I reach my destination. I must look like an idiot walking down a major New York thoroughfare glancing timidly and furtively over one shoulder, then the other, giving side streets a wide berth, and generally acting like a fruitcake. Or maybe people just think I'm a junkie. Probably. To my shock and gratitude I arrive unscathed at the *16 Magazine* offices and meet everyone there, including Gloria, who, I later understand, takes an instant "liking" to me. Some quick photos are taken, they conduct a rather in-depth interview about my musical beginnings in Australia, and I'm herded back to the hotel, then to the airport, and onto another plane, this time pointed for London, England. I'm going home!

I'm somewhat nonplussed when the *16 Magazine* article is sent to me in England a few weeks later and the photos show a rather tired-looking me along with an article entitled "Rick Springfield: Is He Too Tall to Love?" Huh? It details what my favorite color is (blue), where I like to go on a first date (bowling . . . *bowling*?), and what kind of girl I like. ("Sporty"?) I don't remember answering any of the questions in the article, and I wonder where the in-depth stuff about my music went. Only much later will I grasp the full ramifications of this teen-press path I have been set on.

I don't sleep on the plane to London, either. It seems to me a bit obscene to kip out in public, and anyway, I'm pumped up from everything that's happened. My life is moving so fast, I don't want to miss a second of it. We land and the only two things I remember feeling as I step through the open door of the airplane into a brisk, misty English morning are (a) I am HOME, and (b) What's for breakfast? (Bangers and mash, I hope.)

But there's something different about London that I can't quite put my finger on. I get the feeling much later that is has to do with the mass influx of immigrants and the beginning of the melting pot most Western countries will experience. It's a natural progression, for any country in the free world worth living in, that travelers from across the seas bring with them their own magic but slowly erase some of the original identity of the new land they are now part of. I see it in Australia these days, too. It's not a bad thing; it's just change. Inexorable change. Maybe it will help prevent wars over the color of a flag, but I doubt it. And nothing will ever stop us all fighting over the true name of God.

Where was I? Oh yes, home.

I am beyond peeing myself with excitement to be back in England. I end up at the Earls Court flat of Michelle O'Driscoll, God bless her (though at this point I'm still not sure which side she bats for). Michelle has moved to London sometime before me and says I can stay with her and another Aussie girl who is her flatmate while I'm recording my first solo album. And that's why I'm here. To record, in England, my first long-playing record.

I haven't slept since the flight from New Zealand to Los Angeles and have now been awake for forty-eight hours straight. I drop my bags in the bedroom I'll be sharing with Michelle's cute friend and flop down on her couch while she starts telling me all the things I should be doing now that I'm in the big leagues. I stare, exhausted, at the carpet with my face in my hands and suddenly the carpet turns into a fully functioning, clear-as-crystal, three-dimensional street scene. I marvel at the guy riding the bike straight toward me and am about to tell Michelle to come and have a look when I realize I'm hallucinating. I drag myself off to bed and sleep for fourteen hours straight.

The next afternoon I go knocking on the door of Del Newman, the arranger who will be doing the strings for the album. I've talked to him on the phone and he has a rich, deep, Very British voice that makes him sound a bit like a stuffy English bank manager. I'm a little concerned. But when he opens the front door of his flat, I see a thin, 6'4" black guy with a wry smile on his lips. He's seen the look I now have on my own face before. Del is of African descent (born in London), with a lean face and long rangy body that looks like it would be at home on the African savannah. He's wearing jeans, slippers, and a big woolen sweater with elbow pads, and is smoking a pipe. Clouds of sweet tobacco smoke drift through the cozy, firelit living room. He is charming and easy to like. Del is currently writing all the orchestral arrangements on the Cat Stevens records that are bouncing up and down the charts. He is a real gentleman and offers me tea.

Del's favorite line is, "I think a nice deep brown sound would be good here, yes?" He means the deeper part of the orchestra—double basses, cellos, and the low end of the violas. He is a trip and also an excellent arranger. He plays me a half-finished demo he's just received: Simon and Garfunkel's "America," which he's also arranging. Again, I am duly impressed. Even more so than I was riding in Robie Porter's Cadillac.

We are to begin recording at Trident Studios right away. Is this really happening? Yes, sir, little Ricky. And you better watch out.

Michelle writes me a poem that I still have with me forty years later. It refers to, basically, taking the high road in my pursuit of success; something I come to find is not always an easy choice. Its opening lines are:

Now begins your race with the devil
Do you understand the demon of evil?
I'm not referring to any mortal man
This demon being is greater than . . .

These simple words have become more and more poignant as I've followed my path. But at the moment she gives me the poem, I think she means "don't get a big head." She doesn't, and she is much wiser than I, at that time, give her credit for.

Robie joins me in London and the battle and the sessions begin. He isn't a great producer, per se, but he does have an ear for a good tune. And no, I don't get to score with Michelle's cute friend, even though we share a bedroom.

We walk into Trident Studios for our first day of recording and in the control room sits a thin young man with an angry red scar running through his left eye and down the side of his face. Robin Geoffrey Cable has just gone through the extremely disconcerting experience of waking up in a hospital bed in London one morning, unable to remember anything about himself, his life, or how he got there. The hospital staff gently informed him that he was in a near-fatal car accident and has some residual brain damage. He has to be told that he's a recording engineer and has the Number 1 album on the charts right now, Elton John's *Madman Across the Water.* "Who's Elton John?" he asked.

In another of many path-crossings with Elton and his circle, my album is the first one Geoffrey engineers after his recovery. He is brilliant. He is also deeply depressed and troubled about the loss of his memories. We become friends, and I think we see in each other a very similar darkness, though from different circumstances. A brother from another mother . . . but with the same father.

We record the ten songs I have written—mostly ballads—with the great English session musicians and singers and even the London freaking Symphony Orchestra, then we pack up and get ready to head back to the U.S. to do my lead vocals now that the expensive part of the recording is finished. I see myself as a ballad writer at this point and figure that any success I have will most likely come from one of the ballads that seem so easy for me to write. Wrong again.

Michelle is heavily into the English music scene of 1972 with skinny little English blokes like the guys in Roxy Music and even skinnier and smaller ones like David Bowie and even skinnier and smaller still, like Marc Bolan of T. Rex. I get up one morning and stretch my 6'2" self and Michelle tells me I have a big ass and I need to be much "smaller." So I begin buying way-too-small shirts and pants for myself that I squeeze into in order to look the part of the waiflike English rock star. Photos from that era show a very skinny me trying to appear even skinnier, especially in the ass area.

I've also taken to wearing makeup, as is the fashion of the day. I say "makeup," but what I really mean is Magic Marker. I'm too embarrassed to go to a cosmetics counter and ask for actual women's eyeliner, so this is my compromise: a big black felt-pen mark along both lower eyelids. I get a lot of looks at the LA airport when we arrive back, not all of them good.

I move into a ground-floor apartment in the same building as Robie's on Poinsettia Avenue in Hollywood. The building has *colored* lights out front that illuminate the palm trees (wowee, Sport!), and I proudly write to my friends back in Oz just so I can list my return address as: Hollywood, California, USA!!!! That alone makes the whole trip worth it.

In what will be typical of my few years with Binder/Porter, I have seen no money from advances or whatever, but my rent is paid. I still have to buy my own food, and I make regular trips to the Ralph's supermarket on the corner that's *open 24 hours* and buy the first of my many TV dinners. I write an enthusiastic letter home: "Mum and Dad, it's amazing. They have whole dinners you just take out of the freezer and stick in an oven, and in thirty minutes, you have a meal PLUS dessert!" I can't anticipate it, but I'm about to make myself very, very unwell on a steady diet of these "miracle" TV dinners. Kind of like existing on regular servings of Australia's barren topsoil.

We finish the vocals and some guitar solos in a local LA studio and the record is done. Unfortunately, the recording tape's journey from London to LA has produced thousands of unwanted pops and noises, so a new guy is brought in to laboriously edit the million and one clicks out of the finished mixes. He's a young guy named Keith Olsen. I think chopping out the unwanted blips and bleeps from my first album was his first real gig at a big studio.

We take photos for the front cover and they shoot me through not one but *two* windows of the photographer's house, probably to make me look younger and prettier than I am. We call the album *Beginnings*. To my horror, they also remove the hair on my arms in the big gatefold center photo, because they think my hairy ape-man arms will scare the little girls.

The teen press machine revs up, the single "Speak to the Sky" is released on Capitol Records, I take to the road and go on an endless parade of meetings and dinners with all the rack jobbers (people who stock the records in the stores), the promotion guys (people who try to get the record played on the radio), the radio program directors (people who choose whether or not to play the record), and of course the DJs (who actually play the damn thing) and tell them all how freakin' awesome they are and what a fan-fucking-tastic job they're doing for my humble little single, "Speak to the Sky." I end up kissing ass beyond my wildest expectations. If I wasn't so young and eager, I'd be totally embarrassed for myself.

"Speak to the Sky," a nice pop tune with a bit of a message, sails into the *Billboard* Top 10. But my *album*, with songs about a guy committing suicide ("The Unhappy Ending"), a wife who keeps her failed marriage together for her kids' sake ("What Would the Children Think?"), and a homosexual wanting to come out of the closet—no, not me—called "Why?" is hardly young teen fare and lands with a soft thud in the lower 30s of the Top 100 chart.

Gloria Stavers starts calling Steve Binder and Robie Porter to scream at them. "We're giving Springfield all this fucking publicity in our teen magazines, so where's his 'Doesn't Somebody Want to Be Wanted'? Where's his 'I Think I Love You,' dammit!" (These are hit songs by major teen heartthrob David Cassidy. Not the last time someone will compare me to this guy.)

Capitol smells that it's on the verge of young teen blood and kicks things up a notch with radio contests, "Meet Rick" opportunities, and more dragging my apparently teen ass all over America on radio promotional tours. Since I'm illegally working in the U.S. on a visitor's visa, it is advised that I not put a band together to go out and actually play real music, as it could bring unwanted attention to my illegal status, or so the lawyers say. Meanwhile I am making trips to the American embassy with scrapbooks full of clippings about how fabulous I am—but not so fabulous that I'd put an American out of work—so I can get the highly valued "green card" that will allow me to stay and work here as an alien resident. Or I could do it the easy way and marry an American girl. But I am terminally single at this point.

In fact, the only fun for me on these lame radio and promotion tours is the sex I am having with young, pretty, and very American girls. The '70s are the *real* "summer of love" when everybody is doing everyone. The '60s were just the warm-up act before experience, better drugs, and what appear to be no real consequences to the lifestyle emerge. The '80s would be the consequences, but here in the early '70s it's all fun and games ('til someone gets the clap).

In St. Louis I have sex in my photographer's hotel room with one girl, then move into the living room of my suite and bang the little schoolteacher who just can't get enough, then continue on to my bedroom where a girl has wandered in (yes, all doors are open) looking for the photographer (who I say has gone to bed), so I fuck her, too. Being young has its downside but also its upside (as it were). I crash and get up at 8 a.m. to catch a plane to Dallas and begin it all again.

Honestly, I have no idea what bearing any of this has on my record's success, but the powers that be seem to think this is working (the promotion and meetings, not the fucking). I take a young and beautiful Susan Dey out one night on a date; Marie Osmond and I stare at each other across a restaurant dining room table; a very young Valerie Bertinelli and I roll around on someone's apartment living room floor while her TV sister, Mackenzie Phillips, watches; but the real sex is left in the hands of the unsung heroines at parties and record and radio events. I am getting distracted by it.

A second single, "What Would the Children Think?" is released, and I'm booked on *The Sonny and Cher Comedy Hour* to perform the song and also to be involved in some comedy skits. They don't even ask if I can act . . . or maybe they've read some excellent reviews of my star turn in *Captain Scuttleboom's Treasure* that perhaps I missed. I handle myself okay on the show, I guess, but I'm starting to get serious self-doubts about all this attention paid to the way I look. Guess who steps up and into the vacuum . . . my Darkness. He whispers to me late at night from my apartment bathroom mirror—always the darkest mirror in my house—"Is that a zit on your face? Why, yes, I believe it is. And it's big! You remember that radio guy last week who said you weren't as good-looking as your album cover? Do you think he's right?" He continues in a siren's voice that drags me down. "Those circles under your eyes make you look so much older, too. And I know you've always thought you had a big . . . ugly . . . nose."

I start getting more zits, and I'm seeing them show up more and more in photos. I'm feeling the pressure of trying to be something I know very well I'm not. I do more teen press, and it starts to dawn on me what direction my career is taking. And then . . .

ABC television takes a poll of all the teen magazines and asks them who they think is going to be the next David Cassidy. Oh no . . . they think it's *me*! At this point it seems like lunacy to throw away the tons of free press I've had in *Tiger Beat* and *16 Magazine* and countless other teen fanzines, so I bite. "What'cha got, ABC?"

What they have is a brilliant and novel idea for a Saturday morning TV cartoon. It will be part *Yellow Submarine*, part *The Hobbit/Lord of the Rings*, and I will write a song per episode and play myself in this remarkable, groundbreaking show. I meet with some of the artists who worked on *Fantasia* for Disney and we talk about Tolkien and the Beatles at their psychedelic best. Scripts are written, artwork is done, and then the network gets a hold of it. And what comes out of their boardroom after all this cutting-edge, imaginative homework is another Xeroxed piece of absolutely run-of-the-mill shit called *Mission: Magic*. (Quentin Tarantino did tell me he used to watch it as a kid and loved it. Oops, sorry, dropped that one without a warning—my bad.)

It has a place in kitschdom today, certainly, but truly, what were I and my management thinking? That this was a good career move and a way to some real music street cred? Hahahahahahahahahahahahaha-hahahaha. It ran for two seasons, I wrote some cute pop songs, and you can now get it on DVD. Nothing in the digital world is ever forgotten or forgiven.

After almost eleven months in the U.S., I have to go back to Australia. My tourist visa is up and I can't risk pissing off those who will one day deign to let me stay in this land. I must go out of the country for a few weeks while a temporary work visa is issued (still no frigging green card). So I board a jet, this time pointed the wrong way . . . back to Australia. But inside, I realize that I need a breather and am looking forward to going home. I miss my family and Cleo and would like to taste some good old Aussie meat pies once again.

All the press has had some effect at home, too, and I am besieged with requests for interviews to brag about how well I've done in the U.S. Of course I say everything is going splendidly and, yes, I am going back soon . . . to my apartment . . . in Hollywood. Cleo is gray and runs up to me like I just came home from a weekend away. Dad is looking a little more chipper and is clearly happy to have his younger son home. I hug him and he feels a lot bonier than I remember, but Mum says he eats like a horse and has been able to take himself, by train, a few stops down the line, to the institute for the blind, so he can read to some of the permanent residents and also sing to the old ladies, who love him, of course. He is a good man, my dad. Even in his nightmare he is doing something worthwhile. They say they're proud of me, but I see worry in my mum's eyes.

One day, I pick up the phone and call Tania, my old high school crush . . . she of the painful "blue balls" episodes. She's still at the same number. Her breathy voice answers and I'm shocked into silence. I mumble a hello and tell her I'm back in Australia. She says she knows. I have a hotel room in the city for press and meetings, and she agrees to meet me there later that night. When she arrives she is everything I remember. Beautiful, shy, soft-spoken, and with an appealing dark, enigmatic quality that I can't quite name. Our affair is finally consummated on the sacred ground of the bed in room 720. It is the longest I have ever waited to have sex with anyone, and it is an unforgettable experience burned into my memory for that reason. She is hot, sweet, soft, angelic, dark, beautiful, and my sixteen-year-old self's dream finally come true.

I head back to the U.S. two weeks later and get ready for round two. Tania and I write letters of passion and longing that finally falter and stop. Years later I hear that she has realized she's gay and is now living with a woman somewhere in Sydney.

Robie has Louis Vuitton luggage, drives a Caddy, and has been married for five years to a beautiful, if slightly insane, Frenchwoman named Colette, so I figure he must be fairly wealthy. It escapes me that he is also living in my apartment building in central Hollywood. I move on up to the second floor to try and get away from the recurring nightmares I am having of "bad guys" breaking into my ground-floor bedroom while I'm sleeping, to rape and rob me. Obviously I'm still feeling a little threatened by America.

Not to mention the angry Hispanic guy who wants to beat me up for dinging his car while opening Robie's heavy Cadillac door. Robie has driven me to an emergency room for one of the myriad times I slice my hand open on something, and when I come back out, Robie and his Caddy are gone and the aforementioned angry Hispanic guy is demanding money from me because the guy I was with (Robie) said that I was the one who dinged his fine automobile. I can't believe Robie—the fucker has just taken off and left me here at the mercy of this highly agitated and burly dude. I hightail it back into the emergency room, jump a fence, and walk all the way back to my apartment building to avoid (a) forking over cash to this guy or (b) having a confrontation I am certain not to win.

Although I don't always like Robie, I do always like his dog, a goofy

Irish setter named Yan. I dog-sit for Robie and Colette occasionally, and because Yan will sit and stay really well, I dress him up in coats and hats and scarves from my closet, take photos of him, and generally pee myself laughing until his parents come to pick him up. He is a champ and sits there with the dopiest expression while I snap away. I will draw on this harmless and silly shit years later when I tire of putting my own face on my album covers.

Capitol Records agrees to go for another round and I get a second chance. I've been writing nonstop, listening to all things English and determined to break away from the teen image that has been thrust upon me. When I go to Disneyland I'm recognized and pestered for photos and autographs. Most of these young girls don't even know I'm a musician, such is the power of the teen press, but they do have posters of me on their bedroom walls, and the truth is, at this point, I'm famous for nothing other than being famous. Kind of a '70s version of Paris Hilton.

My future wife, eleven years old at this point in time and living in Wisconsin, is a big fan of Donny Osmond, but she also has a poster of her future husband and the father of her two sons on her wall in all his androgynous, nonthreatening glory. Truly, truly weird.

And then Jerry Lewis, thank you very much, steps into my corner. My publicist and good friend Fred Skidmore asks *his* good friend Jerry if he can do anything about "getting this Springfield kid" his green card. I have spent $10,000 (or so I'm led to believe—honestly, I never see a dime) on useless lawyers, and I've lugged even more scrapbooks full of articles on my super-specialness to the embassy, plus letters of endearment from the likes of Dick Clark and the president of Capitol Records, and still nothing.

Jerry, God bless him, makes a phone call and I am a "resident alien" at last!!! Now that I'm legal and can finally work in America, we head to England again to record my second album for Capitol. The songs are more light teenage fare that the twelve-year-old readers of *16 Magazine* can readily identify with. Songs about fear of failure ("Why Are You Waiting?"), dead women coming back to life ("Misty Water Woman"), young girls getting pregnant out of wedlock ("Weep No More"), a girl caught up in drugs ("The Liar"), and my love affair with an eighty-year-old woman ("Born Out of Time"). Yes, I'm in love once more, but with no chance whatsoever of consummation. Fred, my publicist, a man twenty years my senior, has turned me on to old Greta Garbo movies. I watch them all, have posters and photos of her all over my apartment, and am highly pissed at fate for the bad timing of our births. There's nothing I can do except fantasize. And write a song or two.

Off to London Robie and I go to hook up with Del Newman again, but in a different studio and with a different recording engineer. Although I'm staying in a tiny hotel this time, I go to see Michelle as soon as I arrive. Not wanting to go through the whole hallucination/sleep deprivation thing again, I ask if she has any sleeping pills. She gives me a big blue pill (am I Alice?) and advises me to take it just before bed. The next thing I know it's two in the afternoon of the next day, all the lights in the apartment are on, the faucet is running in the bathroom, and I'm lying facedown on the bed, fully dressed. It's amazing what we are prepared to swallow in the '70s.

We record the eleven new songs quickly and, apart from some frustrated tears from me now and then, it goes pretty smoothly. Again we're working with great English musicians and singers and of course the London Symphony. I've given up trying to get laid in England—I don't know, maybe they can sense my desperation, or did Heather Flint put the word out that I'm a geek?—so we hotfoot it back to the U.S., where I continue to have much better luck in love and Heather Flint's warnings have no influence.

I come up with what I think is a cool concept for the album cover. Having always loved comic-book art, I decide to have an actual comic book artist draw me as a superhero on the cover and further illustrate the songs on the inside gatefold. I name the record *Comic Book Heroes*. It's released with some fanfare on Capitol and gets a great review in *Rolling Stone* magazine, but the general public evidently looks on the comic book theme as childish and very, very teen. Comic books? Teen?

Wha . . . ? Then Capitol gets busted for payola (really?) and somehow I end up as the scapegoat. I still don't understand what happened, but we are squarely handed the blame, and it is claimed that management has been busing in loads of kids to buy my record to get it on the charts. We try to fight it, but the word is on the street.

Steve and Robie pull me from Capitol, and Columbia Records snaps me up. I later learn that I've been sold to Columbia as the next—yep, you guessed it—David Cassidy. So *Comic Book Heroes* comes out a second time, this version on Columbia. More promotional trips to Europe and all around the U.S., more teen press . . . but to no avail. The record dies a quick death. What is going on? I should be famous by now, at least according to all the movies I've ever seen and that life insurance guy, goddammit!

The constant diet of TV dinners hasn't helped my mood and is playing havoc with my system. I am tired and emaciated, and my face has broken out in painful red lumps. I look like some teenager's nightmare, and I feel sick all the time. I eventually seek a doctor's advice and he tells me to start going to restaurants and eating real food.

Things are starting to truly unravel. The Darkness speaks to me late at night from my bathroom mirror. Whispering balefully, in my own voice, he tells me, "Your record really flopped, huh? And you're not getting any younger. I think the teen fans see you as an old guy now." And, intentionally or not, I have spent three long years cultivating this frigging teen image. I can't just throw all that away, can I? I book a flight to Melbourne for a few weeks away.

It's great to see my family again, but I'm under the gun. I don't tell anyone that I'm going to see a plastic surgeon in Melbourne. This surgeon looks at my soft, unwrinkled, unlined twenty-three-year-old face and says, without a hint of sarcasm, "Yes, I can help you. I can get rid of those lines and bags under your eyes. It will make you look years younger." I go under the knife, sure that this is the cure for everything. Is it the thousand and one schools I went to, the roots I could never lay down, the girls I couldn't connect with, the animals I failed to stand by, some confirmation I didn't get from my mother? God knows at this point, but I am desperate and on the verge of losing it again.

I wake up in a strange hospital bed, my head heavy from the aftereffects of the anesthesia. Afternoon light filters through the blinds. I struggle up to the mirror (why are they always in a bathroom?) and gaze on a nightmare face that looks as though it's gone a few rounds with Snowy from the Moppa Blues and some of his fellow inmates. My eyes are black and swollen and there are stitches poking through the flesh of my lower eyelids. Dried blood is caked in the corners of my half-open eyes, and I feel like shit. I stumble to the phone and call the one person on whom I can always depend, my brother Mike. When he arrives he is shocked and alarmed by what he sees. He helps me to the car and drives me home. I wait while he goes inside and breaks the news to our mum. I lie on the living room floor for two weeks with cold compresses on my eyes, and when the swelling and bruising has subsided, I don't really see any difference, apart from the still-red scarring. "Nice try, numb-nuts," says the Darkness.

HOLLYWOOD HIGH LIFE

1974–1978

Three weeks later, I fly back to the States, where nothing is mentioned about what I've just done, except by Fred, my publicist and friend, who says, "You look better." I think I actually look a little worse, but I appreciate his supportive words. My face has still not quite recovered from the procedure and there's a puffy red incision line under each of my eyes. I'm depressed because I don't know if the marks will dissipate with time or be there for life. *God*, I'm a fucking idiot!

Lynne Randell is an Australian singer who now lives in LA and is married to an American lawyer. She has an exceptional voice but has never cracked it here in the States. She is cute, blond, and a bit of a wild one. Out of the blue, ostensibly because we're both Aussies, she calls me up and invites me to a porno movie. I'm still too young and horny to see the fault in this adultery, and anyway, I figure it's up to the husband to keep the wife happy, so I accept.

Halfway through the movie she grabs my hand, leads me out of the theater, and drives us back to my apartment, where we proceed to screw our brains out, fired up by the hard-core movie. It's my first encounter with a girl who gets turned on by porn, and my mind is blown. Girls like this stuff?

I become Lynne's illicit boyfriend, along with, honestly, half the Los

Angeles music world, but there is no fidelity implied or expected. In fact, she often invites me over to her house when her husband is away and arranges trysts for me with other girls, all fueled by a new drug she has also turned me on to: LSD. Acid is a pharmaceutical that lifts my spirits, throws a lights-up on the Darkness, and makes me laugh like a fool. And a "trip" lasts a hell of a long time. A lot of bang for the buck.

Another Elton John moment occurs at one of Lynne's alcohol- and drug-fueled parties. A young pretty boy who's arrived with Elton corners me in an upstairs bathroom. It's the mid-70's, with rumors of rock stars like David Bowie and Mick Jagger dabbling in homosexuality and musicians generally pushing the androgynous envelope, it's actually cool to be gay. I think, "Maybe I should take this kid for a test run and see if I like it." But I gather my very stoned wits and move back into the party, thankful that the drugs haven't fully kicked in yet. Lynne always seems to have celebs at her parties—Judy Garland's daughter Lorna Luft with Peter Allen—and I meet Dusty Springfield (she of my first-ever concert as a kid). She runs up and hugs me and says, "My long-lost brother!" It's a funny moment (and cool for me) because "Springfield" isn't *either* of our real last names.

Lynne also has had a momentary fling with one of the members of Led Zeppelin (ain't tellin' which one), so they all show up one night and head to a vacant bedroom with some lucky or unlucky girl, depending on how the night turned out. Lynne also mentions a brief affair with Jimi Hendrix, which further stokes the fires of my drive for fame. At times she appears to be the new Michelle in my life, pushing me to go further with my now-stalled music career. I play her songs I've written and she bemoans the teen direction I've taken. She's seen me in Zoot in Oz and says she always thought I would pursue rock and roll over here, not the teen dream. I tell her that's what *I* thought too!

Due to Lynne's constant prodding and goading, I begin to contemplate a way out of the teen-magazine-lined dead-end path I've been following. Meanwhile, Gloria Stavers of *16 Magazine* takes to pushing the erotic envelope in the pages of her periodical. Steve Binder tells me that

Gloria, who is quite a bit older than I am, has confided in him that all she wants is a weekend with me in a motel room, so I'm a bit nervous when she asks me to take off my shirt and unzip my pants a little at the next photo session in New York. I'm not quite sure what age group she's aiming for with this approach, but I'm pretty certain it's not twelve-year-olds. When the photos are printed in the magazine, incensed mothers from across the country write to the editor complaining about the terrifying impropriety of it all. So now, not only are the kids not buying my records, but their mothers think I'm a deviant. It's time to get a band together and leave this shit behind.

In 1974, I move to Malibu with my very first American band, which I assemble through the age-old process of advertising and auditions. Our new digs are an unfurnished house that Steve and Robie have rented—possibly with my advance money. We set up our gear in the huge living room, drag in a few mattresses, and get to work. The house is in what at the time is the very unpopular, very remote, very un-chic Point Dume area of equally undesirable Malibu, just across the street from Bob Dylan's ungroomed compound, and that's pretty much it for the neighborhood. The house looks out across a wide, overgrown canyon with redwing hawks circling lazily overhead. It's beautiful, but it feels like the boonies. We practice day and night, stopping only to eat or to have sex with any visiting female. It is a veritable young lad's dream.

I write a bunch of new songs, much heavier and more guitar-based than those on the previous albums. The band consists of seriously good musicians, and I'm anxious to break away from the teen rep I've been saddled with. We are young men full of testosterone and drive, the music is the reason we're here, and the sky's the limit. We focus on music twenty-four hours a day—except when girls show up. Lynne brings girls, clothes, a guitar, and underwear for me, and she's really starting to push for me to leave Binder/Porter. I feel it's time, but I'm terrified of being alone in the States. Almost everyone I know is connected to them in one way or another.

My band and I start playing gigs . . . for free, anywhere there's an audience. In an unfortunate choice of stage wear, I make the giant miscalculation of thinking that a Fred Flintstone–style caveman outfit would really help things along. I don't know if it does, but it gets a lot of laughs from the band. I drop it pretty fast.

I move back to my apartment in Hollywood, and Columbia agrees to finance one more album. Into the recording studio we go again, Robie and me, this time to Crystal Studios in Hollywood. My band and I work long hard hours tracking and overdubbing, and I begin to see a stronger, truer direction for my music. Unfortunately, Columbia does not. When they hear the finished tracks, all at least four or five minutes long, with extended and complex instrumental jams, double guitar solos, and a church pipe organ stuck somewhere in the middle, they flip out and pull the plug. I hear the "We thought we were getting the next David Cassidy" line yet again.

My record dies an orphan, landing with a bruised thud on the Hollywood sidewalk after a year and a half of loving care from me. If I didn't know it already, I learn it now: this game is not for wusses. The album, tentatively titled *Springfield—Rocks Off!* (yikes) is put in a warehouse somewhere, along with the crated Ark of the Covenant, never to be seen or heard again. The letter arrives to inform me (just like in high school) that my services are no longer required at Columbia Records, thank you very much, now fuck off.

This is a big blow to me. I dive deep into the darker side of life. I do things with Lynne and the people she brings around that are downright destructive, illegal, and bad for all concerned. A beautiful young girl named Suzette who I am involved with through this scene commits suicide. It is the end that Lynne will choose for herself as well, many years down the line.

I think now about the unhappy results that some of my exes have met with and wonder if it's me or just that I'm attracted to a certain type who gives off a dark signal. I hope for my soul's sake it's the latter. I think I have a lot to answer for in some of my dealings with girls/women through this period and even beyond. There are so many higher roads not taken. It unsettles me still. I decide to break it off with Lynne, who unfortunately has a key to my apartment. I come home one night and my place is trashed. The guitar she bought me is gone, as are the clothes and underwear. The threads I don't mind losing, and I still have my main guitar, but I could really use the underwear. I never see her again, and I wish I could have made peace with her before she died.

Looking back, I see that despite our own issues and the fact that we were troubled spirits, Lynne was clearly the catalyst in getting me to abandon the *16 Magazine*/teen-dream path once and for all. She was most certainly in my corner as far as my music went.

Post-Lynne, I refocus on my goals and where it is I want to be in my life. "My aim is to win" becomes my mantra, and I scribble it everywhere: around my apartment, on streetlight posts, the back of my hand, even public restrooms. In the '70s, without knowing it, you just might have seen it somewhere. Once more it's musicians to the rescue. I go back to my band and we continue doing gigs. None of them is meaningful in any way, but no record company dismissal is going to stop me from playing, goddammit. I am sure of one thing: I love playing live. I connect to it on a level that goes deeper and is more meaningful than merely having a good time with a bunch of strangers. It is the only true way I connect 100 percent with humanity. Relating to dogs is very easy for me, to humans much less so. And this gigging is my avenue to the social need I have for community but am ill-equipped to pursue in a "normal" setting. And lucky for me, I don't need the nod from a record company to play live.

One night, we're playing at the Whiskey A Go Go on Sunset. It's a far cry from the one in St. Kilda, although I think I get paid less. I do two sets, and in between them a girl comes upstairs to the dressing room to say hi. Linda Blair is the hottest young actress in the movies right now and has just come off the tidal wave of adulation and press from *The Exorcist*. She sits on the floor with me while I dry my hair, and we talk. She's sharp and funny and pretty hot in a perky, bright-eyed way. She invites me to the Rainbow club up the street after I'm done with my last set and says she and her sister Debbie will buy me a drink. I don't know how old she is but I soon learn she is only fifteen. I am twenty-five.

I'm drawn to this girl. Sitting at the Rainbow drinking (I don't think either she or her sister is of legal drinking age, but again, it's the '70s, so who cares—obviously no one) she puts her hand on my thigh. I light up like a Christmas tree. She is pretty, sexy, and very famous, and apparently she has the heater on for me. We end up at my apartment—more specifically, my bedroom—and most specifically, my bed. I am her first lover and she is an enthusiastic learner. She's an adventurous girl as well, which is probably why the world's biggest Hollywood starlet (at this time) lost her virginity to a penniless musician in a $180-a-month apartment.

She leaves for the East Coast the next day. I'm in love, and we spend hours talking on the phone every night. I speak with her mom Eleanor, who becomes our cheerleader and defender when the media gets hold of the story. We plan for me to come out to their home in Connecticut over Christmas, which I do, and I end up breaking my foot Christmas morning running up and down the stairs trying to wake everyone up. I spend the rest of the holidays in a leg cast.

Linda goes from coast to coast on business trips and always stays with me when she's in LA. We share a love of dogs and sex—separately, not in combination. Most of the time we don't leave the apartment. She's invited to premieres and Hollywood parties, and we go as a couple, blindly and innocently to the media slaughter. We're actually really shocked by the incensed articles in both teen and regular press about our affair. Either we have zero understanding of what makes the press tick, or it's a really slow month for news. We're pilloried for the whole age-difference thing, but eventually the media relents and backs off—whether they get bored of it or used to us is anyone's guess. Because of the manner in which Linda arrived in the public's consciousness—as the little girl in *The Exorcist* who infamously said "Let Jesus fuck you"—and her later roles as a teenage alcoholic and a sixteen-year-old rape victim in a women's prison, I guess it's almost assumed that she's headed for trouble. So when it shows up in the form of an Older Guy (and a musician no less), I'm not actually brought up on charges.

At one point during all of this, I finally get the cojones (thank you, Lynne) to pick up the phone and call Steve Binder and Robie to tell them I want a divorce. Steve, who I've always liked and even loved for his commitment, just walks away. Robie, on the other hand, throws a quarter-million-dollar lawsuit at me! At this point I'm digging quarters out of my plastic Goofy bank to put together the finances to eat once a day, and he wants $250,000? I'm also about to be evicted from my cheapo apartment/love nest.

My girlfriend, who happens to be wealthy, comes to my rescue. For this moment in time alone, I owe Linda my eternal fealty and quite possibly my future career in America (so blame her). She rents an apartment for us (okay, for me really, since she still lives mostly with her folks on the East Coast), fills it with furniture and even a TEAC 3340 four-track tape machine on which I can record demos of my songs.

I begin writing and recording furiously, when she isn't there to distract me. I've passed through the pain of being without a record deal for the first time in five years and concentrate on my goals with a single-minded drive. Unfortunately, I am not evolved enough to leave well enough alone, and I continue to have sex with other partners when Linda isn't around. But to be honest, so does she. I don't know it at the time, and in true double-standard form I would have been crushed if I'd been aware of it. Meanwhile, I have to break up the band for obvious financial reasons, and we each go our own ways.

Linda and I are together for a year, but she just comes and goes, and I feel we're slowly drawing apart. I'm smoking a little dope, taking acid, and also nailing a female drug dealer for free Quaaludes (my drug of choice back then), but Linda comes over from visiting "friends" even more stoned than I am, so I tell her that it's *she* who has the drug problem (!) and I break off the relationship. To be honest, although I initiate it, I can see she wants to move on too, so it's kind of mutual at this point.

Our lives follow different paths, but we never totally lose touch and I'm glad to say that we're friends even now. I got a Christmas card last December (2009) from her saying "Happy Holidays and watch out for stairs."

Now I am truly on my own in Hollywood. Any friends I had are all attached to Binder/Porter, my band is gone, and Linda and her family are out of my life. And . . . he's back! Just like that, my old friend the Darkness returns, pulling me down in a way that's getting to be typical of our on-again/off-again, possibly bipolar romance. He's happy to see me, the supercilious fucker.

I'm struggling to pay the rent. My parents sense that something is wrong and send me a couple of hundred bucks to buy a plane ticket home to Australia. I spend it on rent and food. I never mention it and they never ask, but I can tell by the tone of my mum's letters that she's getting really worried. I think about what I would do and how I would feel if I went back to Oz now, having basically failed in my mission. I couldn't do it—I couldn't go home. But survival is getting tougher. I make some inquiries about jobs at markets and the like, but I have no work history at all, zero references, and no résumé, I'm still recognizable ("Hey, honey, isn't that Rick Springfield bagging our groceries?"), and I have no other skills. ("Do you need a guy to play guitar for your customers while they squeeze the produce, maybe?") I'm getting more and more depressed by the day.

A little while later, I'm at a club watching a band and some guy leans over and says, "You're Rick Springfield, aren't you? You were good, man. You should have gone farther." I think to myself, "Is this it? Is this really the death knell of my so-called music career?" Around this time I get a fan letter from some kid in Nebraska saying that she'd love to come to Hollywood and visit me at my mansion. What a sorry joke. Mr. Darkness is back with a vengeance, and he has really missed fucking with me. "Little bit of a hiccup here, pal? What'cha gonna do now? Go home and say, 'Man, it's tough in America.' That wouldn't look too good, would it? Not after all that press and everyone saying 'All right, little Ricky's gonna make it . . .' You know there's a gun store just down the street. You've been in there looking at all those big, heavy pistols, I know. It'd be real quick. And pretty painless too, Sport."

I can't believe I'm actually contemplating this. Suicide is always an option. I count out the coins in my stupidly happy Goofy bank. Guns are at least in the low-hundred-dollar price range, aren't they? This all seems familiar somehow. Almost expected. It's like the possibility has never really left me.

I have exactly $37 left to my name. Not enough. Not nearly enough. I continue to exist. But I'm not happy about it. Neither is Mr. D. His default position for me is "miserable," but he'd prefer "dead."

I'm not sure when I see the article, but I do see it. I've picked up a newspaper from somewhere and there's a story about a singer who's just begun to find success. Bob Seger talks about his early, tough days in Detroit and the battle he's fought to get where he is now. I cut out the article and tape it to my kitchen cabinet door. It gives me a tiny jolt of inspiration every time I see it. I start reading a book called *Psycho-Cybernetics* that someone recommended a while back. It's the latest in positive thinking and using visualization to reach goals in your life. It becomes my constant companion, and I read it and re-read it. In the continual seesawing that is my emotional state, I'm now trying to focus on my path again. In fact, my "positive thinking" is rapidly evolving into a mania.

I look now at the entries I made in a diary through this part of my life. They all read, "I must make it! MY AIM IS TO WIN! There is only one result—SUCCESS! I WILL succeed!" On and on and over and over. It's a little frightening to see the obsessive repetition: it reminds me of

Jack Nicholson in *The Shining*: ". . . all work and no play makes Jack a dull boy all work and no play makes Jack a dull boy . . ." At least he had a focus, right?

I cross a line here, mentally. It isn't real healthy, maybe, but at least it's in the opposite direction from thoughts of blowing my head off with a handgun. Where I am now is bullshit, I tell myself. And I know that I cannot rely on anyone but myself to accomplish my goals. I walk the Hollywood streets some nights just to get out of the apartment. It's on one of these walks (they become runs, actually, as I finally start to take care of my body—apart from the occasional acid trip) that I bump into Colette, Robie's now ex-wife, walking her dog Yan, the very snappy dresser. She asks me what I'm doing. (I later find out that she's asking because she's trying to decide whether or not to take "half" of me in her divorce from Robie. Thank God, that's a bullet I dodge.)

I tell her I'm not doing much of anything, which at this point is true. She suggests I check out the acting class she's taking at a workshop here in Hollywood. By this time I've forgotten my ignoble beginnings as Captain Scuttleboom and I agree to do just that. Praise the Lord, my mum calls me to say some residuals have come into my Australian bank account from *Mission: Magic*. Almost $2,000, which back then translates to nearly twice that amount in 1970s American dollars. (There actually was a reason for doing that stupid-ass show, besides giving a young Quentin Tarantino something to watch while his mom made him breakfast!) It's these residuals that begin to pay for my new acting classes at the slightly bizarre Vincent Chase Workshop. Vince is proud to be a forty-year-old virgin and announces it at the slightest provocation. He is, we all believe, a nonactive gay man and has obvious crushes on the hotter young men in the class. He also has fits of rage that make everyone go very still, like field mice in the presence of a circling hawk.

While my music career is in the crapper, I can at least make some money acting. It doesn't dawn on me that most of the actors in the class are waiting tables in lieu of working as actors. Ignorance is bliss. But it

My mum and dad in Sydney on one of their first dates, before I was even a gloomy little gleam in their eye.

The Springthorpe family with our first car. Why am I wearing a dress? Because we've just gotten back from christening me Richard Lewis (not Howard Lewis).

Two years of age and already depressed. No, not really, but judging by the look on my face, I *am* possibly post-tantrum.

I'm the bug and my brother is the exterminator. Our mum made these charmingly coordinated costumes. What was she trying to insinuate?

My kindergarten class in Bandiana. I'm the one in the middle row, third from the right, clearly ignoring the guy with the camera who's yelling, "Everyone, look at me and smile." Can you spot Vicky the Erotic Poop Queen? She has a look that says in twelve years she'll be Trouble.

England in 1960. I think I see the Darkness in my eyes even then.

The beginning (and near end) of my acting career: the coveted lead role in *Scuttleboom's Treasure* and another fine outfit whipped up by my mum. I think all "official" photos in our house were staged on these stairs.

Harold Hare, the grinning little bastard that got me in trouble when I was ten.

Back in Oz and in love with the guitar. At thirteen I had no inkling of what would take place inside this shed in the not so distant future. At this moment, however, it was just a wonderfully white-trash backdrop for a swingin' cool shot of me with my first guitar and my one "hip" outfit.

Vietnam, out in the boonies, 1968. In-ground bunkers like this were set up around a camp to guard the perimeter against the enemy. Dude, I'm just a freakin' guitar player. Don't shoot me.

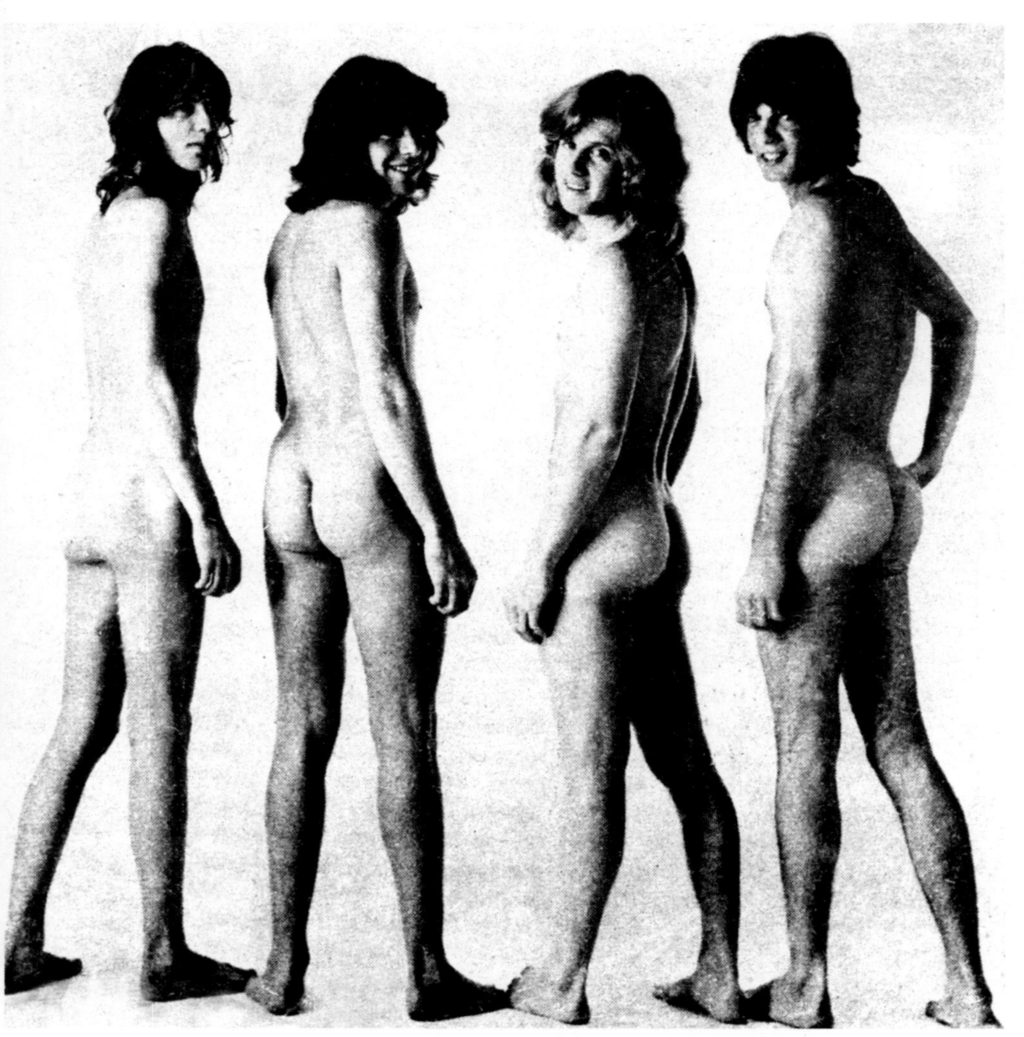

The boys of Zoot, 1970. Whose bright idea was *this*? Oh yeah, mine. Sorry, fellas. The flip side of this photo is even funnier.

Photograph © Glenn A. Baker

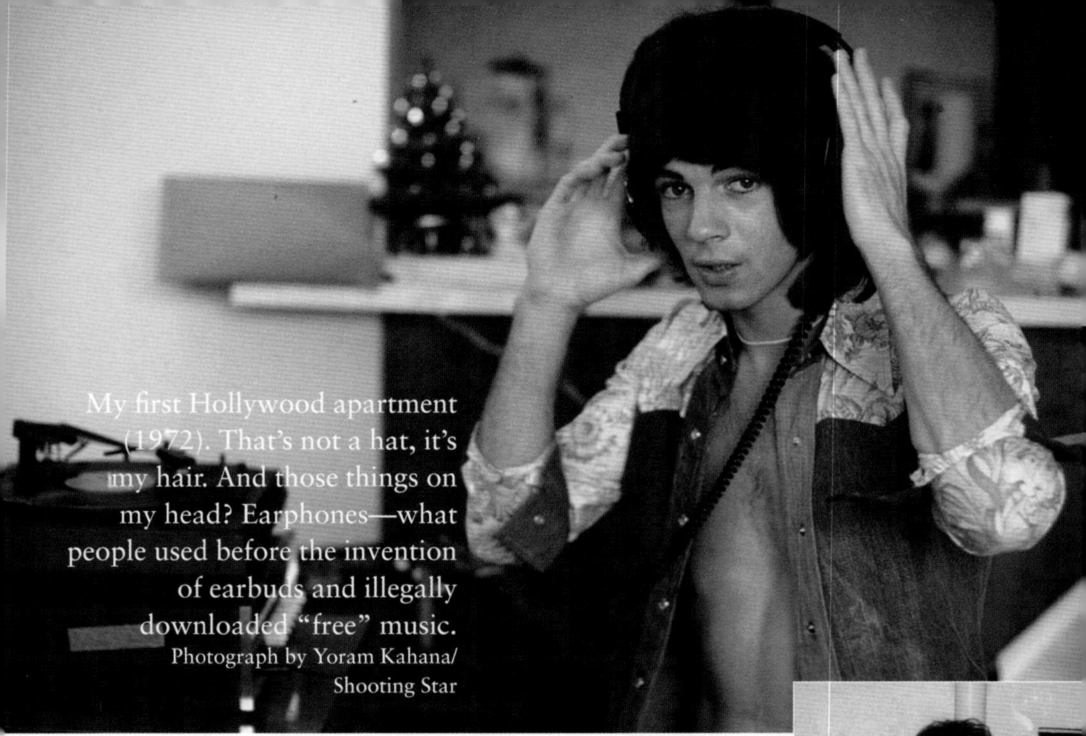

My first Hollywood apartment (1972). That's not a hat, it's my hair. And those things on my head? Earphones—what people used before the invention of earbuds and illegally downloaded "free" music. Photograph by Yoram Kahana/ Shooting Star

Good to go. Melbourne, 1971, just before heading to the US of A. You can't tell but beneath those shades I'm pretty damned excited—even though I'm leaving everyone and everything I know behind. Photograph by Jacques L'Affrique

Young lad loose in Hollywood circa 1974. Proof I *did* love Greta Garbo and that at one point in the '70s, you ju couldn't wear enough denim.

LEFT: The severely balls-flattening white silk pants, white two-inch-heeled shoes, and "R"-for-Ricky lightning bolt sweater I'm wearing comprise the first of two stunning ensembles designed by yours truly. The sexual double entendre—cooked up by some teen magazine—is purely intentional, of course.
Photograph © Michael Ochs Archives/ Getty Images

BELOW: Linda and me hiding out in my . . . okay, *her* Hollywood apartment in 1975.
Photograph by Michael Montfort/Globe Photos, Inc.

It's hard for me to reconstruct my logic now, but at one point in my career I thought this loopy outfit was the right look for me. Thank God the only things in this photo I still have are my hair and that Gibson guitar, which I would eventually use to write the opening riff of "Jessie's Girl."

My only concession to disco: satin shorts. In the backyard of 1216 Maryland Avenue with Ping and Pong, my two chickens—trying to make up for the beheading of so many of their Aussie brethren by treating them well and not eating them. This photo is also proof that at twenty-seven I could actually grow facial hair.

Lethal Ron and me outside my first house. Joined at the hip. We don't know it yet, but Barbara will be moving in with us soon.

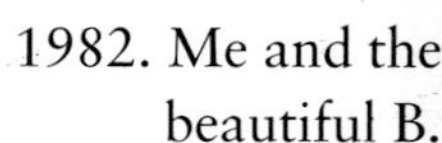

1982. Me and the beautiful B.

No *real* doctor ever had this much time to coif his hair.

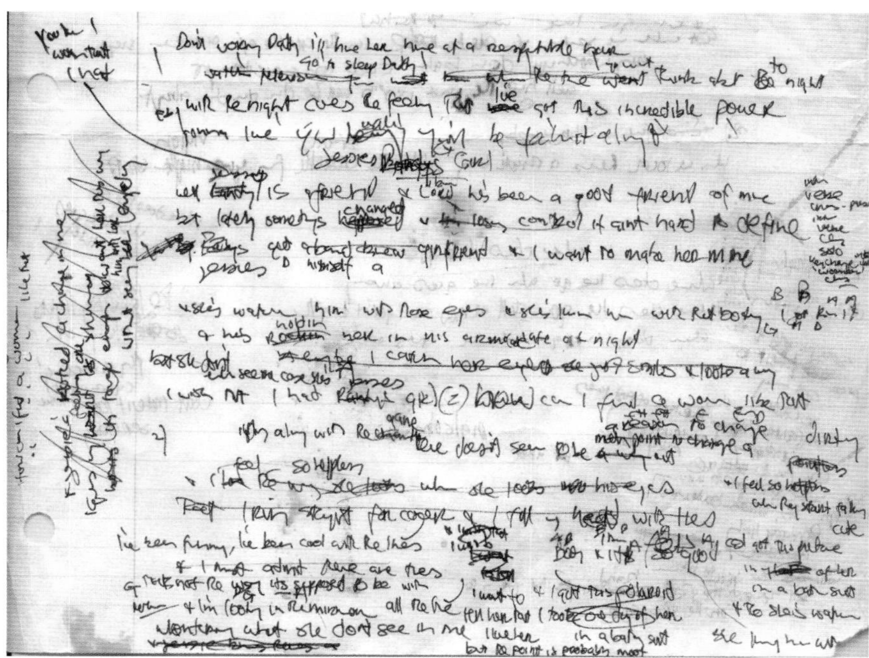

Probably one of the single most valuable pieces of paper I own: the original lyrics to "Jessie's Girl." I guess paper was a luxury back then because I wrote "Love Is Alright Tonite" and "Red Hot and Blue Love"—both from the *Working Class Dog* album—on this same sheet of paper.

From playing cover songs for twenty people one day to playing my own music in front of twenty thousand the next. It's a bit of a mind-fuck, to be sure, and, yes, that is a REDFENDERSTRAT I'm holding. For years I tried to believe this could really happen, but when it finally did, it was hard to absorb.

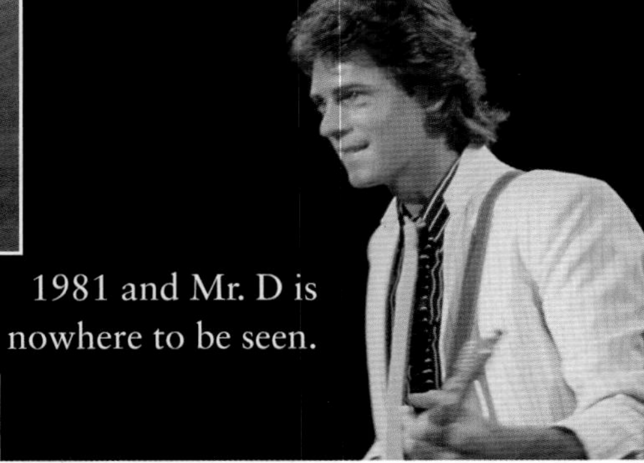

1981 and Mr. D is nowhere to be seen.

The original photo of me that made it to Ronnie's shirt for the album cover of *Working Class Dog* along with Polaroid out-takes. Proof that while I needed perfect lighting, hair, and makeup for *my* close-up, Ronnie did not.

Record store signing in 1981, according to the Miss Teen America sashes. Were these two my bodyguards? If so, then it was kind of like having the hens guard the fox.

Me and Ronnie at RCA. Is it any wonder I put this handsome hound on the cover of my album? What a ham.

B and me leaving my mum's house after our wedding. You'll win a prize if you can spot my mum in this photo.

Live Aid, JFK Stadium, Philadelphia, 1985. One of rock and roll's finest hours. I was performing in the stateside part of this landmark event. The other half was taking place simultaneously in London's Wembley Stadium. Given the estimated four hundred million viewers who tuned in across sixty countries, it's surprising the world's TV satellites didn't all spontaneously combust. Photograph by Paul Natkin/WireImage/Getty Images

Hawaii, with Liam at fifteen months. I could have stayed like this forever.

Shortly before my momentous walk around the pool. Smiling with my mouth but not my eyes.

Liam and I hanging with his new bro, Joshua, just after his birth. Little Mr. Center of the Universe, the sequel.

Sahara, drawing you in.

The *EFX* show. Somehow (in the minds of the writers of this MGM show) I was supposed to be P. T. Barnum who had just landed in E.T.'s spaceship, wearing Sgt. Pepper's jacket and playing Elvis's guitar. At least I didn't have to dress up in a fat suit like the guys behind me. It was a pretty cool show just the same. Photograph by Liz Engel

Taking the Pete Townshend windmill one step further: the rose decapitation. Don't try this at home. Photograph by Rhonda Hunt

A recent concert shot. Playing live is my favorite way of connecting with other human beings. The emotional experience of a concert is a communion. And as an aside: What's the point of getting a tattoo that only people you have sex with can see?
Photograph by Rhonda Hunt

My old mum and me in our backyard. Is there a family resemblance? I think so. She's closer to one hundred than I care to contemplate. I do hope that "family resemblance" includes the longevity gene.
Photograph by Jay Gilbert

B and me out
on a recent date.
My soul mate.

Gomer and me.
My other soul mate.
Photograph by Kym DeGenaro

www.Springthorpe.com.
COUNTERCLOCKWISE FROM LOWER LEFT: Joshua, Liam, Barbara, and me.

becomes much more than a long-shot way to make some money. I fall in with the community of actors, and once again I get a reprieve from my darker leanings. I set the imagined handgun back down.

Although I don't realize it, I am in desperate need of the family connection that is so missing in my life. Doug Davidson, a nineteen-year-old actor at the workshop, steps into the breach. Like me he is a child/man, and we connect immediately and often laugh ourselves silly over lame things that occur in class, much to the chagrin of our occasionally apoplectic acting coach, Vince. Doug takes me to meet his family in prestigious La Cañada-Flintridge, just west of Pasadena, where he is still living at this juncture.

His is a warm, funny, loving family, and I'm adopted without a question or a doubt. His mom, Corinne, was a child vaudeville star in a dancing and singing troupe called the Kaitlin Kiddies, and she encourages my pursuit of music and acting. Doug and I go through all his cool toys and settle on his BB gun and a few plastic soldiers. We take them out to the driveway at night, set little bonfires all around, and proceed to blast away at the enemy with hundreds of BBs, screaming and laughing 'til the neighbors call and ask Doug's parents to bring us inside. "And can they *grow up*, for Chrissakes?"

Then Doug's older sister, Diana, arrives. She has been a model in New York and has come home to rest from the pressures of the business. She is also a gifted actress who began her career, at twelve years old, with a role in Disney's *The Horse in the Gray Flannel Suit* (you might have missed it). She is also (uh-oh) really beautiful, with huge blue eyes and high cheekbones, and she has a warped sense of humor. She starts taking acting classes at Vince's with us and is fascinated by my heavy English/Aussie accent, which she has great trouble understanding. We eventually hook up romantically, though it's more her doing than mine. Because of my relationship with Doug, there's a slight "sister" quality to her that I can't completely shake, and the sexual side of our relationship never truly lifts off the ground for me.

Diana is striking looking but (by her own admission) has had an odd array of boyfriends. One paramour, hooked on heroin, admits to her one day that he is a "junkie." "Oh, I love horses!" she replies. Diana, in her innocence, thinks he's said "jockey." Another is an antisocial one-eyed bird keeper at a zoo. Even with all my idiosyncrasies, I must seem like a "regular guy" by comparison. She is a soft girl, and it's easy for me to get my way. So I continue to see other girls whenever I can.

Diana, Doug, and I are the Three Musketeers, and we hang out and go everywhere together. Doug, although a handsome, hetero guy, is a late bloomer and at twenty, is still a virgin, and there are no girlfriends in the picture yet. Sorry, Dougie. You have the right to strike this fact from the book before publication. (If it's still here, then he's okay with it!) For a long time it's just the three of us. Very tight, very similar in our views of life and art, and very committed to the time-honored (yeah, right!) craft of acting. They also like some of the songs I'm writing. Doug still has cassette tapes of every home demo I've made tucked away in his house—potential eBay and/or blackmail material.

Diana moves into the apartment below me. I've never lived with a girlfriend up to this point (Linda spent at most a couple of weeks at a time with me), and I like my space to get away and write, to see another girl when I feel like it, and to go to the bathroom without worrying who's in the next room. Still, on most nights the three of us are at my place or their parents' home in Pasadena 'til the small hours of the morning.

Believe it or not, the dreaded lawsuit Robie, the sadistic swine, has waged against me is still going on and I actually have a lawyer—Ivan Hoffman—who is working very cheaply on my behalf, God bless him, to try to counter the allegations in the 150-page legal document that Robie's lawyer keeps updating every week. Ivan knows I'm still looking for some type of representation (Anything? Anyone?), and he says there's a studio owner out in Van Nuys named Joe Gottfried who is interested in meeting with me. I ask Ivan if this guy knows I'm Rick Springfield and not David Cassidy, or even someone who wants to be the next David Cassidy. He says he knows, and he relays that Joe likes what he's heard of my music. A meeting is set.

Around this time, Doug and his father, Don, are doing work with kids through the YMCA. Doug invites me to go on camping trips as "counselor" for these young kids—a lot of whom are from troubled homes. I don't know anything about kids and am not particularly interested in hanging with a bunch of twelve-year-olds, but he says I can play guitar around the campfire at night and just be a "cabin leader"—someone who makes the kids go to sleep on time and get up for breakfast. It's actually an amazing experience, and I come to be particularly close to some of the kids in my "care."

One is a slight, blond boy named Chris who lives with his mother. I become something of a father figure to him (God help him), and he actually cries when it's time to go home from a camping trip on Catalina Island. We stay in touch, and some years later he enters the Marine Corps. I can't imagine this soft, sensitive little boy being inducted into the brutal life of the Marines. But we all grow and change—except me.

I seem to be stuck in a sort of permanent adolescence. Even now.

Music has always been a young man's game, and I am one of a peculiar subspecies: I'm a songwriter. As a songwriter, it's natural for me to stay open and receptive to everything that I and the people around me are feeling, doing, saying, and fantasizing about. It's not a skill set that every job requires; for many people it would be a headache they don't need. I think it's desirable for certain careers: artists, writers, actors, therapists, dog owners (hahaha), and some rather spectacular mothers. I need to stay sympathetic and connected to the emotional roller coaster that most "grown-ups" have become desensitized to—but that they still want to hear about and be reminded of in the songs they listen to and the books they read. One consequence of this openness is that I remain pretty naïve and gullible, despite the things I've gone through. The result: I am frequently deceived (which is probably only fair since

I've done my share of deceiving). To this day, I'm still surprised at some people's ulterior motives when they are revealed to me.

But on the whole, and especially back then, this permanent adolescence serves me well on the path I've chosen, so I'm at peace with it. Only down the line, as I take on more adult responsibilities and find them harder to shoulder, do I realize how ill suited it leaves me for some of life's roles that I desire most.

CHAPTER TEN

THE AMERICANIZATION OF RICKY

SAN FERNANDO VALLEY
1978

The Hollywood party scene I now find myself in, courtesy of my new actor friends and associates, is the usual drug-taking, drinking, sexual free-for-all that we've come to know and envy after everybody but me has written their autobiography. But honestly, I'm sure the parties are no different than the ones everyone else is going to. It's just that these are actors and musicians, so most people assume that they have the advantage of getting all the "good stuff." It ain't necessarily so. There is no rhyme or reason to these parties, and I meet all the other wannabes who are swimming at or near the bottom. A few, like Michael Biehn, Shaun Cassidy, and the Hudson Brothers, will have their own successes later on.

I am also pretty naïve about the strengths and effects of the drugs I've been taking on and off. At another of the endless Hollywood parties that seem to be going on all night and every night, a friend gives me some psychedelic mushrooms. I take them home and put them in the freezer as he suggests. A few nights later I decide to give them a whirl. I chop a good-sized piece off one of them, swallow it, and wait for the fireworks . . . nothing. So, thinking they must be a little weaker than windowpane—the chemical version I'm used to—I cut up and ingest more of the magic mushrooms. And wait. Nothing. So I call my friend, and he suggests drinking some hot tea to thaw them out in my stomach since I'd been dumb enough to eat them straight from the freezer. So I drink tea. And wait . . . Nothing. I eat some more of the 'shrooms and drink more tea. Dammit, nothing. "Fuck this," I say to myself, and I do a hit of the windowpane I have in a drawer and settle down to watch TV. Ten minutes later it all kicks in.

I think I'm underwater and the ferns in the corner of the room are really seaweed. I begin to back myself off the couch and up the wall, feeling increasingly uncomfortable and disoriented. Everything is turning freaky. An ad for a pot roast on the TV looks like a raw, bloody, severed human thigh. I am most certainly losing it. I get up and walk to the kitchen. It's even worse. The linoleum is rolling and buckling like ocean waves. I manage to dial the guy who gave me the mushrooms and croak out, "I'm too high. Help me." He says he'll be right over but to take some Valium. It will bring me down.

My hands are shaking uncontrollably as I pour out a handful of Valium and swallow them. I drink water but it tastes like liquid iron and chemicals. I pace and moan and it seems like forever 'til there's a knock at the door and my friend enters. He looks cartoonish, like a gnome. His nose is too big and his eyes are tiny steel black balls set deep in his head. He grins and it looks like a threat. We go outside and walk around the block. It's Christmas, and the lighted decorations run the length and breadth of Hollywood Boulevard. I am stunned. It looks to me like there's a fortune in jewels hanging from the sky. I've never seen anything so astonishingly beautiful and glittering in my life. We make it back to my apartment finally, and I am off hallucinogens for life.

Acting class is getting interesting, and of course there are lots of really pretty people. Though I am officially with Diana, I am still running amok whenever I can with some of the other girls in class and at the "actor" parties we all go to. Richard Chamberlain, who is a past and current student of Vincent Chase, occasionally hosts some of these. Richard comes to class sometimes to "work out."

He's friends with Elton (here we go again), and at Richard's parties

I regularly play a couple of the newest songs I've written, on his piano, before Elton gets up and sings some of his new stuff. Am I actually opening for Elton John? This is around the *Captain Fantastic* period, so it's a high point in his career. (His album, I mean, not me opening for him.) His group and entourage are all good English folks, but I stay clear of the bathrooms when there are young, pretty-boys around. I do make my way there, though, when I find a girl who is game, and more than once the door opens and I am busted *en flagrante* with my jeans at knee level and the plucky girl sitting up legs astride me on the bathroom counter top, breathing heavily. Have to remember to lock the damn door.

Despite these apparently self-assured moves in and out of party bathrooms, I still don't have much self-worth or confidence, mainly because of the lack of success with my music. If just "having sex" could have been a career option for me, I would have been much happier at this point in my life. As it is, sex offers only a momentary reprieve from my severe lack of self-esteem and my severe lack of a career. I am determined to change that, so I take up martial arts.

I choose the only martial arts dojo in walking distance (I still don't own a car and in fact haven't even learned to drive). Shotokan is a hard, external version of karate that focuses on strong stances, balance, and power punches and kicks. The sensei, a tough Japanese master, teaches me to guard my ribs in a fight by punching me hard enough to crack one. I get the same treatment from the black belts at the dojo that I used to get as a neophyte musician in my first bands. They give us white belts a bunch of good-natured shit. I'm a diligent student, and as I progress through the ranks up to black belt, I begin to tap into the internal strength I've been seeking—so much so that I start doing things I would have avoided before, like purposely crossing a street to walk past a gang of loudmouths near Hollywood High School or walking down the darkest street I can find at night. It also improves my confidence at the Vincent Chase Workshop and I start to take acting seriously.

I also make another choice here: I change my accent to mid-Atlantic American. At last Diana can understand what I'm saying. My decision is driven mainly by the idea that when I start auditioning for acting roles, I want the American accent to be natural and not something I have to think about. But I know there is a deeper, slightly darker reason as well: I'm shedding all vestiges of myself as an Australian, because I'm still haunted by the experience as a twelve-year-old returning native son, of looking out at the Melbourne wharf and seeing all those Aussie bumpkins lining the docks as we anchored. I don't fully realize this at the time, but I know now it is in there. Even with the new accent, I'm still uncomfortable with who I am. It's a slightly schizoid thing that I'm now talking with an American accent but still thinking in my old accent. I dream in it too. I try not to focus too much on what this might say about other mental tricks that I may be playing on myself.

Joe Gottfried is the owner of Sound City, a recording studio that isn't doing much business right now but will gradually and steadily become one of the hottest rooms in town through the coming decades as Fleetwood Mac, Tom Petty and the Heartbreakers, Santana, Foreigner—and much later Nirvana and Queens of the Stone Age—commit their hard-earned cash to cutting audio masterpieces there.

Joe is a good-hearted guy who loves the whole entertainment business but doesn't really know a thing about managing a music career. He says he wants to sign me. I look at the very expensive Neve recording consoles in studios A and B, picture myself cutting some tunes for free, because my manager owns the place . . . and sign on the dotted line. I am more or less back in the music business.

But as Mr. Darkness likes to point out in his inimitable fashion, "Things can't always be bright and shiny," so of course Cleo, our family dog, takes this opportunity to kick the canine bucket. I write her a song called "Fare Thee Ever Well," which I later rewrite under even darker circumstances. And my old mum calls three weeks later to tell me that Norman James, our sweet struggling man, has developed colon cancer.

I catch a plane home to be with my family. Five or so years after his first death and despite the addition of cancer, my dad is doing pretty well. Mum is, too, although I can see she has serious "caretaker's stress syndrome." She feels guilty for resenting having to care for a husband she loves. She gets fed up with his repetitive questions, his constant forgetfulness, and his childlike pigheadedness. She yells at him, then reproaches herself even more harshly. It's a no-win situation for her, and now she has to begin to chart the unknown course of his cancer treatments. It's in the early stages, so there is hope that something can be done to arrest it.

We are all brokenhearted at the loss of our old girl Cleo, Dad included. We bury her, in her basket, at the back of the yard, under the shade of the tree she loved to rest beneath during the hot summer days. I realize again that I prefer the company of dogs. They are truly good, unconditionally loving beings, and they have never abandoned me, even though I have abandoned them. I do feel guilty for leaving Cleo while I journeyed to another land, as I had done to my best furry pal Elvis so many years before. And now, suddenly, there is a possible end point to my sweet old dad's life. I know I made the choices I did because it was my path, but it doesn't make missing precious years with the ones who truly matter any easier.

My parents are happy (relieved?) that I finally have a new manager. I don't tell them I think he might be a little green. But I am feeling positive. Any move forward is a good move, and I must get back, despite the fact that my father has cancer. He understands. They both do. I think I do, too.

I jump on the next flight back to the States, where Joe has a surprise for me. We're meeting with a small label named Chelsea Records in two days, and they want to hear my songs. Again, I pull my demos together.

Wes Farrell is famous to me for having co-written the song "Boys" on the Beatles' first album. He is a suave, handsome, white-toothed American entrepreneur, and his new label Chelsea is looking for talent. He likes the songs he hears, we sign a deal right then and there, and just like that I'm back in the music biz. *Wait for Night* is the title I come up with because it sounds vaguely like the name of an old '40s movie. Being an "actor" now, I'm into that sort of shit. People and relationships at the acting class are great fodder for songs, and I feel this is my best writing so far.

I've found an amazing engineer named Mark Smith who will make the record with me, and in another brush with Elton John and the people attached to him, Nigel Olsson and Dee Murray, Elton's drummer and bassist since the beginning of his career, have just left the band and want to cut the new songs with me. I think this is a frigging great idea. I've met Nigel at a couple of parties and we've gotten along well. We cut the whole album at Sound City as a three-piece band. They also sing background vocals on the songs, and, truly, it sounds amazing. I am over the moon. It's also the very first time I've triple-tracked electric guitar parts. The songs sound huge! Again I think the ballads are my best songs on the album.

I pose for an appropriately movie-esque photo for the front cover (although I'm getting sick of putting my face on every record I make), Chelsea prints up copies, and Wes cleans off an area of wall space in his office in anticipation of the first gold record we will get. I can almost see the shiny record on the wall, and I like that visual.

I meet Susan George, the hot English actress who played opposite Dustin Hoffman in the Sam Peckinpah film *Straw Dogs*, in Wes's office and she says she thinks the album is really good, so I jump in the sack with her. It doesn't occur to me 'til later that maybe Wes had designs on Susan, too, and maybe banging the record company owner's prospective "shag" isn't the best way to endear myself to him. It's hard to stay straight on my career path, when I keep shooting myself in the foot with my dick.

When the album is finished, I put another band together, Nigel and Dee being a little too expensive as a touring band for me at this time. The drummer I choose is a fresh-faced hard hitter from Detroit named Jack White. We can't know it then, but he will remain the drummer in all my bands for the next thirty years. We have similar issues with women and get into more than one bloody fight on the road over who has the seeding rights to which girl at any given time. It's a good, solid band, except for the bass player, who keeps falling asleep at rehearsals and leaving early to meet a friend. I don't know it at the time, but he's a heroin addict. Eventually we replace him with Robbie Levin, a really fine player but an even better entrepreneur. While I'm paying Robbie $100 a week to rehearse, he's making $50,000 a month selling T-shirts and will eventually make millions through an expanded clothing line and a vacation resort in Idaho—but he'll retain the unquenchable desire to be a musician: it never, *ever* leaves your soul, no matter how much money you make doing something else.

Chelsea releases *Wait for Night*. It gets great reviews, the single "Take a Hand" hits the charts, the band gets a pretty serious string of gigs, we start touring, and then . . . Goddammit!!! Wes Farrell divorces his wife. His wife happens to be Frank Sinatra's youngest daughter, Tina. I think Frank calls in his loan, because Chelsea Records folds like a house of Las Vegas playing cards. *Wait for Night* is DOA.

Am I in the wrong business? Is this a sign that I should have kept to the "electrician" backup plan like my mum wanted? Or—and this is where my insatiable drive kicks in—am I being tested to see how bad I want it?

Well, I want it. Bad.

I'm very career-driven and impatient for success. But that impatience doesn't make the success come any sooner, and it flows into other areas of my life where it doesn't belong. I make spur-of-the-moment bad decisions that leave me feeling even worse, not better.

My band and I happen to be in Portland, Oregon, the moment the call comes through that Chelsea is out of business and all my blood, sweat, and tears have been for nothing (again). Portland happens to be the home of "The Flying Garter Girls" (FGG for short), a group of women led by a twenty-five-year-old groupie who recruits young, hot girls and schools them in the very fine art of satisfying the many bands that come through the area. I head to the hotel bar to give my band the bad news about Chelsea, and the Flying Garter Girls are there, gossiping about a new band they've just serviced (well, honestly, I don't think they serviced the *whole* band: Queen). I'm angry and dispirited. I should be calling home to reach out to Diana—a good woman who supports me with her whole heart and would probably talk me down off the ledge. Instead, I decide to drown my sorrows in the instant gratification and temporary high of the FGGs.

I would say at this point that I am as driven sexually as I am career-driven, even though my music career has stalled once more. However, I'm not the only one in my life who is driven, because who should climb into my hotel bed with me as I am shaft-deep in one of the Flying Garter Girls? Yes, it's Mr. Darkness, and he hisses ominously that I'm now zero-for-three in the record business. "Starting to get a bit of a rep as a loser, mate."

But I do go home and begin to regroup and rebuild. It's in my nature now: to keep going, to never give up. I have another phrase in my head, no doubt inspired by all the goal-attainment books I've read: *There is more than one way in.* Maybe I've been going about this all wrong. So Diana and I decide to rent a small theater and put on a one-act play starring . . . us. If no one will hire us, then we'll bloody well hire ourselves. We begin rehearsals and start looking for a cheap theater.

A few weeks later, an envelope drops into my mail slot. It's a check from a music residual collecting agency made payable to me, for $3.50 . . . no, wait . . . $35.—No, wait . . . $350. NO, WAIT! It's $3,500!!! There is no way this money is mine, so I call up the agency and, judging from the sound of her voice, an older lady answers. I tell her my name and that I think they must have mailed this check to me by mistake. She answers, "Honey, just cash the check." So I do.

The play we choose is a short one-act called *Lunchtime* by Leonard Melfi. We invite every casting person on the face of the planet to the crappy room-turned-into-a-theater that we've found up an alleyway off Fairfax Avenue. It runs for a week, and all sixteen of our friends show up. But no casting people. Not a fucking one—even though they all said they would. No one, that is, except for a wonderful man named Milt Hammerman, who is head of the contract players division at Universal. I guess he likes what he sees, because he signs me to a contract deal at Universal Studios. Diana is thrilled for me but hurts for herself, and this is why I never date another actress or musician. Careers tend to advance at different speeds, and it's a huge pressure when a couple's careers move out of step.

I start guest starring in Universal's big '70s TV shows. *Battlestar Galactica, The Rockford Files, The Incredible Hulk, Wonder Woman, Turnabout, The Eddie Capra Mysteries, The Six Million Dollar Man, The Nancy Drew Mysteries*—the list goes on and on. Well, not really. That's pretty much it.

Diana, who is a much more accomplished actor than I am, is waiting tables at a local restaurant. She also narrowly escapes being raped one night, and after a transvestite is shot to death outside the apartment building we're both living in, we sagely decide it's time to boogie to the 'burbs. I swallow my doubts about living full-time with a girlfriend, and Diana, her sweet dog Sasha, and I move out to the slightly smoggier but slightly safer area of Glendale, California, where we rent a minister's two-bedroom house. We get some chickens (I leave their heads fully attached to their bodies this time), paint and decorate, and generally become quite the little suburbanites.

Since I'm making my only money from acting, I throw my energy into it, but an actor's life is filled with days, weeks, and months of waiting, so I continue to write songs and silently keep my radar aimed at the vast, open, and very empty field of incoming record deals.

My mum is now confident enough managing my father that she books a trip for the both of them. She wants to see her relatives in England as well as visit me, so they hit the skies. My mother says later that all through Europe my poor dad—who I'm sure she dragged to every musty old castle in the vicinity—kept asking, "When are we going to see Rick?"

They finally arrive, and I unwittingly put them up in a motel whose regular clientele are hookers and their johns. The next day my mother tells me what an odd room they're staying in. "Why would anyone put mirrors on the ceiling above the bed?" I move them to a Holiday Inn.

They stay for a few days, meet Diana's family (my mum thinks Diana is her future daughter-in-law, and at this point I guess I believe that, too), see the tourist sights, hit Disneyland, and all too soon they're ready to head back to Oz. Dad is sweet and seems quite adjusted to his life as a five-year-old, but I still see the tension on my mother's face from constantly having to watch out for him. I kiss my dad good-bye at the airport. Even in his present state he is still my champion. I have always felt his warm, steady, unwavering love. It was the thing I clung to when my mother and I were at war in my teens, and it's what I cling to even now. In his diminished capacity, without all of life's distractions running through his tangled mind, his support is clearer and more focused than ever before. I feel it in a way I can't truly articulate.

Since my manager Joe (whose office is under the car ramp to the roof parking for the studio, which speaks volumes about the competent hands I am in) owns Sound City, I suggest we make a record "on spec." This means we'll record a whole album's worth of songs at the studio's expense and then shop the finished product, giving us a better shot at a label deal. Joe, to my great surprise, agrees. Clearly, there is an upside to his inexperience as a manager, God bless him.

Tom Perry has just come off recording Boz Scaggs's *Silk Degrees* album, which has yielded a few good hit singles and launched Boz into the musical stratosphere. Tom agrees to produce the spec record, and away we go again. I have written what I think is another strong batch of songs, and we assemble a band and start recording. Tom is also dating the recording studio manager, a bright and funny Englishwoman named Jemimah. One day, while we're slaving away over a hot studio console, Jemimah brings a young girl who she's just befriended into Studio A; she's hired her to answer the phones over the summer holidays. This petite girl is wearing a white shirt, tight black jeans, and a loose-fitting man's black tie. Looking very much like a French schoolgirl, she's introduced to all of us, amid the collective sound of various musicians' jaws hitting the floor, as Barbara Porter. She is so extremely hot that I say a brief "Hi" and turn back to the console to continue working while everyone else in the room tries to chat her up. Why should I risk certain rejection?

Despite my healthy young male desire to procreate, or at least go through the motions, and my pretty good success rate in that area, I'm still a complete dope when it comes to actually communicating with a woman. The reason I've been so fortunate in the sexual arena so far is that because I'm a musician, girls have generally approached me and struck up a conversation to convey their intent. This way my pathetically fragile ego hasn't had to step out onto a limb and risk getting my hand slapped (again).

So I blow this girl off. She leaves. She is also only fifteen. I tell myself I'm not going to jail no matter how hot a girl is, and I think I do a pretty good job of convincing myself.

Lucky for me, I don't have the final say in the matter.

CHAPTER ELEVEN

SO LONG, CHICKENS; THANKS FOR THE EGGS

THE BURBS: GLENDALE, CALIFORNIA
1979

My fourth attempt to make a record that the fickle record-buying bastard public will buy is complete. Joe shops it and sets up a meeting with the one record label interested: Mercury. I go away on my final trip as a YMCA counselor, up to the Sacramento River, with a co-ed group of kids. My meeting with the label is on the day before the YMCA trip ends, so I'll have to come back to LA early. The group of counselors is also co-ed. We're camping out in the middle of nowhere and the night before I'm supposed to leave—at 4:00 the following morning to make my meeting with Mercury Records—I crawl into the sleeping bag of one of the female mentors and have at it. This late, late at night romp causes me to wake up waaaaaay past my planned departure time and I jump into the tiny motorboat they've arranged to take me back to Sacramento, still pulling on my pants and tying my shoes.

We hurry, attempting to make up for lost time, so of course we get lost. Really lost. Really, *really* lost. At one point, in the still pitch-black early morning, we see a set of red and green lights up ahead. Only at the last possible moment do we realize it's a fairly good-sized ship. We get out of the way just in time as it barrels past us, almost swamping our little boat. I eventually make it back to LA (by car), but I have missed the meeting with the record label. And they don't want to reschedule, either.

I hear a loud report: I look down at the bullet hole in my foot and my still-smoking penis and realize I've done it again. Shit!

My old friend Milt Hammerman of Universal Studios' contract-player division has his assistant call to tell me the contract-player program is cancelled and I am out of work. Mum calls to say the cancer has now spread to my dad's lymph system. Diana's pet rabbit calls to say it's just dropped dead. I wait for the train to hit me but it doesn't come. My old friend Mr. Darkness does, though.

Down I go.

"Nice one, dipshit. Home run," I hear his mean susurration. I cry out of frustration, disappointment, and fear. I stop writing songs. I feel like it's over. The meeting with Mercury that I've just blown was hard for Joe to land, because every record company now believes they have a handle on who I am, or was—an ex-teen-idol wannabe. The "Speak to the Sky" guy who had the cartoon show. I know I'll go insane and the Darkness will completely take me over if I don't keep myself busy, so I buy some modeling clay. I start sculpting figures of aliens, spaceships, even a sinking *Titanic*, and glue them to mirrors. I set up stalls at swap meets and try to convince people, who are really out looking for cheap T-shirts, to buy my crap instead. Diana takes five minutes one Sunday to whip up two dozen Raggedy Anns and Andys that she cuts out of my sculpting clay with a cookie-cutter and joins me at the next Pasadena Rose Bowl swap meet. Her cookie-cutter dolls sell out. I sell one mirror. I am really starting to wonder what it is exactly about my creative output that people are resisting in droves.

I spend the next year or so growing a beard and hanging with the chickens in the backyard. I am becoming somewhat domesticated. I start writing a few songs, but they are unfocused and one is even (God help me) a stab at disco. It's difficult to get motivated, having had no real success for a long time and with no clear goal to reach for. I want my music to be heard, but there's no record deal on the horizon, and singing my songs on a street corner with an upturned hat isn't going to do much for me. If it weren't about connection and the desire to excite people with something I've created, I'd just write the damn songs, demo them up, and stick them happily on a shelf in my music room.

Diana's parents are Protestants and regular churchgoers, so I start attending their church with them, something I haven't done since my mother forced me to go at gunpoint. After my first visit, we're in line shaking hands with the minister who gave the service. He's saying quick "Thank you for comings" and "God bless yous," but when I reach him, he holds my gaze for a moment as though something has caught his attention. "You should think about entering the clergy," he says out of absolutely nowhere. It shocks me because, although I've never been a devout Christian, the idea of devotion has always appealed to me. I'm so disheartened by the lack of progress with my music, I've actually been wondering if the priesthood might be a next-best option for me. I've long sought a deeper connection with this world and the people in it—something beyond the mindless "How you doin' today?" And I accept that if we're open to it, there is a spirit, Supreme Being, collective consciousness—whatever the name—that offers guidance and communion for us all. And I've told no one about these thoughts or about my possible plan to become a priest. How could this minister intuit them?

The minister's comment and the implied knowledge behind it are my wake-up call. I don't choose the priesthood, but I rise from my somnambulant existence and start the process, again, of turning my situation around. And it's true that as miserable as it always made me each time I changed schools, it did endow me with a special resilience. A real-time experience of turning a situation around. There's a great saying that has stayed with me through the years (and I've needed it): Every dark situation brings with it the seed of an equal or greater opportunity. The "seed" meaning, you have to work for it. It doesn't come on a plate with garnishings. And the thing about hard-won lessons is that they're surer to stay with us because of the cost of learning them.

My persistent (some would say "insane") effort to become successful with my music is more than just not wanting to go back home a failure.

It's always been more. I truly feel that success will make me well. Will heal me. I feel this in my core. It's the drug I need in order to finally be happy and to know that I'm okay. I need it. And I will have it!

I put together a band of musician friends who, like me, need to make some money. We start a weekly gig at a local restaurant/bar playing other bands' hit songs. The girls haven't been much in attendance through my "bearded chicken-man" period, but now that I have a guitar in my hands, they are back. I love the guitar. It gave me a voice as a young out-of-sync teenager, and I still feel that it's my way out of the insecurity, insignificance, and general discomfort I feel in my own skin. And right at this moment, in a back room of the restaurant where we're performing nightly, that skin is getting some much-needed attention.

During a set break, in a back room at the restaurant, Diana catches me with a female customer one night and is mortified (a) that I'm doing it, (b) that I'm doing it in public, and (c) that I don't seem to care that she's caught me. The truth is, although I love Diana, I'm increasingly feeling trapped and uninspired by the relationship. I think I'm trying to break up with her, but I keep flip-flopping on whether it would be the right thing to do or not. I also sense that I'm too much of a coward (shit, my dad was right) to take the initiative. I don't want to lose the closeness I have with her family. Plus, I'm crazy about her dog. But I also find myself thinking now and then of that young girl (thankfully getting older by the minute) who's now answering phones full-time at Joe's studio. She of the Brigitte Bardot pout—Barbara Porter.

Playing the restaurant/bar gig begins to give me a germ of an idea. I'm also inspired by the new rash of LA clubs that seem to be opening up, and the press, attention, and followings that unknown bands like the Knack—soon to be famous for their monster hit, "My Sharona"—are garnering playing these clubs. It's 1979 and I can smell the heady stink of the early stages of putrefaction emanating from the almost-corpse of disco. Thank God! And I feel like the all-powerful and roaring electric guitar is due for a rebirth. I start writing for real, with the thought of assembling a great band to play my music and start gigging around LA.

Besides, we've just been fired from the highly prestigious restaurant/bar gig, so my nights are pretty much my own now.

I'm never higher than when I'm in the throes of a serious songwriting binge, and I'm on one now. While Diana is at work, I have all day to write, play with the dog, write, play with the dog, write, play with . . . well, you get it, right?

Each morning, while I'm waiting for Diana to leave, I get nervous like I'm meeting a clandestine lover. And she's waiting, in my music room. My muse. We all have one. (A muse, I mean, not a clandestine lover). The spark of creativity that's there to ignite the fires of creation. It's fucking awesome, and when it happens with me I get warm and flushed and quickly adopt the thousand-yard stare . . . I am not here. I'm . . . *there*. It doesn't happen every time; in fact, it doesn't happen a lot of the time, but when it does, it's a drug that I want to hit again and again.

When I'm really connected to writing, another mind enters the process, and that's when things are revealed that I couldn't possibly have come up with on my own. It's that all-powerful spirit/Supreme Being/collective consciousness thing again. It gets behind me and propels me forward, and ideas manifest that normally would not, if I were, say, just sitting on the couch watching *Dancing with the Stars*. Songs also isolate and freeze a moment in time. I hear a song, whether it's one I've written about a particular event, or someone else's song that I have a connection with, and all the memories associated with hearing or writing it come rushing back. To me, the creation of music seems almost like magic. It's the white rabbit that's pulled from the top hat.

I call Jack White, the drummer from my aborted 1976 *Wait for Night* tour. He rounds up some players, and we meet at my manager Joe's Sound City Studio (where Barbara is still answering phones—I ignore her, of course). I bring a couple of the new songs I've been writing and the other guitar player brings some of his. We rehearse all afternoon in Studio B. Jack keeps saying, "Hey, let's play that 'Jessie' song again man, that's cool." The other guitar player tries to steer us back to his songs, but Jack won't have it. I'm pleased with his reaction to my new music. We end the rehearsal and plan another one later next week.

I continue writing. I like the path the new songs are taking. It will be simple to play them in the clubs with just guitars, bass, and drums; the choruses are pretty catchy, so people might grab on to them faster; and they are concise—all under three minutes in length—so if one isn't going over with the crowd, it's okay folks, keep your seats, another one will be along shortly.

I'm revitalized with my new songs and also by what's happening to the music scene in general. There's a powered-by-punk shift away from the orchestrated dance music and ballads of the era. People are starting to get rowdy again. And the volume on the mystical electric guitar is slowly being turned up.

I go back to acting class to kick that into working order. Vincent Chase is still at it. He asks me if Diana and I are going to get married. "I guess," I answer, half-resigned to the inevitable. Then I meet Jennifer of the Cartesian-philosophy-conversation-that-never-happened. We stay out all night and end up at her apartment and I know it's over between Diana and me, finally. She and I begin the long, drawn-out finale to our relationship.

A dirty, scruffy, black-and-white bull-terrier-mix mutt is walking aimlessly around the Glendale library parking lot one morning, dodging cars and looking nervous. Diana, because she is a good woman, picks him up, puts him in her car, brings him home, and sticks him in the garage, for me. A last gift from her to the man she thought she'd marry. I name this dog Lethal Ron for reasons mentioned earlier.

My mum is writing to me, worried because the doctors are sticking my dad with needles and drawing his blood to try to find out why he isn't getting nauseated or losing his hair from all the chemo he is enduring. It is a mystery to everyone, but she doesn't want them prodding and poking him to discover the answer. I push thoughts of my dying father out of my mind, for now. I know he would understand.

Then Joe calls to say he has some label interest in me from RCA. What?

I am determined not to screw up this last chance. I look somewhere other than to God for my strength. We're still not cool because of the way he's treated my sweet old man. Instead, I look to my very powerful "positive thinking" path and begin a heavy-duty self-awareness program called Lifespring. Eighteen hours a day for five days, I and thirty-five other needy, desperate losers subject ourselves to all kinds of techniques designed to get past the protective bullshit we've constructed over the course of a lifetime and to target our vital inner core. Our days ping-pong between moments of self-revelation, brutal honesty, and heart-opening exercises. There *is* a spiritual leaning to the whole program, but it's safely far away from any particular denomination, so I don't feel alienated by it.

I rise from the week transformed, affirmed, and with a new best friend: Ernie. Unbeknownst to me, Ernie is gay and has developed a thing for Yours Cluelessly, though of course Mr. Guileless here doesn't pick up on any of that. I find the balls to ask Barbara out on a date (lucky me, she's just turned eighteen, so no jail time is required) and when she agrees (really?) we go to a movie and end up at my manager's old house, where I'm living for a while, thanks to his benevolence.

Barbara is bright, sweet, funny . . . and burning hot. After a few beers, I make a move to get her into bed . . . she resists. I move, she resists. I move . . . okay, you get it. She tells me she's only ever had sex once before and that I know who the guy is. "Oh, no! Is it Bill?" I think in alarm. I've only just started working with Bill Drescher, an in-house engineer at Sound City, planning the recording of the new album for RCA. I know he's taken Barbara out a few times and has a giant crush on her, but I didn't think he'd actually beaten me to the punch. This could put a serious crimp in matters, as Bill and I are looking at long hours together, locked up in a windowless studio, making the record. "Bill?" I sputter. "No," she says, "it's not Bill." I relax, but only a little. I still have serious and truly lame, jealous, don't-piss-on-my-lawn issues. Someone has been sleeping in my bed! And I haven't even slept in it yet, though I am getting the feeling, as Barbara reveals more, that it is a distinct possibility tonight.

Shyly, but with a slight hint of pride, she says, "It was Peter Frampton." "Peter Frampton, the singer?" I exclaim in horror. Frampton, who is a longtime friend of Jemimah the studio manager, has recently been recording at Sound City and has been Barbara's girlhood crush since she was thirteen. It all fits—dammit!!! Who am I to deny a young girl the fulfillment of her teenage rock-star crush? But I do, and I'm incredibly resentful, mainly because he's successful and I'm still sucking mud at the bottom of the pond. It shouldn't matter, but it does.

The Darkness checks in briefly. "Gonna be pretty tough to measure up to a famous guy, huh, Rickyboy?" I'm feeling strong now, so I push him out. We do end up in bed, Barbara and I. It is the most amazing night, and I will never forget it. We wake in the morning and I think we're in love. My brand-new, furry soul mate Lethal Ron has propped himself up against the outside of the big bedroom window, looking in at us with a slightly perplexed expression. He's never been locked outside my bedroom before and is probably wondering what exactly is making that shape next to me where he usually sleeps.

From that very first night, this girl gives me a feeling I've never had before. (No, I've had *that* feeling before—I'm talking about one somewhere in and around my heart.) The last thing I want right now is a new girlfriend, but I find myself wondering what she's doing wanting to phone her. I stop calling other girls because I want to be with her. This girl has really gotten to me. We start seeing each other regularly, much to Ernie's chagrin, is a good friend nonetheless, and when I sign the deal with RCA and get a $5,000 record advance, I buy a house and he agrees to move in and pay me rent so I can shoulder the burden of a mortgage.

I begin recording at the studio where Barbara still works. She sleeps over at the new house a lot of the time. Before long, I decide I want her to move in. When she questions me about Ernie and his designs on me, I'm astonished. "What? Ernie's not *gay*!" She starts laughing; she thinks I'm joking. And then it dawns on me: he's been making my bed for me, cooking for me, cleaning the house, giving me back rubs whenever I want them—duh! I know now what it will mean to Ernie when I tell him that Barbara's moving in. And I'm right, because he says that if she's moving in, then he's moving out. And he does. Now it's me, B (my shorthand nickname for her), and Lethal Ron in our little love nest on Broadview Drive, Glendale. Yes, I am definitely in love.

B's mom, Pat, is a little concerned about this thirty-year-old gentleman (me?) who her young daughter is living with. She wants to meet me. She says later that she was expecting some older guy in a leisure suit telling her he's "quite fond of young Barbara." In other words, someone with his act together. When I show up, an immature might-as-well-be-adolescent with a record deal, Pat understands why the relationship is working. Although there is a twelve-year age gap between B and me, it's obvious to Pat that I'm really the younger one in the equation. She sees how connected we are, not to mention that we can't keep our hands off each other. Pat is our supporter from that moment on and sees the romance in our relationship that she knows she's missed in her own. Now I love Barbara's *mom*, too.

I get the call to come in and read for *General Hospital*. I've always been a nervous auditioner when it comes to trying out for acting roles. I feel judged (which I am) and under the microscope (again, true). It has very little to do with the art of acting, this reading process, and every actor has to go through it. But something has changed in me since I've begun seeing B. She likes who I am, at this moment. She loves our little house and will later confide that she thought we would live there forever. I don't need to be anything more than I am right now, as far as she is concerned. I see this in her eyes and hear it in her voice. Her complete acceptance gives me great strength and confidence and a "don't-really-give-a-shit" attitude, so I go in and kill the audition and land the part. Barbara is responsible for that. Her unconditional and perfect love make what is about to happen to me possible.

It's nearing Christmas, and my mum asks me if I could come home for a visit. So I leave my new girl and new dog and fly to see my old mum and old dad in Australia.

CHAPTER TWELVE

WHAT'S THE POINT OF BEING A DOCTOR IF EVERYBODY DIES?

OPPOSITE ENDS OF THE EARTH: LA AND AUSTRALIA

1981

I'm beginning to feel like a visitor in my homeland. Going back to Oz has less of the sensation of a homecoming; it's more like I'm looking through a box of old photos from a dusty attic. In my upstairs bedroom, I rummage through songs I wrote when I was a teenager (thankfully they'll never see the light of day), drawings I made, poems I wrote, and dumb things I collected, and I go to sleep in the same bed I've always slept in at my parents' house. Downstairs my dad battles the cancer and my mum picks up after him like he's her child. No one talks of dying. I long to ask my father how he's dealing with it, but how do you talk to a five-year-old about death? Instead, we pull out the tinfoil Christmas tree my mother bought years ago in order to save a few real trees, decorate it, and quietly slip our presents to each other beneath its aluminum branches.

My dad always wanted a pocket watch. I give him an antique one that I bought for him at the Pasadena Rose Bowl on one of the days I was out there hawking my mirrors. I spent way more than I made that day. I've had his initials—NJS—engraved on the inside along with the sentiment, "To Dad, love, Rick." I feel like something is missing in our house now that Cleo is gone and I go to a shelter and get them a puppy—with paws the size of snowshoes—that my mum names "Flora," another frigging name from another century. (Flora will soon grow too big for their yard, and my mum, already overwhelmed with my dad, will decide to give her away four months later. My lifelong atrocious luck with the family-dog combo holds true to form.) We take photos and I hug and hold my dad and wish him healing. He says "Go get 'em, son." I board the plane that will take me back "home." I can't bring myself to say "Good-bye, Dad," so I say "I'll see you later."

I wish it were true.

Barbara is waiting for me at LAX with Lethal Ron in the car. I'm excited to be back. "Lethal Ron" soon wears out its welcome as a name, so I shorten it to Ron, then lengthen it to Ronnie, then modify that to Arnie, then distort that to Arnfarn, and so on and so on. It seems my old man's trait for endlessly evolving loopy dog nicknames is alive and well in his second son.

And his second son is definitely in love with the feisty little firecracker of a girlfriend he has miraculously managed to keep interested in him. So I do the right thing and go meet Barbara's dad, having already met her mom. Her mom loves me; her dad, not so much. I figure one out of two isn't bad.

The album is complete, but I have a concern about something. I'm giving serious thought to releasing the new record under a "band" name, as I'm worried about all the baggage that goes along with "Rick Springfield." I'm gun-shy about my own name (or at least, Pete Watson's version of my own name) after all the teen-idol crap from the '70s. Joe and RCA talk me into keeping the RS moniker on the album, but I'm adamant that I won't have another "beauty" shot of me on the front cover. Instead, I tell them that I'm dressing my dog up in a shirt and tie (thank you, Yan the snappy dresser), putting him on the cover, and calling the record *Working Class Dog*. RCA thinks I'm joking. I am soon to be the new face on a national TV show that's fast becoming a summer phenomenon and I want my dog on the cover? I'm determined not to be swayed this time. I'll mock up a cover and show them what I mean.

I measure Ronnie's neck—eighteen inches around—and head off to a big-and-tall men's store to get him a shirt. The conversation goes something like this:

Me: I'd like a white dress shirt with an eighteen-inch neck, please.
Sales guy: Certainly. And what length sleeves are we talking here?
Me: It doesn't matter.
Sales guy: Well, just give me a ballpark number. Is he a thirty-inch sleeve—a thirty-five?

I know he's not going to let up.

Me: Twelve.
Sales guy: Twelve? Twelve what?
Me: Twelve inches. His arm length is twelve inches.

We stare at each other for a moment or two. Somewhere in the distance a lonely cricket chirps and a train whistle blows.

Sales guy: How 'bout a short-sleeved shirt, then?
Me: Sounds good.

More to their credit, when I show RCA the mocked-up cover, the suits get the idea and we are off and running. We do a hilarious photo session with my patient dog, who's dressed for hours in the shirt and tie. I tempt and reward him with dog cookies and at the last minute I shove a black-and-white photo of me in his shirt pocket as a kind of joke to the RCA art department, who are still insisting that I be on the cover.

In the photo we finally choose, Ronnie's smiling broadly and looks like he's having a blast. But now the label is having concerns about the album itself. Although everyone can sense disco is wearing out its welcome (thank the gods of music), as are the big syrupy ballads, no one can guess that they will both shortly be replaced on the radio waves by rock and roll. RCA is hesitating to release *Working Class Dog*, for fear it will fall on deaf ears. I start getting anxious too. I know the album is good, but honestly, I just don't want all our hard work wasted again.

Another week goes by and RCA pushes the album's release to the following month. This happens again no less than three times. I am freaking out. Thank God I at least have the TV thing starting up soon. For the first time in my life, I'll have a pretty decent and regular income, and that eases some of the frustration I'm feeling about the record. RCA finally sets a release date for *WCD* and assures me they will keep to it. I'm relieved, excited, and truly happy.

Then my mum calls to say my father's cancer has now metastasized to his brain. They've shaved his head of all the hair he was so proud to have kept through his many chemo treatments, in order to focus the radiation more directly on the tumor. She sends photos. He's sitting in his chair in our tiny TV room, smiling sweetly and looking like a big bald baby. Because I'm not living there with them, I can conveniently shift the pain and fear back a little in my awareness. I must get on with my life.

On March 3, 1981, I go into the *General Hospital* set for my first day of shooting. I am beyond nervous. The show has been running for years, with pretty much the same cast, and everyone is in the flow and has their cliques and friendships. Oh, no, it's the first day at a new school again! I struggle through day one just as I've done so many times before in other settings, and, as has always happened, it gradually gets easier; I make friends and begin to find my place. I'm elated to be working regularly. After two weeks on the show, people are starting to stare at me on the street. It's unnerving at first, and unexpected. I am learning that this is the power of TV. I keep checking myself in store windows to see if I have an errant booger or maybe my fly is open.

Meanwhile, RCA finally keeps its word and, without much fanfare, they release *Working Class Dog*. Again the promotion department of a record company kicks into overdrive on a record of mine, but things are feeling different this time around. As I fly to New York to do radio and press, word starts coming in that stations across the country are playing different cuts from the album. I've never had this happen before. Usually you have to kiss their ball sacks morning, noon, and night just to have them play the damn single, but stations are picking their own favorites and playing them and writing about them in the trade papers. And something else is happening. I'm starting to get decent amounts of fan mail at ABC, something TV producers take big note of. Gloria Monty, *GH*'s producer/Svengali and the woman who hired me, starts putting my character into more episodes.

RCA releases the first single. No, not *that* song. With nine of the ten tracks on the record written by me, they release the only one that isn't—"I've Done Everything for You." I think they figure it will have a better shot because Sammy Hagar's name is attached to it as the writer. I'm okay with it. I think it's a good song. I would have preferred that one of my own be the single, but all that matters is that we launch the album with a hit. The thing is, radio doesn't pick up "I've Done Everything for You," and although other tracks from *Working Class Dog* are being played, "I've Done Everything for You" isn't making the rotations. It bombs.

Then something magical happens. A gift. Word starts coming in to RCA that radio is starting to get strong "phones" on a particular song off the album. And in a move that couldn't happen today because of radio's tight playlists and corporate fingers in the pie, the radio stations of America choose the single, and that single is "Jessie's Girl." RCA releases the song, and it begins its tortuously slow climb up the charts.

RCA gives me $1,500 to shoot two videos. For what purpose, I don't know. I write up a script and storyboard the "Jessie's Girl" video, but I leave the "I've Done Everything for You" video to the cameraman/director, Mark Stinson. We shoot everything in three days. It's guerrilla video-filming at its finest. At 3:00 a.m. we're shooting the opening scenes to "Jessie's Girl" in a Hollywood alleyway with the song blasting through portable speakers when someone yells that the cops are coming. We toss our gear into the van and tear off into the night. It's so fucking cool.

Our big expense in special effects is the twenty-four bathroom mirrors I break in the middle section of the song. No one, including myself at this point, understands my reasoning for smashing the mirror in a bathroom setting. They certainly don't know about my adolescent years spent staring into that depressing thing. And that it's precisely there where the Darkness lives and breathes. Looking at the video now, I see a lot of real pain on my face in that scene as I splinter the mirrors with the headstock of my guitar.

I walk onto the *GH* set one morning and everyone's talking about the "Jessie's Girl" video. It turns out that the night before, heavyweight champion Larry Holmes defended his title against Leon Spinks. The fight was broadcast on cable. Lucky for me and for Holmes, Spinks was knocked out in the third round. When the fight ended much earlier than expected, some desperate TV guy had gone scrambling for anything to fill the empty airspace and his incredibly-lucky-for-me fingers landed on my videocassette. So everyone has seen it. And then MTV calls to say they'd like to interview me and play the video. "What is MTV?" I ask. Nobody seems to know, but it's press, so next time I'm in New York I find myself in a tiny hole-in-the-wall in a not-great neighborhood talking to a kid named Martha Quinn who looks like she's twelve. She asks me questions about the video of "Jessie's Girl." I believe she is the first to ask the questions I've answered more than any other: "So, was there really a Jessie's girl?" I'm suddenly flying all over the place doing TV and radio interviews and playing "Jessie's Girl" for whoever will listen.

I soon find out that it's more than blue-haired little old ladies who watch *General Hospital*. Our audience includes colleges full of young adults, high schools full of kids, houses full of stay-at-home mothers and, yes, blue-haired little old ladies as well. Stars watch it, too, they tell me when I meet Elizabeth Taylor (when she guests on *GH*), Sammy Davis, Jr. (who approaches me as we walk down the red carpet for the first *Night of 100 Stars*), Brian Wilson (when we do a gig with the Beach Boys), and Little Richard (who sits with me at Sound City one night, singing to me and trying to convince me to record a song of his), just to drop some more names. Come on, you know it's expected.

Gloria Monty sidles up to me one day on the set and says, "I hear you're a musician, too. We'd like you to sing on the show." I've already started to hear that a few of the album-oriented stations have stopped playing "Jessie's Girl" as soon as they found out I'm on a soap opera. It's the double-edged sword that Keith Olsen warned me about. I refuse to sing on *GH*, as I will later refuse to allow the licensing of Rick Springfield lunch boxes and girls' swimsuits, and as I'll say no to doing Converse ads and singing on a McDonald's commercial. I need to keep my music separate from the degree of cheesiness attached to "Daytime Drama."

Jack White, my spirited drummer, has rounded up a few musicians and we're all busy rehearsing for some upcoming shows that promise to actually have an audience that actually hasn't just wandered in off the street, when Joe breaks into the rehearsal room carrying some glasses and a cheap bottle of champagne. "Jessie's Girl" has just reached Number 1 on the *Billboard* charts and is looking like it could become a worldwide hit. Cheap champagne never tasted so good. I am on the way to what I always felt was my destiny—that thing I believed I was saved for when the rope came unraveled long ago in the backyard shed. But there's still a painful detour I have to make just up ahead.

I come home from *GH* one evening and the message light is blinking on my '70s-style PhoneMate answering machine. I hit the playback button and my brother Mike's voice, broken and dire, comes out of the small speaker. "Rick. Call home. Dad is gravely ill." I call Mike back. On the other side of the world, my champion sleeps in a stark hospital bed, drugged against the pain. Mum has been sitting with him night and day for two weeks, but she needs to go home so she can get some clean clothes and check on the house. She dashes out, hoping to be back by her husband's side within three hours. My dad, I think, has stayed around at this point because he knows his wife is desperate not to lose him. But it's time to go.

And an hour after his best girl has left the hospital grounds, my father, my champ, my sweet old man, leaves this world forever. Eileen Louise Springthorpe, née Evennett, arrives home to the phone ringing, answers it, and hears the words she has prepared herself for years to hear, but they still shatter her. Our man is dead for the second and final time. Normie at last makes it home. I am woken in the early hours of a Friday morning by my brother's second phone call. He tells me Dad is gone. I am at least twenty hours away from my family in Melbourne, and I'm scheduled to be on the set of *General Hospital* in three hours. I think about what my dad would do in my place. His work ethic would say, "Finish your job, Son." His heart would say, "Take care of your mum." So I do both.

I book a flight home to Australia leaving that afternoon and I arrive on the ABC set at 8:00 a.m. as I'm supposed to do. The only one I tell is Gloria Monty, who moves my scenes forward in the daily schedule so I can finish early and get to the airport in time for my flight home. It's still all so raw and new that I just can't talk about it, because I know if someone comes up to me and hugs me or offers words of condolence, I will crumble. So I make my face into a mask, finish the scripted scenes, and get myself to the airport. *General Hospital* gives me four days to fly to Australia, attend the service for my dad, and then fly back to resume my shift as Dr. Noah Drake. I take the fourteen-hour journey home once again. I'm in shock, as are Mum and Mike, even though we knew it was coming, and my two days at home go by like moments spent in someone else's life.

We have a service at my mum's church, then family and friends convene at our house to talk, to cry, to miss him together, and to prove to ourselves that life goes on. The doorbell rings, my brother answers, and I watch through a fog as our dad's ashes, all that remain of him, cross over our threshold one final time. We rent a little fishing boat to take us out on the bay the following morning—it's gray and stormy, the sort of sea my dad loved—and we cast his ashes into the waves that are threatening to overturn our craft. For lack of any initiative from the rest of us, Mike steps into the breach and does the deed, intoning "Ashes to ashes, dust to dust." I don't know what these words mean, but I have nothing to say myself. I'm numb. My champion is gone, and I begin to lose what small remaining faith I have in God.

My spirit commences a long, slow spiral down. Meanwhile, forces already in play on the other side of the world are conspiring to launch my usually sub-sea-level ego toward the stratosphere. In America, *Working Class Dog* is actually climbing the charts. It's the kind of success I've been longing to savor for what feels like my whole life. I've fought for this overture to success for so long that to just roll into a ball and fully absorb my father's death is not an option. If four days is all I'm given by *GH*, then four days is all I will allow myself to grieve. After that, I will again grab the brass ring that is about to yank me up. My champion would understand.

But on the plane on my way home, I end up curled in a fetal position on the floor in front of my seat with my stomach writhing and twisting. My body is trying instinctively to roll me into that ball, but when the plane lands, I straighten myself up and walk down the jet bridge to my new life.

CHAPTER THIRTEEN

WE HAVE IGNITION

ON THE ROAD

The '80s

I feel better once I'm home with Barbara and Ronnie, but there are schedules to meet and work to be done, so I'm soon on another plane, this time to New York.

If I thought I was doing pretty well with women up until this point, I am in delighted awe at how I am suddenly doing pretty fucking amazingly well. And I see no problem, nor do I feel any guilt, in continuing with my "musician's lifestyle," even though I have a girl at home that I am truly in love with and by whose abandonment I would be crushed. Looking back, sometimes I'm amazed at my disconnect. But possibly my behavior can be excused, for a short while at least, based on the "kid in a candy store" defense, Your Honor. Although there is enough sex for me on this New York trip, I experience something completely new and alien. I am really missing Barbara in a deeper way than just companionship and familiarity. I make a decision, though based on my antics in New York, it seems almost ludicrous. But it is heartfelt.

I arrive home, euphoric. After dealing with Ronnie's over-the-top welcome—"Oh my God, it's YOU! You're really home! WhoooHoooooo! Ring the bells, break open the champagne, alert the fucking media. This is INCREDIBLE!!!"—is there any wonder we keep our dogs around?—I sit Barbara on the bed and simply ask her to marry me. It's a question I have never asked anyone before and only plan to ask this once in my life. Praise Jesus, she says yes or the toilet would have flushed on my life right here. She doesn't know what she's getting into, and frankly, neither do I.

We call our respective mothers. Hers is ecstatic, mine sounds miserable. I realize my mum is having trouble with more than the fact that her son is marrying someone he's only been dating for a couple of months, a girl she's never met; my father has been dead only four months at this point. I immediately arrange for my old mum to come over and stay with us in our little shack. She does. She seems a bit down when we greet her at LAX, but I don't recognize the Darkness in her at this point. I just think she's understandably missing Dad. Things are happening so fast in my career that I don't have time to sit and contemplate my own belly button, let alone my mother's. I go back to work.

Fans of Noah Drake, my character on *General Hospital*, and fans of "Jessie's Girl" put together that it's the same guy behind both—so the rocket fuse is lit and we have liftoff. I am not holding on when the afterburners kick in and am almost thrown when, instead of four fans at a record signing, there are suddenly 4,000 threatening to smash and overturn the police car I'm in. And instead of twelve people at a gig, there are 12,000. I am high as a frigging kite from this dramatic and unexpected leap forward. It is what I have been waiting for and feared might never come. And yes, the Darkness is nowhere to be seen. I believed that success would heal me. Apparently I am correct. But the Darkness is just biding his time, the son of a bitch.

I'm filming *General Hospital*—a show that is now drawing twelve million viewers a day, five days a week—then jumping on a plane Friday night and flying out to meet my band in some part of the U.S., playing a show that night, flying to another city Saturday, doing a show, flying to a third city Sunday, doing a show, then getting up at 3:30 Monday morning to catch another plane back to Los Angeles in time to walk onto the set at ABC for the next week of *GH*. I'm on the phone doing radio interviews at lunchtime and from my home at night, and in my dressing room between filming scenes, I have a keyboard, guitar, and tape recorder and

I'm writing songs for my next album. I am going sixteen hours a day, seven days a week. It's a brutal schedule, but I'm up for the challenge and never want it to stop.

We play theaters, colleges, parks, and even three nights at Carnegie Hall, and all the shows are sold out. The noise level of the audience is insane and it's sometimes hard to hear the band, even with the stage monitors cranked up full. I'm distressed that the teen magazines have picked up on me again. I'm not doing any interviews with them so they're taking old ones from the early '70s and surrounding the articles with new photos. It seems that "Is Rick Springfield too tall to love?" is still a burning question in the minds of young America, at least according to the much older writers of teen magazines. Jack White does an interview with *Tiger Beat* on the sly and I am pissed. I'm trying my damnedest to stay away from these magazines that earlier in the '70s almost spelled my doom.

I'm starting to have to fight this credibility issue on several fronts. Because young girls are the most vocal and most observable force at my shows, record signings, and radio and TV appearances, some members of the press start to get the idea that I'm a soap actor who some clever producer found a song for and got to sing on key for three minutes and fifteen seconds. Even when "I've Done Everything for You" is released a second time, followed by "Love Is Alright Tonite," both of which are hits, there is this undercurrent than I'm merely a synthetic musical confection designed to ride the coattails (or surgical scrubs) of Noah Drake. People's confusion about who I really am is highlighted for me when on a plane trip (again) to New York, there is a mid-flight request over the intercom for a doctor. The whole cabin looks at me. I want to jump up and shout, "It's a fucking TV show!"

Not everybody is enjoying my career, though. I wake up one morning and walk outside to see obscenities and references to my possible alternate sexual orientation spray-painted on the driveway. Another morning, I'm on a run and a woman swerves her car at me, missing by inches. People in my camp—yes, I now have a "camp"—are starting to tell me that I should live in a bigger house with more security and that maybe my crap heap Ford Fiesta isn't the ideal vehicle for a young rock star. Okay, not in so many words, but I'm being swayed from the fact that I really couldn't care any less at this point about a fancier house or more expensive car.

I remember meeting a friend at a party in the early '70s, who'd just had a big hit with the song "Baby Come Back." He was telling me that the first thing he did was go out and buy a Ferrari. Six months later he was asking me if I knew anyone who wanted to buy it. That stuck in my head, and although it's a relief not to have to worry about paying the electric bill every month, for me, money is just a way of keeping score of how well I am or am not doing. What it's really about is the joy of writing music people want to hear, playing to people who want to celebrate with me; of being in a career I'm passionate about . . . and having sex with lots of strangers. (Yep, I'm still doing it. Hard habit to break.)

I find a bigger, more expensive house, more to please my manager Joe than anything else. It's in Toluca Lake, in full view of the Universal tourist trams that ride around the park on the overlooking mountain, and my house becomes one of the regular attractions on their tour. Ronnie is not pleased, and he barks and barks and *barks* until he sets off the house alarm that my camp has also talked me into buying, and the cops arrive. At least the car I get is cool, a 1948 Buick Roadmaster. Ronnie and I tool around LA in it and are often sighted and chased. I soon realize that driving through LA in a 1948 Buick Roadmaster is not unlike riding around with a neon sign that says "Hey, look over here!" I get another car this time, one with a lower profile.

Money can't buy happiness, but it can sometimes buy cool things that can get you pretty close. On B's twenty-first birthday, I wake her up in our back bedroom in the early hours of the morning and hand her one end of a long string. I tell her to follow it. (My mum and dad did this to my brother and me one Christmas morning when we were kids and living in England. I've never forgotten it.) Barbara, sleepy eyed but exhilarated and laughing, giddily follows the string as it leads her out the bedroom, down the hallway, through the living room and the kitchen, and out the side door and gate to the front of the house, where the other end is tied to the grill of a brand-new black Mercedes 350SL coupe. She squeals with joy and jumps into my arms. The whole thing is caught on tape by my tour manager, hiding in his car across the way. Needless to say, the strings my brother and I were handed did *not* lead to a brand-new German automobile that chilly Christmas morning in 1961, but the string idea stuck with me nonetheless. The only downside is that I have set the bar really fucking high for all future birthday mornings.

My mum's sister Pat comes over to the U.S. to see her big sis. Pat is worried about how my mum sounds on the phone even after having spent three months with us. I haven't yet heard the word depression relating to me or anyone I know, so I'm confused when Pat tells me she thinks my mum is "depressed." She says she was feeling the same way about losing my dad and a doctor gave her some pills. The Rolling Stones song "Mother's Little Helper" leaps into my head, and I have sudden images of my gray-haired old mum stoned out of her brain, stumbling around the house, high on happy pills. Pat gives Eileen a few of her pills and in a week my mum is looking and sounding much better. The old kick-ass energy she has always owned is back in force. I'm pretty amazed and recognize this as a significant event. Maybe science is the answer to all our ills. But I have no time to analyze this; too much else is going on.

I've just been nominated for a bunch of Grammy Awards (including Best Album Cover—yay us, Ronnie), and it's time for the next album. *Working Class Dog* has gone double platinum (in record biz parlance that means it sold more than two million copies), and RCA wants another one, please and thank you. I have managed to write enough songs (even more than enough, so we can cut the chaff) in my dressing room at *GH* and in my music room at home, so I play the demos for Keith Olsen, who wants to produce the whole next album. We pick out the best songs, but there's one Keith doesn't like, that I resist dumping. It's a song about my fear of Barbara doing exactly what I'm doing on the road: having sex with people who aren't your significant other.

I've had the title "Don't Talk to Strangers" on a piece of paper on my piano for a while, and in fact it was the original title of "Jessie's Girl" before I got into that song and fleshed it out. The song "Don't Talk to Strangers" chronicles my sexual insecurities about Barbara that no amount of fucking on my part can erase. Keith doesn't like "Strangers" when he hears the demo and rejects it, so I go home and re-demo it, convinced it should be included. To our eventual mutual pleasure, I win. Keith, the little shit, is still not a fan of my guitar playing at this point, so this time he hires Chas Sanford—who will eventually co-write a bunch of hits himself, "Missing You" being the biggest—to play most of the guitar. Years later, Keith will walk into a session I'm producing, see me playing slide guitar, and comment, "I never knew you played slide guitar," to which I will answer, "You never asked."

Keith does have an ear for talent, though. Tom Kelly and Richard Page and I do all the background vocals: Tom will later co-write "Like a Virgin" and "True Colors," and Richard will soon have his own success in the band Mr. Mister. Keith also brings in a new kid who has just arrived from Albuquerque to play the solos on the record. Tim Pierce will eventually be in my touring band and on my records all through the '80s and will later become one of the go-to guys in the recording studio world, playing on pretty much everything you hear on radio and TV.

It's actually fortunate that Keith takes the reins for now—even though I'm anxious about giving someone so much control—because I'm still on the TV show/touring/interview treadmill that I've been on since this all started and my recording time is severely limited. I'm there for most of it but not the final mixing. And when I hear Keith's finished mix of "Don't Talk to Strangers," I'm ecstatic. It sounds like a freakin' hit. The background vocals session for that song was quite memorable, too: me and two other very happy guys singing the "Don't Talk to Strangers" chorus over and over because there are two naked girls in front of us on the studio floor going down on each other. Now this is how I always imagined it would be. There will be other times when sex during the recording process will be *de rigueur*, but this is my first experience of it and I feel like I'm in some kind of rock-and-roll heaven.

We complete the album, and I call it *Success Hasn't Spoiled Me Yet*. I come up with another loony cover shot featuring my mutt, Ronnie—this time he's in a limo with two female poodles, enjoying the fruits of his labor—and the new single, "Don't Talk to Strangers," is released to radio saturation play. In lieu of a raise in pay from *General Hospital*, I ask for extra time off so I can tour more extensively.

With the help of Jack White, who's still on drums, I put together my new band: Tim on guitar, Mike Siefret on bass, and Brett Tuggle on keyboards. Brett and I discover a special camaraderie out there on the road, where we will laughingly dub ourselves "the Boner Brothers," and eventually seek an answer to the BIG question: Why can't we stop having illicit sex? It will take a few world tours to get to that point, however. We hire a tour bus, print up a book full of tour dates, and hit the road. The Springfield School Bus for Undisciplined, Very Naughty Girls is about to touch down via the interstate at a town near you. But as we start doing bigger and bigger shows, something unexpected begins to happen to me.

I swear I'd rather swim laps in a vat of rat piss than step onto another bus tour, after spending five years on one.

But during this period of the 1980s, with the things we do on these buses, it is A-freaking-okay with me. The shows are shriek-fests, with daily newspaper reports, after we've left town, of people needing medical attention for heatstroke, cuts, and bruises—and the occasional girl with her jaw stuck in the open "scream" position. The band and I are "living the life" as has been ordained by the thousand and one bands that have gone before us, and no one is complaining. But the concerts themselves are occasionally starting to have an unforeseen debilitating effect on me.

As insane and otherworldly as life on the road is now, everything I'd ever dreamed it could be—sold-out shows around the world, audiences singing "Don't Talk to Strangers" in Swedish, German, Japanese, and Chinese; an old and patient companion who has been biding his time, waiting for his moment once I get used to mine, is about to step in and make his presence known.

"The Great Escape" is our code phrase for running offstage and straight onto the bus after the last song and taking flight into the night before anyone realizes we're gone. I sometimes run directly to the back bedroom of the bus and sit alone in the dark, my ears ringing, still sweating and breathing hard from the show as the bus bumps its way onto the next interstate. And before the audience has even started to file out of the arena we just left, I begin to berate myself for not truly connecting with the fans who came to celebrate and dance to the music. I don't know how I know this—it's just something I feel. Maybe it arises from inside me or maybe it comes from them, but I sit there beating myself up and trying to figure out what I can change so it doesn't happen again. It leaves me feeling so empty. Only then does that old "friend" sidle up next to me on the couch and throw a duplicitous arm around my wet shoulders. He just couldn't stay away, he says. "Missed you, Boyo."

"Wow, they really liked you didn't they, Ricky? That was pretty damn cool. You've waited a long time for this. What a shame you didn't give them your best though, huh? You and I know it was kind of a half-assed performance you put on back there, and no amount of money or adulation can really change that, can it, big boy?" The Darkness has finally hitched a ride.

I change, dry off, and go up front with the rest of the partying band to grab some wine and chase him off. Most of the time Mr. Darkness doesn't drink. Sometimes I stay in the back until someone comes looking for me, and then I moan about what a shitty show it was, perhaps fishing for some faint praise so I can feel momentarily better, and whoever I'm moaning to says something like, "Are you kidding? It was fucking great. The audience went crazy." And as I move up front to grab a glass, Mr. D.

always has an enlightening parting shot: "How long before the audience finds out that you're faking it, d'ya think?" I have a drink, crawl into my bunk, and pull the curtain closed. The tour bus rumbles on through the night.

Other than these visits from the companion who refuses to die, everything is soaring. We're selling out everywhere we play, movie and TV producers are sending scripts, RCA is ecstatic to have a current artist selling millions of records for them at last, and T-shirt sales are so through the roof that the things start showing up in photos of Midwestern teenagers on the pages of *National Geographic*. I play live on the Grammy show and then win one of the awards I'm nominated for: Best Rock Vocal for "Jessie's Girl," although I'd have preferred for Ronnie to win the album cover category. I give the Grammy to my old mum, as I do most of the platinum albums and awards that are starting to come in from other countries. I never display this stuff in my own home and never will. I feel it's past tense and just looks like cheesy ego crap. But it's okay for my mum to display it and tell her friends how great and awesome I am—I'm totally cool with that.

I now own several companies: touring, publishing, and even a landholding company, all named after my very groovy dog Ronnie. There's Ron's Band Corp. and Super Ron Music, the Lethal Ron Corp., and Ron's Land Corp. He has become synonymous with my newfound success. We continue to play and screw our way across America, Europe, and Japan. One day in a hotel in Osaka, I find the Japanese version of Gideon's Bible in a bedside drawer. It's a collection of teachings from the Buddha. I steal it. It's a very un-Buddhist way of acquiring the book, I'll grant you, but God works in mysterious ways. I begin to read it in hopes of replacing the faith I was raised in with something else.

I grew up with the concept of God as a punishing father who whipped me with failure and guilt when I was "bad" but who required that I get down on my knees, grovel, and thank him from the bottom of my unworthy soul every time something "good" happened. I didn't get it. But at least there was a degree of comfort in believing that an all-powerful entity was up there somewhere and I could pray to him when I felt like shit or needed something. But now he's taken my dad way too early and broken my mother's heart. It's impossible, given the teachings I learned as a young boy, not to hold this vengeful God responsible. What remaining faith I have left is slowly leaching away as I travel the world with my band and look for fame to heal me.

So it's only natural, as my faith in my Christian God slips away, that I seek a path of spirituality that will sustain me. I begin buying (hey, I'm no longer stealing them) and reading every book I can find about alternate divine paths. I don't want to resolve my lack of faith into total atheism. Whether God exists or not, I would rather choose to believe in something, and have that belief at my back, than to think that it's just me out here amongst the black sky and white stars. Books like *Think and Grow Rich* have given me an unshakable conviction that there is something, some power around me that is more than just me. So I go shopping for a kinder, gentler God.

Barbara sometimes flies out to join me mid-tour. She is beautiful and alive and innocent of all that goes on while her back is turned. But the pressure we're both under and that which we put on ourselves is not an easy thing to plan our approaching wedding around, and the big day is pushed farther and farther away until it hits the back burner. One other gift the Darkness has cursed me with is a reckless and wicked temper that flares when I'm feeling stressed, and Barbara gets the brunt of this because she's the only one really in the center of the storm with me. Neither of us knows what we're doing or how to reconcile our deepening relationship with all that's going on around us. It's insane for us to even try. We often turn on a dime from loving partners (the crew calls us "Ken and Barbie") to a couple of kids having a full-blown tantrum, with the added touch of smashed hotel furniture and screaming profanities, all fueled by large amounts of alcohol.

We're in an expensive New York hotel one night when one of these raging fights comes down. After some table lamps are smashed against walls, and chairs and bedside tables splintered, I angrily pack a suitcase and charge out into the hall to go get myself a separate room. Four house detectives are lined up with their backs to the corridor wall, with looks of "What the fuck do we do now?" on their faces. I smile and say "Oh. Hey," and slowly back my way into our suite and close the door. These battles get progressively worse as new lines are drawn in the sand and words that should have been left unsaid are spat out in self-righteous anger. I know there are many reasons for these fights, but the one I'm the most keenly aware of is my infidelity, of which Barbara has a dawning understanding.

I approach one of my business people and ask him to arrange a meeting for me with a therapist, so I can try to work out a solution to my disloyal behavior. I go to the meeting with the gnawing pangs of guilt I should have been feeling from the very beginning but never have. I understand that being in love with Barbara and wanting her to stay in my life doesn't jibe with me trying to fuck every girl I meet. I am earnestly looking for guidance. I spill my guts to this guy, hoping to find some healing ground, but all he says to me is "Look, screw around if you want to. Just don't tell her." It's years before I discover that it was all a setup. It was prearranged by my camp that he say that to me so I'd get on with my career and keep making everyone lots of money without any disturbances caused by my trying to address this issue and have a real life. I know that what he's advised is wrong, but for now I take his counsel anyway, and the Darkness smiles a Stygian smile.

The three singles released from the *Success* album are all written about Barbara: "Don't Talk to Strangers," "What Kind of Fool Am I?" and "I Get Excited." All three become hits, and my second RCA album outsells my first. MTV has exploded into the living rooms of the world, and the $1,500 original cost of my first two videos doesn't even cover the catering bill for the next one. Everybody wants to direct a music video, and I meet with William Friedkin (who directed Linda Blair in *The Exorcist*) to discuss the possibility of him shooting a video for the *Success* album.

I'm not a big fan of music videos. They seem like just a bunch of cheesy mirror posing and cheap special effects with no real cohesion to any of it other than the music track that they're supposedly illuminating. Until Michael Jackson gets hold of the medium and utilizes it properly, it's all just a big, money-sucking, stroking wank. Luckily a video only takes a day to shoot, so there's no harm, no foul, and people can't seem to get enough of the damn things. I still focus on the music, although every now and then, when I'm writing a song, I do get the odd vision of a staggeringly beautiful and meaningful scene from the video I could film—and push it firmly out of my mind. The rocket burns on.

We are booked into seven sold-out nights at the Universal Amphitheater and will shoot my first live concert video there. The night before my week begins, Barbara and I go to see Frank Sinatra open the place. He says something about "this kid Ricky Springfield will be in for seven nights starting tomorrow," and I secretly wish my dad could have heard him say that; he loved Frank. I comfort myself with the assurance that he did hear it, somewhere—out there. The final track on the *Success* album is a five-line, one-minute and thirty-second song about my dad's death called "April 24th, 1981," the day he left us. It's an adaptation of the song I wrote for Cleo when she died, and it's all I can manage to get out, so fresh is the wound, but it marks a change in my writing.

From this moment on, my songs start to become much more personal. I feel I have no real choice other than to write this way. My friend Doug Davidson will later tell me, "Your dad deserved a whole song," prompting me, three years on, to write just that and have the most cathartic songwriting session of my life, finally doing some serious grieving for my father.

The unexpected thing about emotional pain is that it deepens our colors; I can feel something shift inside me. My songwriting starts to reflect more complete slices of my life rather than wishful fantasies. I also see that, though my writing is becoming more personal, moving inward, it's also moving outward at the same time, connecting to others by virtue of the fact that we are all human beings and have the same basic life issues.

The ride continues. I'm nominated for a couple more Grammys for my second album, though not for Best Album Cover, bugger it! I see Elton at my second Grammy show and he says, "You've come a long way from the 'most popular guitarist' award." We laugh. Is he following me?

We're one of the few bands that actually come off the road in better shape than when we start the tour. There are drugs on the road, of course (though it's no longer something I'm into), but for the most part, we become workout junkies. Clearly my father's death has inspired me. I've seen how people often develop a specific anxiety about whatever disease kills their parents. I'm sure my dad's health was wrecked decades earlier by the stress, atrocious food, disease, and near-death experiences in the jungles and mountains of New Guinea, where he fought the Second World War. And war takes the lives of more than just those who don't come home from the front. Since I'm not fighting any world wars right now, I focus on what I eat and how I maintain the general health of my body.

I read a book called *The Save Your Life Diet* and stop eating red meat for years because of it. I've already sworn off chicken because of the chicken-head-detachment-and-subsequent-boiling-of-the-feathery-body-to-loosen-the-plumage summer back in my golden youth. And to supplement my healthy (I think) diet, I begin working out with weights. I've already been running daily for several years now. The band and I work out at the gyms in health clubs and in the hotels we sometimes stay at.

We book into these hotels on the days off so we can recuperate a little. It's a much-needed break from life on the tour bus. One day in a hotel Jacuzzi I meet a woman who is nonplussed at the attention I'm getting from people walking through the pool area. "Are you someone I should know?" she asks innocently enough. I tell her who I think I am, and she seems intrigued. "Hmm. I don't think I've ever heard of you before," she says, and follows with, "Do you think I could come to the show tonight?"

She seems nice enough, very mature, and possibly even of some breeding. I tell her I'll get her a couple of tickets. "No, just one will be fine," is her answer, and she goes on to say how she's just lost her fiancé in a terrible car crash. I feel bad for her and say if she needs anything to just let me know. Anyway, long story short, she informs me at another show (yes, she starts coming to them regularly) that she is an heiress to the Marriott hotel chain; would we like it if she gets us free Marriott hotel rooms everywhere we travel? "That would be cool," I answer, and I'll be damned. She does it. Even to the degree that when we arrive at a Marriott in New York and they can't find my reservation, she gets on the phone and says, "Let me speak to the manager." I have my room in five minutes. Even my name at this point couldn't move them that fast. She asks if she can ride short distances with us on the bus, and I say "Sure." In only a matter of weeks, she insinuates her way into my inner circle. One day she surprises me with the gift of her dead fiancé's ring. I would just like to say here for the record: I did not have sex with her.

The tour ends, and a few months later, to my absolute surprise, the FBI comes looking for her. They tell us they're after her for writing bad checks to cover all the "free" hotel rooms she'd gotten for us. And to add insult to injury, she isn't related to the Marriott family in even the most remote way. She'd been a fan right from the beginning and had planned the whole thing, including the "chance" meeting in the hotel's Jacuzzi. She'd conned us all. I want to find her and hire her. Anyone who could pull off the "swindle of the decade" that she pulled was someone I wanted working for me. Never did find her—and I hope the FBI didn't either.

CHAPTER FOURTEEN

SEX, MORE SEX, AND ROCK AND ROLL (NO REAL DRUGS TO SPEAK OF)

AROUND THE WORLD IN 80 WEEKS

1984–1985

General Hospital is a mixed blessing. It's certainly been the liquid hydrogen to my music career's liquid oxygen, and together they've ignited to launch the space shuttle of my livelihood to this point. But the soap opera joyride is starting to drag a little as far as I'm concerned. Music has always been my priority, and I've gotten a bit sidetracked with what now feels like the burden of this acting gig. It started out well enough with our young hero arriving early, bright-eyed and bushy-tailed, nervously struggling to remember his lines and dutifully playing the new stud on the show, doing what he was asked, and showing up at functions to play the network game. And certainly people's attitudes on the show start to change as Noah Drake gets more popular—the *GH* stars treat him with a little more respect; the young ingénues try to catch his eye—and although the attention is fun and a bit head-swelling, it still feels like a side gig: something to facilitate my music. To a degree it's a barometer of success as well. Scenes are added each week for Dr. Noah, thanks to the positive feedback from fans about the role I'm playing, but that's the difference to me. It's a role. Whereas the music I am writing, recording, and playing taps very solidly into the real me.

The backstage dramas that play out behind the scenes on the *General*

Hospital set seem like episodes from the show itself, but I feel removed from the action, with my one-foot-in/one-foot-out attitude toward this gig: There's the child actor who gets fired and asks me, with tears in his eyes, "What am I supposed to do with my life now?" And the older leading man (he played a doctor opposite me in my first-ever acting role on a *Six Million Dollar Man* episode) who's been a regular on *GH* and approaches me to intercede on his behalf with Gloria because she's thinking of dropping him from the show. The Daytime Emmys that everyone but me attends. The ego struggles between some of the stars, and the bruised self-esteem that ensues when one character gets more airtime than another. And, of course, the almost daily photo sessions for the daytime magazines that I mostly manage to duck.

Fortunately, I don't compound the issue by nailing any of the actresses on the *GH* set, though there is a lot of sexual innuendo that goes on amongst the young cast. Apart from a brief, erotic moment in front of a dressing room mirror with Demi Moore (sorry, she was just too hot), I have a hands-off policy while I'm on the show. I'm not quite sure why this is the case with me regarding acting gigs, but I have never (okay, almost never) had sex with an actress I'm working with. I feel no similar compunction when it comes to music. I think because I started acting later in life, it's the adult in me that shows up for work, whereas music started when my hormones were just beginning to rage and the arrested adolescent set the tone early. Anyway, I think it's time to leave the show.

I've been on *General Hospital* for almost eighteen months straight when some serious movie offers start coming in. Talk about the one that got away: the producers of a film called *The Right Stuff* are interested in seeing me for the part of one of the astronauts, but I've just been offered a shitload of money to do a film starring me! (Hang on a sec; maybe it *is* about the money.) At this point my inflated ego is relatively unchecked, so I decide I'm ready to carry my own movie. I'm so damned desperate to believe all the great things people are saying about me and to me that I actually begin to believe some of it. The movie that's offered is called

Hard to Hold. After I read the script, I toss it in a corner of the room in disgust and call my acting agent.

"The script is rubbish," I tell him.

He says that what I read is just a first draft. They'll fix it.

"I don't think I should play a musician in my first film. People will think I'm not acting," I counter.

He says that they're offering me $1.5 million to do it.

I sing "Do-re-mi-fa-so-la-ti-do." And Universal Pictures has themselves an actor/musician.

Gloria Monty, the *GH* producer, is as tough as Kevlar and wears iron undies. Most of the cast and all of the crew are terrified of her. But for some reason she's sweet and gracious to me and even takes me into her confidence when she's diagnosed with cancer. I like her. I tell her I'm leaving the show.

"Yes, I know," she says.

We hug and I thank her and tell her I'll stay in touch. She comes to see me now and then at different gigs, but we never work together again. I go to her service when she passes away many years later and cry on the drive home. It's as much for myself as for her, because I understand how close I came to never reaching what I was reaching for. She helped to lift me out of the obscurity that, but for one more roll of the dice, I might have been consigned to. And she saw something in me at a time when maybe I no longer saw it in myself.

On the road again, I write the songs for what will become my next album: *Living in Oz.* Since I'm doing most of my writing on the tour bus between gigs, the songs have a lot more energy. I'm focused on writing strong stage songs. I'm also writing more about what's really going on in my head. Now that I've reached a certain degree of success, I feel like I can stretch out a little. Writing about sex for sex's sake is taking a backseat, and instead I'm looking at my past ("Allyson," "Me and Johnny," "Like Father, Like Son"), how I'm dealing with fame ("Motel Eyes," "Living in Oz," "Human Touch"), and how it's all affecting my relationship with Barbara ("I Can't Stop Hurting You," "Affair of the

Heart"). I produce the sessions myself with Bill Drescher because I want the guitars to be louder, the drums bigger and more ambient, and the vocals edgy and blasting, an approach Keith Olsen avoided on the previous record. In other words, I want everything to be louder than everything else. (Sorry, that's an old, dumb studio joke.) We finish the record, I leave *General Hospital*, and the filming of *Hard to Hold* is about to begin. We're also starting up a new tour, now that the new record is done. Ronnie is not featured on the cover this time (though he is on the inside sleeve) because I feel this album is very different from the last two and I want the cover to suggest that. My reviews are not always stellar, although even in a glowing review I'll find the one negative and obsess on that (or should I say, the Darkness will do it for me—glad to see Mr. D is still with us. I'd be lonely if it weren't for him hanging around, trying to kill me) and the bad reviews demoralize me and my fragile ego. I've since come to understand that reviews say much more about the person writing them than they do about the artist being reviewed, but that future knowledge doesn't help me right now. *Living in Oz* is reviewed in the *Los Angeles Times* as an album about "nothing." Even our most earnest and heartfelt works can be summed up, by others, as meaningless crap. It's good to know. Thank God no one listens to this guy, because the album and singles are hits and even more of my money is thrown at the production of lavish videos.

The script for *Hard to Hold* hasn't changed all that much by the time we start shooting the first scenes, but I'm feeling confident that I can make the movie into something really worthwhile. My expectations are shaped by the control I have had in the recording studio. I believe this will be a similar undertaking. It's not. And I learn the hard way. There are a writer, a director, an editor, other actors, the director of photography, and the studio heads. They all have their say, and it starts to feel like we're designing a racehorse by committee and will shortly end up with a very lumpy camel.

During the filming I write more songs, this time for the *Hard to Hold* soundtrack album. But time is tight and I have to do it on the set. It's a challenge getting a vibe going on a song when everyone keeps yelling for you to shut the hell up, the cameras are rolling. I write a song called "Love Somebody" in the penthouse suite of the Fairmont Hotel in San Francisco between shooting scenes with Patti Hansen (Keith Richards's girlfriend and, later, wife), and the song has elements of her personality in it. I also think the song is a plea from my brain to me to stop all the fucking around, which I'm still doing—on the set, in my dressing room trailer, and in hotel rooms.

Keith Richards (looking astoundingly like Dracula) pays a visit to the set one night to visit his girl and check up on me, vis-à-vis his girl. I'm flattered that he would even think there might be something going on between us (there isn't), but I'm more excited just to talk with him. I was fourteen when a girl told me that she thought I looked like Keith Richards. It was the coolest thing anyone had ever said to me. That old moment keeps jumping into my head as we're talking, and the fourteen-year-old in me wants to stop the conversation and scream (in a high, my-balls-haven't-dropped-yet falsetto) "Oh my GOD! It's Keith fucking Richards!!" But I manage to restrain myself.

Filming and recording of some of the new songs continue. I meet a couple of fans outside the studio one night who are excited when I invite them in as we finish up mixing the song "Love Somebody." They expect to hear the song once and then we'll get crazy and party, but the recording business is slow and tedious and they're soon bored shitless. Truly, for the uninitiated, attending a recording session is about as thrilling as watching a vacuum cleaner being repaired. "We gotta go," they say and split. To quote a line from *Hard to Hold:* "It ain't all tits and champagne."

When we finish filming, I hit the road.

The new stage show begins with the opening bars of "Affair of the Heart," the first single off the *Living in Oz* album. The heavy bass riff is pulsing through the darkness from the giant array of speakers that encircle our stage, and you can literally feel the tension in the arena building. At the end of a crashing chord from the band the spotlights arc on and reveal yours truly, standing on a small, table-sized elevator platform, fifty feet in the air. The first night we play, the piercing screams that follow are of such a volume and high frequency that I completely lose my equilibrium, drop to my knees, and start to tumble over the edge of the dais. I am still fifty feet above the stage. I grab at anything, terrified I'm going to fall, and a hand finds a hold: I ride the damn thing down to the floor on my knees. Not the cool and rocking opening moment I was hoping it would be. The next night I wear earplugs and it works waaaaay better.

College kids are starting to show up for us at festivals and outdoor shows, with my song titles painted all over their cars and Winnebagos. Promoters who thought I would be toast by this time stand open-mouthed on the side of the stage, stunned by the enthusiastic receptions we're getting. And the Springfield School Bus for Undisciplined, Very Naughty Girls rolls on. Brett, my keyboard player, and I are actually starting to have late-night conversations about what we're doing to our girlfriends. He has a girl who he's serious about as well, and my guilt at my infidelity is leading me to examine my behavior a bit deeper. Not stop it, mind you, just try to understand it.

By now I've reasoned myself into believing that there is no God. I've read and listened to a ton of opinions on the subject and have done a lot of navel-gazing myself during sleepless nights alone in my bunk on the bus. So there is no help from God for me at this time, by my own design. Brett and I, trying to find some understanding of our natures, zero in on our loving but withholding mothers. Maybe they are at the root of our neurotic sexual appetites and lack of self-control . . . maybe. We're looking to blame someone. But we also discover that we were both pretty sexually aware at a very early age. That might have something to do with it. Whatever the cause, I resolve to change my ways but am powerless to alter my course when presented with an opportunity. Which is often. Very often.

Doug Davidson marries his long-time girlfriend, Cindy, at a ceremony in Santa Barbara and I'm in the wedding party. Barbara and I drive up during a break in touring, along the coast in a '63 Corvette Stingray I've recently bought. The wedding is a hit and everyone has a great time, toasts are made, tears are shed, jokes are told at every wedding party member's expense, drinks are drunk, and then Barbara and I get back into the Corvette for the drive home. It's now been nearly four years since I proposed, and we have yet to set a date. Considering this, there's nothing like going to someone else's wedding to get that shit really stirred up. I've been busy over those years, admittedly, but I've also been dragging my feet even though I truly love this girl. I'm clearly confused about my commitment, given all my disloyalty on the road. We've already broken up and gotten back together so many times that whenever she comes in the front door, our crazy housekeeper (a Chinese guy we call "T") doesn't know whether to welcome her or alert me that there's an intruder.

We're arguing on the drive home from Doug and Cindy's wedding and I make a decision. Maybe it's powered by alcohol, but I like to think I also have reasonably good intentions—although, looking back, it's hard to say precisely what they were. I pull the car over to the wrong side of the freeway and confess everything I've been doing on the road. Barbara is crushed. She tells me she's moving out and that we are over, you fucking bastard. We drive the rest of the way home in silence except for her soft sobbing. I feel a sense of relief, like I've done the right thing. When we get home around three in the morning, I watch as she packs up all her things one final time. She looks defeated as she walks around the house gathering up all the small mementos that are precious to her. She says nothing to me, kisses Ronnie on his head, and moves out of the home we have built together. I don't have the same sense of relief as I did when Diana and I split. It's altogether a different feeling. When Diana and I broke up, I was sure that what I really wanted was to be unfettered and live my life the way I want without any unrealistic commitment to another human soul. But now that is apparently not the case. Already I'm having second thoughts.

Barbara moves in with her mother. She lives in an area of Glendale where the serial killer the press call the "Night Stalker" is just getting his career going. A couple is murdered a few weeks later on a street just over from where Barbara is now living. I'm freaked when I hear this. And so are they. I go to their apartment and suggest that Pat move into my old house on Broadview Drive and that Barbara move back in with me.

There's more to Barbara moving back in with me than just distancing her from Richard Ramirez's killing ground, however. I want her back. Now I need to prove to both of us that it's not just going to be business as usual. We talk about marriage for the first time in a long while, but we still don't settle on a date. I leave for a three-week tour of Japan amid a rash of promises to commit and pledges to change. Japan has always had its own set of rules as far as we touring bands are concerned. It's really difficult to know if you've offended a girl over there by asking her to suck your dick or if, although there is a lot of cultural shyness in Japan, she would really love to. The authorities are very, very anti-drug, and yet there are graphic porno magazines full of young girls covering themselves in their own shit—I'm not making this up—for sale at the local grocery market where moms shop with their kids.

We've sold out three nights at Tokyo's Budokan Hall, and although the audience is screaming and yelling and is as wild as any in the world, the promoter tells me that Japanese law forbids me from jumping off the front of the stage and joining the crowd during the show because it's considered sacrilegious for the soles of my shoes to touch the same floor that thousands of kids are jumping up and down on at that very moment. Then they take us to a bath house so we can screw our brains out. Amid this strange dichotomy, I'm not sure if my promises to Barbara are actually legal in this part of the world. C'mon, I'm joking. Well, sort of. It's a hard drug to quit cold turkey, this sex thing. The shows are a blast. And there are girls. I satisfy my old obsession for a while by hearing about and occasionally watching crew and band members have their fun in the hotel rooms around this country . . . but temptation is pulling at me, as is a more sinister yet familiar voice. "Go on, Rickyboy. Barbara's ten thousand miles away. And these girls won't always be around, ya know. It's all gonna come to an end someday. You don't have more than a year left at best, I'd say."

I weaken and, to my ultimate sorrow, I join in.

I call Barbara all the time. I miss her and want to connect with that part of my life she owns, the part that's still any good. She is my rock. My anchor in uncertain seas and in the course I am charting. I have only a vague yet palpable sense of what the consequences will be for me if I stray too far. I want us to work. Maybe she can sense that I'm reaching out to her because out of nowhere she suddenly says, "Let's get married at your mum's church." Sitting on the edge of my hotel bed in Tokyo, I think, "What the hell am I waiting for?" We arrange for her and her family to meet me in Australia. We'll get married at the church that held the service for my dad. My mum freaks out when I call her. She has two weeks to book the church, alert everyone on our side of the family, hire a caterer, and find a photographer who won't sell the photos to the magazines.

She pulls it off. It's as natural as Barbara and I could ever have hoped. In fact, it feels so right that I wonder why we didn't do it sooner. I still haven't grasped how I will adapt to this new level of commitment, assuming I will adapt. And it will be a while before I understand the whole concept and benefit of commitment in a relationship. It's like trying to advance in a video game. I've just entered a room and am waiting for the door ahead of me to open and let me through, but I'm keeping the door behind me still ajar just in case escape becomes necessary. But it's only by shutting off my exit, and being okay with no way to back out, that the door ahead will open. I do get it eventually, although I don't manage to close that back door for some time yet.

I'd be lying if I said I wasn't a little concerned about the fan reaction to my marriage. The paparazzi were much more restrained in the '80s than they are now, but they had already taken furtive photos of Barbara and me walking around our canyon neighborhood and published them with lame, untrue stories about us taking separate planes to destinations so fans won't find out we're a couple. And I've received some nasty "fan" letters containing charming things like drawings of gravestones with Barbara's and my names written on them in what appears to be blood. Apparently these sweet people now want us both dead.

It makes me remember an insidious meeting at our Toluca Lake house between the "lawyer," the "business manager," and Joe, months earlier, when they became aware of our wedding plans. They ganged up on me in my backyard and told me that Barbara's mother had said to them that if her daughter and I split up, she would "take me for all I was worth." Pat has always been our advocate and is a sweet, soulful woman. I know she would never in a million years say something like this, especially not to these idiots. I should have bailed on them all then, but I guess I thought they were trying to protect my interests. They weren't. They were trying to protect their own. And apart from having a drink thrown in my face while B and I are walking through a hotel lobby after a show one night, the fan reaction is pretty minimal.

The only thing I remember about the wedding, and the party at my old mum's house later, is that I have bright purple streaks in my hair (thank you, 1980s), that Barbara's hair is Lucille Ball red, and that I tweak her nose softly when she says "I do." This is the last time I'll see some of my uncles and aunts, as they will soon be joining my dad in the place where all the good people go after they die. And the old folks aren't the only ones at death's door. As I said, I've never been a big fan of shooting videos for my songs, but I have had a director I like very much. His name is Doug Dowdle. Doug is responsible for a lot of the more well-known and heavily played videos I've filmed.

While Barbara and I are celebrating our wedding and all the happily-ever after we believe it will lead to, I get a phone message from Los Angeles telling me I should call Doug in Hawaii. I do, and he tells me in a voice thick and heavy with painkillers that he has cancer (at age thirty-two) and is "on his way out." I am stunned. I have never spoken with someone about their impending death before and I'm scared that I'll say the wrong thing, which, of course, I do. I end our final conversation on this earth with something stupid like "Be well, man. I'll see you soon." He's dead before we even make it back to the U.S.

I am determined that with marriage I can change. I don't realize at this point how dramatically my whole life will soon be transformed, when, right on cue, three months into our marriage, Barbara is pregnant. This is incredible news for both of us, although I have the distinct impression at this point that the baby will be more like a cute performing seal I can take around with me so people can "ooh" and "aah" over him/her and tell me how much he/she looks like me.

Clearly I don't have a clue about what lies ahead.

Meanwhile, back at my 9-to-5: the *Hard to Hold* soundtrack is a hit, with "Love Somebody" becoming my biggest single since "Don't Talk to Strangers." I turn on the radio one day and spin the dial: four of the biggest Los Angeles stations are all playing the song at the same time. This impresses even me. The movie itself does less well and is pretty much raked over the coals by movie critics, although they do seem to think I can act. (Thanks for that.) It is my first real defeat since "Jessie's Girl" launched me into the inky firmament, and I wake up one morning, not long after the miserable failure of *Hard to Hold*, feeling like someone has just slapped me. I shake it off and launch into writing a new record.

Ever since I pilfered that book from the hotel room in Osaka, I've been delving tentatively into Buddhism, Taoism, and anything else that doesn't resemble the fire-and-brimstone religion I was raised on. It gives me some peace to understand that these Eastern paths place God inside me rather than up in the sky, where the punishing Father dressed all in white that I grew up with was thought to dwell. I should say here that, were I on a crashing airplane at this point, I would fall to my knees and pray to the Christian God I've known all my life. And I do realize that those teachings will always be a part of me. But I'm searching for some alternative views. I need some beliefs that will sustain me, and I'm casting my spiritual net out there to try and find a friggin' fish. Most of the new songs, which become my album *Tao*, are about a spiritual search, although I'm light-years from actually finding anything. One song deals with the loss of my sweet old man and my consequent loss of faith in God as I once knew him.

I've been writing lines about my dad's death on scraps of paper for a month or so, but I've avoided sitting down and focusing on putting it all together as a complete song. I know it will hurt. One day I make the decision to finally write it. All I know for sure when I sit at the piano is that the song will be called "My Father's Chair" and will focus on my dad's favorite chair, which stands empty in the years since his death—a potent symbol of his absence for me, my mum, and Mike. I cry and ache all through the three-hour writing session, and when I am done, so is the song. And I realize that this, finally, is my memorial to my dad. Not the flowers I bought or the service I attended or the times I've talked about his loss or the prayers I've offered up for his soul. It is my proudest moment as a songwriter. And as a son.

In the years since, fans and others have let me know that this song has given them comfort through the times when they've lost someone close. The lyrics have been quoted at funerals, chiseled on gravestones, and published in obituaries. These are things I never intended but am gratified to hear about.

When we go into the studio to cut this record, for the first and only time I shun the big guitar sound I've become known for. I've been listening to a lot of European music that hasn't been heard in the States and won't be until all the synth/hair boys break out of Mother England. I'm inspired by it and approach *Tao* with more of a computer/sequencer attitude. Every musician will soon fall in love with the perfect rhythm of the computer. It's not a human feel, but it is flawless, and all of us who have spent hours in the studio waiting for all the musicians to finally get it fucking right are reveling in the tight, instantaneous grooves of the electric drum machine and the keyboard sequencer. The truth is, the first sound we ever hear, in the womb, is our mother's heartbeat, which is where I believe our love of the backbeat comes from.

Looking back, I actually don't think all the perfect beats and the sequencers suited the spiritual theme of *Tao*, but it sure as shit is a modern sound, and I dig it. Mitchell Froom, who will eventually produce Elvis Costello and Crowded House's self-titled '80s album and record Paul McCartney, covers most of the heavy keyboard work on the album, and I play guitar and bass and, for the first time, write the drum machine programs. Live drummers are about to take a backseat to drum machines for a while on the pop charts, and they're not happy about it.

Halfway through the sessions, Barbara (now eight months pregnant) and I find a house we love in Malibu: a sprawling ranch on three acres in exclusive Serra Retreat. One night I'm driving home from the *Tao* sessions to Toluca Lake, the next night I'm driving to Malibu. I haven't had time to assimilate this relocation, and it's almost like I don't want to. After all the moves I've made in my life, I just want it to happen as seamlessly as possible. The act of "moving," even to a nicer pad, is a reality I want to avoid, so I guess I pretend like it's not really happening.

I think it's a sign that I'm losing some sense of reality that I will barely acknowledge this big change in my lifestyle. But waiting on the kitchen table in the dim light, the first night I enter our new, multimillion-dollar home, is a pair of tiny baby booties and a way-too-small-to-be-for-a-living-human-being cotton jumpsuit. It's an amazing moment. I walk into this new house like it's no big deal, but my hands are shaking as I lift my unborn son's jumpsuit up to the light.

And then Barbara's water breaks.

We're sitting in the family room when it happens. I leap up and run out of the room. B thinks I've gone to get some towels and my car keys, but I return with the video camera and start documenting the beginning of the birth of my son. She screams at me to "put the fucking camera down and help me get to the hospital!" I do, and at 7:28 a.m. the next morning—October 27, 1985—Liam James Springthorpe, aka Little Mr. Center of the Universe, is born. And my concept of myself, the world, and the reason I'm here will never be the same again. Thank God.

I'm so excited to show off my new-cute-performing-baby-seal-who-looks-just-like-me that we take the frigging 835-hour flight to the other side of the universe so my mum can ooh and ahh over him too, and so can all my other Aussie relatives. There's been a slight shift in my sensibilities since the birth of our seal—sorry, our son. . . . I'm completely unaware of it at this point, but it presents itself to me when I have a quiet moment to myself in my old mum's house while she and B are out showing off our boy to the neighborhood folks. I look around the old familiar living room and see all the platinum and gold albums, the awards, and the professional touched-up photos I've sent her over the past successful years. They are nailed, hung, placed, and framed everywhere, all over the house. It suddenly looks to me like the inside of a really gaudy Chinese brothel: garish, flashy, metallic, too bright. And on the small table by the fireplace is a single photo of my brother Mike. Just one. Clearly in a place of honor.

The lurid array of "prizes" that I've sent my old mum over the years seems sad. Like I'm trying too hard. All she needs from Mike is the one black-and-white photo. It is enough. He is enough. I know my brother has always been her favorite, and it's okay. I love them both. But I also know that she expected me to shine. And I've tried to do just that for her. But suddenly I feel unexpectedly ashamed and embarrassed.

The awareness of my shifting view doesn't happen right away, however. There's a tour to complete, but I'm uncomfortable about leaving home this time and I miss our new baby all through these travels. We rent a private plane so I can go home at a moment's notice. I'm done with the whole tour bus thing. "Celebrate Youth," the first single off *Tao*, is the biggest hit I've ever had in Europe, and we go there on an extensive outdoor festival tour. The Europeans have, by far, the best outdoor concerts. Some attract 100,000, even 200,000 people. All that human energy is an undeniably powerful force, and it lifts me from the stage every time it's directed at me. It's that palpable. This feeling is part of the reason I love to perform. My extroverted seven-year-old self is here onstage with me, and he's having a great freaking time, too.

Back home in the States, I perform at Live Aid, and it's seen by another 300 gazillion people around the globe. Eric Clapton and I have the same booking agent—a sweet young Woody Allenish New Yorker named Bobby Brooks—and Eric, who's also playing at Live Aid, wants to meet me. Swayed by my Mr. D, whose grip on me is starting to tighten ("He'll only see what a dick you truly are"), as well as by my usual insecurities, I blow Eric Clapton off. Wait, did I mention I was clueless? I did? Several times, right? Okay.

I meet a young arty guy from San Francisco named David Fincher who wants to direct my next music video. He will later become a very successful Hollywood director of hits like *Fight Club, Se7en*, and *Panic Room*, but right now he's a skinny, pasty-faced kid who looks like he's barely seventeen. David says he has an idea for a sci-fi themed video for my new single "Bop 'til You Drop." He adds that he is in possession of a fine, $3 plastic salad bowl which, when inverted and painted gray, will look like a multimillion-dollar space dome. He has some other pretty outrageous ideas, and I'm encouraged. But when I see what he shoots and edits for the videos of my singles from *Tao*—"Celebrate Youth," "State of the Heart," and "Dance This World Away" as well as "Bop 'til You Drop"—I am absolutely floored. They're still the only videos of mine I can sit through, aside from the original one for "Jessie's Girl," which will always have a cheesy/cool appeal for me. David then shoots my next concert video, *The Beat of the Live Drum*, and again does stuff no one else is doing with music videos.

On the surface, it's all good. I have another hit record and a new, cool pad, I'm newly married, and best of all, I have a new, cute, performing baby seal that everyone thinks looks just like me. The truth is that I am stone in love with this little boy, and this love is moving things inside me. But I'm about to be shaken like a rag doll in a Rottweiler's mouth. I wake up one morning on the road and something is crawling inside me like a spider. I've been dodging him or ignoring him and pretending everything is peachy, but the Darkness is truly back to stay. Every nerve in me has been hit so hard and so many times over the past years that they're all numb, and he knows it. I can no longer escape him. And he wants to go back to Japan.

This is my last tour of the '80s, although I don't know it at the time. The Darkness wants some fucking attention, dammit, and he's telling me to dump my career so we can have some quality time together, he and I. I wake up on our last morning in Tokyo to the news that the Space Shuttle *Challenger* has exploded during liftoff and everyone on board is dead. This is another one of those *Titanic* moments, like the death of JFK, where we all have to reassess where we thought we were headed. Sure, we knew space travel was dangerous, but we always believed that "they" had a handle on it. I wake up to the fact that the world is in even deeper shit than I imagined and we are definitely not in control. It's fitting that I chose the Space Shuttle image to describe the launching of my career, because that same career is about to meet a similar end—at least as far as the '80s are concerned.

CHAPTER FIFTEEN

MY DEPRESSION

MALIBU

1986–1989

It's a spectacular Malibu morning. Soft sunlight seeps through eucalyptus branches and splashes across the counterpane of our antique four-poster bed. I wake up in the master bedroom with its arched, old-barn-wood ceiling and look out onto the Spanish fountain in the enclosed courtyard just outside the bedroom's elegant, hand-milled French doors. I rouse myself and head into the Malibu-tiled master bathroom complete with stained-glass window, but I refuse to look in the mirror and greet the dark bastard. I know he's close by. I pee—some things never change no matter how big your house is—and walk down the hall past guest bedrooms, across a few steps, and down into the kitchen. It's "old farmhouse" style, with a domed brick ceiling and a turreted skylight. Gleaming copper pots and pans hang from an old iron ceiling rack with antique farm animal cutouts around the rim. To the right is the dining room, with more French doors opening to a small cactus garden dominated by a twenty-five-foot saguaro. A hand-carved, sixteenth-century European dining table has ten authentic Queen Anne chairs at attention around it, and across the open kitchen counter is the large family room with an old dark-oak bar and a fireplace guarded by two stone angels.

I kiss B good morning, take the mug of steaming tea she hands me, and drop to my knees in supplication before our priceless little miracle, who's sitting in his baby-walker. He smiles at me and hands me his soggy-Cheerio-encrusted Big Bird toy car. Something is pushing me this morning, making me restless. I tell my son he's beautiful and take my tea out past the twenty-foot-ceilinged great room off to the left and through the antique carriage doors that serve as the formidable entrance to our labyrinthine Spanish-style home. I walk out into the sweet morning air. Ronnie comes bounding up the long, pepper-tree-lined driveway, having just put the latest passers-by in their place with a preemptory bark, and gives me a standing double high five against my crotch, making me spill half my tea. The gardeners are already hard at work here in the front of the house, so I make my way, tagged closely by my faithful hound, around the side, past the stables and the half-acre riding ring, to the beautifully laid out pool area.

But there are three of us walking, and I know it. I've felt this confrontation coming for a long time, and although I'm a little unsure of the course it will take, I know the drill. I begin to walk around the pool, but I am pacing more than strolling. I pass the waterfall, the tennis court, and the meditation gardens. It's a secluded and peaceful place, and I'm looking for some relief from the growing unease and discomfort that is beginning to writhe like serpents in my gut. This is not how I imagined I would feel.

Sure, the Darkness has again become a regular visitor on the road and is hovering like a starving vulture over my career in general, but I'm home now. Safe with my family, for Chrissakes, and in the house of our dreams that I've worked so hard to secure. In an effort to calm what feels like the beginnings of a storm in my soul, I start to chronicle my accomplishments, because at this point I still believe I have every reason to be satisfied, content, and maybe even happy because of what I've achieved. Wasn't this supposed to be the magic healing potion, all this really great stuff?

I make my mental list: I have enough gold and platinum albums from around the world to make really cool suits of armor for me, my family, and my whole road crew. I've played sold-out concerts in theaters, halls, arenas, and speedways. A Grammy Award and numerous Grammy nominations, American Music Awards, plus some European and Japanese rock and pop awards festoon my old mum's house. I am famous (good for prompt restaurant reservations), and I'm so wealthy that I can't even count how much money I have (although, looking back, I will wish I'd given it a shot). And to top it off, I married my true soul mate and we've given birth to a baby genius. What don't I get about "things are going pretty fucking well"?

Since the morning, at this point more than twenty years ago, when the rope unraveled in the backyard shed and I fell to the hard concrete floor, I've always felt that *this* was the purpose I was saved for—to go forth (done that), be fruitful (that too), multiply (worked really hard at that), and reach for my dreams. Suddenly I'm not so sure. Is there a grander plan that I'm not aware of? Something that doesn't involve riches, adulation, and fucking?

But the Darkness is pushing me, and I must face something here, even as I try to make light of it all. "You're a pretty funny guy, huh? Well, I tell you what, pal—you can't laugh or fuck your way out of this one." And he's right. Because I've tried. On the road, the high from the craziness only lasts so long now and dissipates as quickly as spit on a hot plate once it's over. And with women, I'm starting to be the person I never wanted to be. I am becoming egotistical and controlling. Mean-spirited and abusive. The gap between the outward appearance of my fabulous-seeming life and my real inner life of self-doubts, insecurities, and guilt has gotten unreasonably wide. I can no longer reconcile the two. It seems to me that as my success and fame have grown, any self-love, confidence, or natural optimism I might have possessed has slid deeper into a pit, herded and whipped by the depression that I've never really shaken.

There are times when I have awakened in the middle of the night and seen him sitting there on the end of the bed, my Darkness. He whispers to me and fills my head with fears and doubts that I can't shake, that keep me tossing and turning until the sun cracks the morning sky. Now as I pace around the pool, trying to take desperate inventory of all the awesome shit I've accomplished, my skin is crawling at the terrible awareness of this reality gap between where I appear to be—successful, happy, complete—and where I really am inside my head: no happier than before I started this journey. And the deeper implications of what kind of a bleak future I may be looking at if I can't reconcile this dichotomy are beginning to dawn on me.

Where do I go from here? Where will my drive to win come from if I now know that winning, of itself, won't heal me as I'd always believed it would? Ronnie sniffs the bushes, blissfully heedless of my growing recognition of this predicament. Mr. D sits in my fucking Jacuzzi smiling knowingly at me and smoking a big fat cigar. He knows I hate them. I begin to visibly sweat. My mind is racing. What have I been chasing this all for, then, if nothing's really changed? Although I've attained most of the goals I set out to reach, I'm still miserable. Success has not changed me. It is not the panacea, and I am not a better person for it as I had hoped I might be. I certainly have not escaped the depression that has dogged me all my life, like I'd been pretending I had. I've changed everything around me that I can possibly change, but I am still the same. After all the mountain climbing, the battlements storming and victorious plundering, it's still the same guy looking back at me from the bathroom mirror. I am not cured.

And I am finally made aware of the "myth of fame." It may seem like an obvious revelation, but honestly, unless you've gone through it, you can't imagine what kind of a mind-fuck it really is to truly understand that, in and of itself, fame is not ultimately transformative.

One thing's for sure: I can't just go on doing what I've been doing. Suicide has ceased to be an option for me now that I have a son, so the Darkness doesn't even consider pushing me in that direction. He knows me well. Besides, I'm sure Mr. D is having way too much fun at my expense right now; why would he want it to end?

I try to turn to God, but I have no connection there, so I get no comfort and no answers. I grab the phone and call Tim Pierce, my guitar player and friend. Tim is a kindred if differently tortured soul, and in his search for his own answers he has turned to Jungian therapy. Tim and I talk regularly about our shit, and when I call he suggests I go check out a man named Robert Stein, a therapist who Tim has been seeing for a while. I balk, remembering my previous encounters, first with the useless "draw-yourself-in-relation-to-sex" guy when I was seventeen, and then the idiot I saw a few years ago who had the winning advice, "Just keep screwing around and don't tell her." But I'm desperate. I read up on Jungian therapy and am attracted to its link to the spiritual side of our existence, something that's totally missing in Freudianism. I ask myself, "Am I really insane enough to go see a shrink?" Then I realize that I'm probably not the guy to ask, but I definitely can't go on in this miserable state. So I give this Stein guy a call.

By the late 1950s, Robert Stein was a young and successful doctor. Happily married, with a house in Beverly Hills, a couple of Mercedes-Benzes in the garage, and two young daughters, he seemed to have an enviable life. But, very much like me, he had deeper psychological issues that spoiled the fun. Incest issues from when he was a child had come back to haunt him. After witnessing some medical colleagues band together to hush up the accidental death of a patient, Stein soured on his profession. Between this experience and his personal struggle with the wounds of his childhood, he decided to close his thriving medical practice, let go of all of his possessions, and move his family to Zurich so he could become a Jungian therapist under the personal guidance of Carl Jung himself. Stein's intention was to first treat himself and then help others. Ultimately, he will write a landmark book entitled *Incest and Human Love*.

I walk into his office at 3:00 p.m. on a Monday in 1986, introduce myself, and tell him I'm in trouble. (I sit in a big leather chair because the couch is taken up by Mr. D, who thinks this is all about him.) I start seeing Stein twice a week, and I acquaint him with everything I have ever done, fantasized, wished, feared, believed. I am finally so ready to deal with this crap that I open up and dive in headfirst. I understand that pouring everything out to this man is nonnegotiable. My sanity is at stake, as well as my family's survival.

Stein's the only person on the face of the planet who I tell everything to: the light and the dark, the triumphs and the train wrecks, the righteous and the reprehensible. He doesn't try to fix me; he just listens, and now that I'm facing my shit I spiral down even further. The Darkness is loving it. But I'm scared, because I came to Stein to feel better, not worse. I tell him I don't need to pay $300 an hour to feel like shit—I can do that to myself for free. He says I must go in and face the "shadow" (his term for the Darkness) and that only by facing it will I begin any kind of healing. I ask him, "Will I have to confront Darth Vader, too?" I don't think he gets the joke. Stein's office feels more like a professor's study. He is intelligent and soulful and he's been through the fire himself, so I feel that my sanity is in good hands—although he tells me that my sanity is in *my* hands! That may be so, but I often feel like I'm the kid doing the math problem and he's the math teacher who already knows the answer but won't tell me because I have to work it out for myself. I continue downward. Life goes on.

Barbara is pregnant again. It's the only good news in our world at the moment, and it draws us together. Our relationship has been struggling as well, under the barrage of my flip-flopping moods, our being new parents, and the general surreal fishbowl we find ourselves in every time we go out somewhere. Then, eight weeks into her first trimester we go to see our obstetrician, who runs a sonogram but says nothing. He wipes the gel off my girl's belly and tells us that there is no baby, it's just a bunch of cells. I think, "Isn't that what a baby is anyway—just a bunch of cells?" But he means something altogether different. There is no heartbeat. No life. We lose this one, and we're devastated. We wonder where the little spirit went.

Late at night, I hear B crying next to me in our bed and I hold her. She says she feels like she's failed. We have that in common, she and I. And everything around us continues to implode. I'm gradually withdrawing from the world. The term "househusband" runs through my mind, and Stein remarks one day that I look like a homeless guy, given my unwashed hair, unkempt beard growth, and ill-fitting clothes. He urges me to go deeper into the shadows and be okay with it. I'm not okay with it, but I know I must confront my fear or the Darkness will win.

My new family and my mental and spiritual state become my only focus, so with the throttle still wide open on my career, I hit the kill switch. I've been seeing Stein for only four months when I make this decision, but I've probably known it was coming for much longer. I call up my manager, Joe, who has only ever wanted the best for me, and I tell him that I'm leaving him and retiring. Others in my "camp" start calling, "Is everything okay, Rick? Do you need anything, buddy?" What they mean is, "What the fuck do you think you're doing? You're our cash cow, bitch!"

I have a lawyer and a business manager who are bloodsuckers of the first order. The lawyer, who is a "friend," has regularly called me up to ask me about my family and chitchat for a while, and, I suspect, bill me for the call. My business manager is an accountant who got his start by having the words "Business Manager" painted on his office door one day. We are "buddies" as well, but when we go out to dinner (which is once a week) and the check comes, he sits back in his chair, folds his arms across his chest, and smiles at me. I always pick it up.

And because we're "friends," I guess he feels he can confide in me. He tells me one day that Stephen Stills (whose money he also handles) has come after him with a baseball bat because Stills has a professional beef with him. I'm sitting with him another time when a young singer in a band, who's just had a big hit and whose money he is also supposed to be protecting, calls him up and asks if it's okay for her to buy herself a Corvette: "Sure, go ahead," he answers. He hangs up the phone, turns to me, and laughs, "She can't afford that."

Maybe I'm not smart enough at this point to notice the flashing red lights and warning bells that are trying to tell me this guy is a frigging moron and definitely should not be managing my family's and my financial future. Meanwhile, as I'm struggling to get my life in order (and am not working or making money in any way), real estate markets around the world begin to implode and collapse. A huge apartment complex in Phoenix that I own starts to go belly-up, only no one clues me in until it is too late. So just as I'm taking a breather from the world and my career, trying to pull myself together, I begin bleeding money like a hemophiliac with a straight razor. For the next two years, as I put my life on hold to work with Robert Stein, my business manager continues to mismanage my finances and I allow myself to remain ignorant. And perhaps the one area of my life that was sound—my finances—slides from solid to nearly insolvent.

There are no real "eureka" moments in this deep therapy I am undergoing, just a gradual, growing awareness of the ways in which demons drive me. There's Numero Uno, Mr. D himself, still taking up most of the couch. He likes being the center of attention, the little shit. It's a long, intensive, and arduous process as Stein and I discuss old fears and current ones, my depression and my sexual demons, my lack of faith and my lack of faithfulness. As I go deeper into therapy, I get to the point where I really cannot see myself going back to that world I left: music, life on the road, the pursuit of happiness and healing through achievement. This is not what I was hoping for. I was, again, looking to be "cured," this time by the magic of therapy rather than the magic of success. I was expecting to eventually pick up my life exactly where I left off. But that isn't going to happen, and I start to get scared for my future as a musician, father, provider, and flesh-and-blood mortal.

I tell Stein I think that maybe my career has stagnated and I now have nothing but loathing for myself. He leads me to the conclusion that my self-worth has been based solely on how successful I perceived my career to be and that if this career is not constantly rising and breaking new ground or giving me something fresh to feel good about, then I must eventually start to feel worthless. The Darkness over on the couch sneers, "He *is* worthless." I understand, fully now, that in and of itself, fame is not a metamorphosis. I am in here battling my sexual demons as well. Marriage and a baby haven't eased this in me, and I feel like I'm one come-hither look away from diving right back in. I know Barbara senses this, too.

Stein suggests that I connect to whatever it is that makes me feel good about myself, away from all the public acclaim and "mountaineering." I know right away what that is: first, songwriting! I get joy from the act and connection to my muse that has nothing to do with the outside world or anyone else. And second, my family, who warm and nurture my spirit. So I decide to write about my family. It's difficult for me to begin. I feel like an accident victim learning to walk again. It's false and strange at first to sit in my music room waiting for inspiration to come. Am I still a songwriter, or am I now just pretending?

One of the first lines I write, "Well, I pick up my guitar, I tune up, I look in the mirror. It's like a stranger in my hands . . ." issues directly from this turmoil. Most of the songs I begin to write come from the same place, and I feel that at least I can still be an honest songwriter, if nothing else. It creates a small well of self-esteem in me. My relationship with Barbara has suffered from all this time I've spent delving into my psyche, and she has an underlying mistrust of me, now that she's aware of some of my sexual issues and adulterous behavior. I feel damned if I do and damned if I don't.

Visitors to our home see none of this, of course, and we've gotten pretty good at the "social face," but this underlying and unresolved battle causes tempers to flare like ignited phosphorus at any moment, and our romantic love takes the hit of its short life. "Honeymoon in Beirut" is the song I write about all of this, and it is nothing if not candid. Using the once-beautiful city of Beirut—at this point torn apart by a war—as a metaphor, it chronicles the contrast between our "great life" without and the breakup within.

Strategy and maneuvers have replaced any love that was here,
We have dinner in silence, and bullets with beer,

I kidnapped and held for ransom the one in me that you love
We wait for the fall and put emotional bullet holes in the wall
And we keep sending signals all is well, wish you were here.

It's Keith Olsen's favorite song, probably because he's going through a similar thing at *his* home, and his battle ends in the divorce that I hope to avoid in mine. Bizarre though this seems, "Honeymoon in Beirut" becomes a big club hit in the city of Beirut.

My best songs come from misery, and at least my Darkness is providing a lot of that. Other songs that start to come are about my newborn son and the rip in my space-time continuum that he has caused. I'm also feeling small and lost because my father is dead and now I am the father. Dads are supposed to have it all together, be the strong ones their children can lean on. I don't feel I am that. In one fell swoop I have become the person that life's buck stops at, with no experienced father to back me up, help me, talk me through it. It's a sudden advancement in roles that I was neither ready for nor expecting.

And so, with Stein, I look at last into the sad death of my sweet old man and the spiritual loss that has followed. I face the anger I still have over losing him so early, the guilt I have over the years I spent away that were his last on this earth, my rejection of the God that gave my mum no time to smell the roses with her man, and my sorrow that I couldn't save him. That he went before I could offer up any solid proof to validate his long-held faith in me. That he died so young, with so much unsaid between us. That I ran from facing the end with him. That I had no time to tell him, he in his well-earned old age and me in my middle years, exactly what he meant to me growing up, feeling sheltered by his strong and loving hand. My sweet and gentle-hearted prince. Throughout the first two years of seeing Stein, I seesaw back and forth between ignorance and awareness of my monsters, demons, and angels, all under the guidance of this man.

B and I then discover that she is pregnant for the third time, and the spirit we thought might have been "lost in transit" is about to come back to us. This is a signal to me. I see that life must go on, even while I'm fighting this depression in private. I can't remain a recluse and expect my marriage, my career, and my life to remain on permanent hold and unchanged. I have to return to the real world and start a healthier pursuit of my needs and desires, despite the fact that where Mr. D and my self-worth are concerned, there is still no cure, remission, or even sullen standoff.

I begin to look at making a brand-new record, so I go find myself a brand-new manager. It's difficult to push myself out of the house after living all this time away from the general populace, but now it's not just all about me anymore: I have a family. And I am the dad. I sign with Ron Weisner, who has just come from co-managing Michael Jackson and Madonna. I think this is a good move. What I don't know is that Ron, who has just lost his wife, Rose, to cancer, is dealing with life-changing issues of his own. I learn a practical way to meditate through TM but keep falling asleep during my meditations. What am I trying so hard to stop myself from seeing during these sessions? It's truly amazing how my mind works to trip me up and confuse me. It will be a long time before I understand why the Darkness keeps making me go unconscious when I settle down to meditate. But it will make sense to me when I do.

Stein encourages me to stay with the meditation process. He also urges me to keep going with our sessions, even though I'm slowly turning back to my life. Through the writing of these new songs, I realize that songwriting has been the only thing that's made me feel valuable without any outside acclaim. The process and the outcome of writing validates itself. Recording is a 24/7 process for me, and I commit myself again. I end the sessions with Stein to concentrate fully on making this new album. I call Keith Olsen to ask if he wants to co-produce the record with me. Keith has been fighting his own devils while I've been away, cleaning up a bad coke habit, and we are an especially good fit at this point in both our lives. I do feel I've gained some clarity in my sessions with Stein, and these songs are all about what I've been finding in there with him.

But when I get back on the treadmill I jumped off a few years before, I find it's just more of the same: distraction, busywork, and ego boosting. I do love the process of recording, but my mental state is still fragile and my sexual shit is not fully under control. During the recording, sex rears its head (so to speak) and I fall again. I need a bigger diversion, so we head to the Bahamas to complete the lead vocals once all the tracks are done. Both the families go, kids and all, and it's an incredible break for Barbara and me. I come back from the trip reenergized and truly ready to get back to my life.

Rock of Life is the name of the album, and also of the song that distills much of what I've been going through with Stein. The single "Rock of Life" becomes a hit, and I go to Europe to do TV and radio. I'm anxious about going on the road again for fear of falling back into old sexual habits, so I'm relieved when I make it home with my integrity intact and my foot bullet hole free. The album is struggling slowly up the charts in the U.S. despite the hit single, so I plan a tour and put a new band together. We jump into rehearsals.

I love machines. Especially machines that go really fast and put my life in danger. I've broken ribs when my Paraplane (a type of ultralight aircraft) crashed on takeoff, and I've broken them again and sustained some pretty bad cuts and bruises on dirt bikes and on my three-wheeled ATV. "All-terrain vehicle" is the name given to the off-road motorcycles that trash the delicate ecosystem, and I've been an avid rider for about six years. I even tool around my neighborhood with my young son, Liam, sitting astride the gas tank. And it is while I am raping the fragile desert in Palmdale one morning, between rehearsals, that my bike flips and the fragile desert hits back.

I go down at sixty miles per hour and pull the heavy bike on top of me, knocking myself unconscious, breaking six ribs, shattering my collarbone, and stripping tendons from my left leg and left shoulder. And I sustain all this damage to my body despite the fact that I look like a fey and fruity gladiator with all the colorful off-road armor I'm wearing. In the ambulance on the way back to Los Angeles I finally get a shot of Demerol and slip into the state I will be in and out of for the next six weeks. My clavicle is so shattered, the doctor will pick pieces of bone out of me for two of the three hours of surgery I undergo to install a permanent titanium brace where the living bone used to be. The morphine drip in my arm is my only comfort.

Needless to say, the tour is cancelled. It will be five months before I can even hang a guitar off my damaged left shoulder. So down, down I go again. The Darkness is still standing.

My business manager is full of good news as well. He finally tells me that the apartment complex in Arizona that has been the beneficiary of a shitload of my money is toast. We have to walk away and kiss all the money he has squandered on it good-bye. But the good news is that my lawyer has a big publishing deal he's working on for me . . . no, wait . . . that's toast, too. Oh, and by the way, you'd better move out of that expensive house of yours before it's too late as well. See ya.

I am torn and miserable about confiding in B, especially because she is carrying our baby, but I know I must. She is the only safe place for me to turn. She cries when I tell her, then toughens up and goes looking for a house for us to rent so we have a place to bring our new baby home to, while I wallow in defeat. Mel Gibson and his wife Robyn come to the rescue and buy our home, but I am broken to have to sell it. I've failed myself and, much worse, I've failed my family. Dad has blown it at his first time at bat.

I'm more like a frightened kid when I go running back to Stein. He helps me to a degree with this unfolding nightmare, and I try my best not to appear like a loser for Barbara's sake, as the added stress could hurt the new baby she's carrying, but I know she's scared, too. She does her best to stay calm for all our sakes, and I'm grateful for her courage and strength. We do nonetheless manage to get into a couple of blowout arguments. Then Jose Menendez, the president of my label, RCA, and a man I have come to know and like, is shotgunned to death, along with his wife Kitty, by their own two sons. (Suddenly my family life doesn't seem so bad.) And while I'm still in shock over that, a new regime moves into RCA. I'm pissed at what I believe is their cavalier treatment of my *Rock of Life* album, so I leave the label. My family and I move into a rental down the street from where we used to be home owners. If it's true that my self-worth is based on how well I'm doing, then you can probably guess where this move is on the list of "The Top Ten Reasons Why I Suck."

I blame my depression for pulling me out of my career midflight and causing all this resulting mayhem. "Gotcha, you little fucker," says the Darkness.

See, I'm right.

Then on the day that we move into this makeshift home, I get a phone call informing me that Bobby Brooks, my sweet Woody Allen of an agent, has just been killed in a helicopter crash along with Stevie Ray Vaughan. At his service I start crying uncontrollably, to the point where people are looking uncomfortably at me. It's for more than Bobby that I cry. He was there on the road with me when I started this journey. In the bus, at the first gigs, cheering as we climbed higher and higher. Saying good-bye to him feels like I'm also saying good-bye to those times, forever.

I finally grow some balls and shake my old business manager, leaving him scot-free for all the financial destruction he has caused through ignorance and mismanagement. Jim Pankow (from the band Chicago) and I have been friends for a while, and he recommends *his* business manager to me. I finally get with someone who knows what he's doing with his client's money. This new accountant has serious questions about how my finances have been managed in the past, and he instigates a lawsuit on my behalf against my old business manager before I put a stop to it. It's not in me to take money as restitution for damage done. *Success is the best revenge*, I hear myself say. It makes me pause. Did I just say that? It's a positive sign that maybe what I'm going through with Stein is doing some good. I translate this to mean that somewhere inside me I haven't given up: there is still a flicker of life, a beam of hope.

Then the sun bursts through the clouds for a brief moment and Joshua Charles Springthorpe (Little Mr. Center of the Universe II) enters our world on the 21st of March, 1989. It is the only bright event in our terrible year. I hurt and feel shamed that we're bringing our new son home to a temporary shelter. It seems like we have no roots. My words, screamed in frustration as a child at my mother when we were told that we'd be moving again, come back to haunt me: "When I have kids, I'm never, ever moving!"

"Sure you're not," says Mr. D.

And gushing money from the severed artery of my trashed career, I slowly bleed away most of my first fortune.

So where do you think I run in my pitiable state? Straight into the arms of a friggin' wannabe actress. I've started attending another acting class to try to get that life going, and it's there that I meet her. She's pretty and blond, but the real reason that I'm attracted to her is because when the class goes out as a group to eat, she turns guys' heads. I'm feeling worthless and emasculated by having failed my family and myself, so what better way to get some integrity back than to fuck this girl that so many men seem to find hot? Makes sense to me. And Mr. Darkness thinks it's a stellar idea. No longer content with shooting myself just in the foot with my dick, I am now attempting to strafe everything I love and want in my life too.

Of course Barbara knows something is going on, and when she confronts me I tell her the truth. Here she is, a sweet and sincere girl who is feeling dumpy and unattractive having just given birth to our second son, and I'm parading this young babe around like I'm a hotshot. It is a testament to B's soul that she only throws a carton of milk at me. It's the lowest point in my life. In a song on *Rock of Life* called "World Start Turning," I wrote the line: "*I made a promise to myself I'll never get that low again.*" But it seems I just have. I've traded all that is true and pure in my world for a quick fix.

I break the affair off and beg Barbara not to leave me. I watch her sitting quietly, feeding our baby Joshua, an air of deep sadness around her. She looks like a little kid in a too-big chair. She is again the eighteen-year-old innocent I first fell in love with, and my heart breaks for what

I've done to her. She could take half of what money is left and run. But something holds her—and me—to this marriage. It's not fear of what's out there or fear of starting a new life with someone else. It's not fear at all. What holds us together is what we both know in our souls: that despite our troubles, we are right for each other. We stay together by choice. Letting go is not an option either of us will choose, but in holding on, we know we have work to do to make things right. Clearly I'm the one with the real labor ahead. I must change. I am forever grateful for B's big heart and her willingness to stick with me when I have put her through so much.

We go into couples therapy with Stein's wife, Lottie, who is also a Jungian therapist. Even though B is fundamentally committed to our marriage and to working through this, I could lose her. I work hard to undo the damage I have so recklessly caused.

It's a long road back from where I've led us, and for a while we can't even get close to a place of true reconciliation. Barbara has justifiable recriminations and I have nothing to offer in my defense. And so it goes until we begin bridging the gap and finding our way to make this the relationship we both want. I resolve to honestly face my shit and not to opt for bedding a pretty stranger every time I need to prop up my ego or assuage my depression. I'm finally feeling up to this challenge, thanks to the small but steady progress I've made with Lottie's husband.

Dammit, spoke too soon. Mr. D. isn't done with me yet—but at least his attack is on another front.

I hit forty years of age, and in the music business, where everyone is in a more or less permanent state of arrested development, I start to feel old and useless. Ugly again, like I used to. The Darkness suggests a little elective surgery. "Yeah, a face-lift. That'd fix you right up, pal. And don't worry about your earlier episode under the knife, these American doctors are *grrrrreat*!" With trepidation I make an appointment and go to see a plastic surgeon. Looking at my sad and tired mug, he says with confidence, "I can make you look years younger." The fact that I could also end up looking like a stretched-lizard-faced freak isn't mentioned.

I'm feeling nervous as the surgery day approaches. I have this horrible feeling I might die under the anesthesia. I can't shake this feeling of death, so on the morning of the surgery I call the doctor and cancel it. I hang up the phone and it rings immediately. I answer and a voice tells me that Joe Gottfried, my amiable old manager, has just died of a heart attack while driving his beloved BMW. I knew someone would die today—I just thought it would be me. I'd always intended to apologize to Joe for the unceremonious way I dropped him when my life started to unravel. He was a good man who loved me and who I treated unfairly in the end. If this is my chance to say something, then: Joe, I'm truly sorry. You were there for me when no one else was. Dammit, I seem to spend my life apologizing for shit I've done—this time too late.

In another case of excellent timing, *The Oprah Show* calls—that's a good thing, right?—to ask if I'd like to participate in a segment they're doing called One-Hit Wonders. That's a bad thing, right? Well, yes, it is. It's especially bad considering the frame of mind I am currently in. The *Oprah* contact is still talking, but I can't make out what she's saying for the blood pounding in my ears. For the first time in my life, I am angry at the fact that I wrote "Jessie's Fucking Girl." Mr. D. has set me up. ("Hey, Sport, Oprah's calling!") only to sucker punch me ("They think you're a one-hit wonder. Hahahahaha"). I don't remember how I get off the call, but I retain enough pride to decline the invitation.

Later, I toy with the idea of sending them an e-mail with the titles of my seventeen Top-40 friggin' hits poetically woven through the missive in a cleverly wry and ironic way, underlining the fact that I am a waaay bigger star than they think I am. But I don't. Instead, I take it in the gut and accept it as further proof that I am a lost soul and a total loser. My Darkness speaks to me again as I fall asleep that night: "Hell of a legacy, bro. After twenty-five years in the biz: a one-hit-motherfucking wonder. Nice."

So for as low as I feel, and as much deeper as Mr. D. would like to take me, I am clear about one thing: I must work on my life with B. If I lose her, it doesn't really matter what else happens to me.

Back in the warmth of Robert Stein's office, I open up and tell him everything I've been up to.

There is no judgment here, and I'm thankful for that. Still, I must face what I've done and where this has all led me and dragged my family along to. I tell him I wish there was some piece of me that could be removed surgically so I'd be free of the Darkness, the sexual shit, and my massive lack of self-approval. He nods in agreement. "Yes, we'd all like that," is all he says. Sometimes I think I'm making real strides in healing all this, and other times I feel like I'm pissing my life away just sitting here talking to this stranger who knows me better than any person ever will, not making any appreciable progress at all. All the crap I hate about myself, all the garbage that I never asked for, that I feel I've been saddled with against my will, that I was born into or predestined to face or whatever the fuck it all is, will be with me until I die, and this therapy and pursuit of a spiritual path are the ways I learn to recognize and own my burdens, my demons, and not let them ruin or destroy my life.

And that life goes on.

Liam, our elder son, is in a private school that caters to future doctors and lawyers. Even at this early age, he is obviously an arty kid, and this school is a bad fit. The powers that be at his school also have their collective heads up their asses and, full of self-righteous attitude; they call all the time about Liam's disruptive behavior and the wild stories he makes up. One week we get a bunch of phone messages from concerned school parents saying things like, "Oh my God, we just heard. We're so sorry. Barbara, if you need anything, just call us." We find out that Liam had gone to school the day after watching an episode of *The Simpsons* in which Homer has a heart attack and told everyone that *I* had a heart attack.

The school calls again to ask if there are any "challenges" or "issues" at home, as Liam seems to be "acting out." I hang up the phone before I puke from "buzzword" sickness, although in fairness to them, Liam is obviously feeling the tension between B and me. But the school isn't working for our son, so we move him to a local one closer to home that's run by moms and doesn't have the Harvard-or-bust mentality. Barbara and I continue going to couples therapy together, and I continue to see Stein by myself.

And life goes on.

We start to notice that Ronnie is sleeping more and more and eating less and less. I take him to the animal hospital so they can run some tests and maybe find out what the problem is. They put him in a small cage, and he looks at me sadly, head lowered, eyes showing half-moon whites. I don't know why he looks so melancholy. I kiss him and tell him I'll see him tomorrow. I do, but not in the way I thought I would. On a bright July morning full of promise the following day, I get a call from the hospital. The voice at the other end tells me he's very sorry, they tried to save him, but Ronnie is dead. I go numb.

I drive to the hospital and a nurse leads me into a small, nondescript room off the main hallway. There, in the same wire cage where I bid him good night the evening before, absolutely sure that I would see him again, lies my boy, on his side with his tongue poking out a little way like he's blowing a raspberry. I kneel down, open the cage door, and put my hand on his side—he's still warm. His eyes aren't looking for me anymore. He's gone. I try to feel his spirit near me, around . . . anywhere. Although I'm still consistently reading about it and searching for it, most things spiritual seem beyond my grasp. So I'm on my own contending with this. The only one who knows how it feels to lose him is Barbara, and I've done my best to alienate her.

I need to know, so I ask . . . "How was his death?" The doctor tells me it was a little stressful for Ronnie. His lungs filled up with fluid and he couldn't breathe, so they put a tube down his throat trying to vent some of it. He died like that. I take his body to the Pet Park I pass every time I drive into town, and I have him cremated, before I've even begun to absorb his loss. They give me a cedar box with his ashes in it. I am in a fog as I take them back to Barbara at home. And as I drive through the canyon, the Darkness wickedly insinuates that I abandoned Ronnie.

"You did that to your boy Elvis too, remember?" he whispers. And yes, I do.

Then the landlord calls and says he wants his house back. We have to pack up and move again.

CHAPTER SIXTEEN

OF HAWKS AND THE ISLAND OF THE LONG WHITE CLOUD

MALIBU TO NEW ZEALAND

1989

Our new rent-a-house in the Point Dume area of Malibu has a large open fireplace in the living room with a heavy oak-beam mantel. It is on this mantel that I place the cedar chest of Ronnie's ashes. It looks too small to contain the mighty life force I knew as my dog. I tell myself it doesn't. It's just the ashes of his corporeal shell. But where is that life force? I light candles around the box and place flowers there, too. I am making an altar of sorts, but there is no spiritual connection, as hard as I try to manufacture one. I can't feel where he has gone, my furry boy.

I hear a strange sound in the back of the fireplace. I pause . . . and hear it again. I finish lighting the candles, grab a flashlight, and rake the narrow beam, yellow as chicken fat, across the sooty black back of the chimney. I see movement in the dark of the flue and jump back in surprise. Heart pounding, I move in and shine the light directly on the source of the motion. A pair of large, bright, forward-facing, predatory eyes peer out of the gloom in back of the fireplace. I look closer and see a flurry of striped, exotic feathers. It's a young hawk trapped in the ashes of the flue, directly behind where I've placed Ronnie's ashes. I suddenly feel like I'm inside a dream. I've just been reading about the Native

American belief that birds are signs of the spirit, because they fly so close to heaven. Probably because the spirit is likened to an animal, it's one of the few images that has registered with me.

My hands are shaking as I dial the number for the area animal control. It's Sunday, so I'm not expecting to get anyone, but a voice answers and tells me that there's a field officer in the Malibu area right now rescuing a seal. He'll be over in thirty minutes. He's there in twenty. He arrives, reaches into the flue and, after a struggle, withdraws his gloved hand from the darkness of the fireplace. Perched wild-eyed and panting open-beaked on his arm is a magnificent red-shouldered hawk. I ask him how long he thinks it's been trapped there. "About two days," he answers. It's the exact length of time since Ronnie left this earth. We take the hawk outside and release him. As I watch the young raptor circle the house and then wheel off into the bright summer sky, I feel a giant weight lift from my chest as Ronnie's spirit soars with this bird. He is okay. I feel it in my soul. It figures that a sign from my boy would lead me back to the spiritual path I fell from when my dad died. Unexpectedly, Ronnie's death has punched a pinhole of light in the cinder-cone blackness that surrounds me.

In that moment, I commit again to a belief in God and the path of the spirit. Light shines on the Darkness and he scurries away like a rat in a sewer. I begin to understand that God doesn't come when you're looking the hardest, but when your need is the greatest.

I've always wanted a tattoo, but I've never been able to settle on anything that would be okay to wear on my skin for the rest of my life. Now I know, so I go to the only tattoo parlor I can think of. When I first moved to the U.S., in 1972, I stayed at the old Hyatt House on Sunset Boulevard for a night. Looking out the window that first morning in Los Angeles, I saw a sign over the store opposite, with a red heart and the words "Sunset Tattoo" wrapped around it. It is there that I go. And I walk out after three hours of pain, wearing across my right shoulder the symbol of a reawakening in me: a red-shouldered hawk. It is the coat-of-arms of my acceptance of God/a greater power/something unfathomable but more than me. And along with all the dogs of the world, hawks now become my totem animal spirit.

I feel a change coming. I should be going down the tubes because of the loss of Ronnie, but I'm actually feeling a little stronger. Ronnie's parting gift has spurred my recommitment to a connection to faith. My beautiful sons fill my days, and I'm there every step of the way with them. Together we mourn Ronnie, our hairy brother, and they watch as their dad cries. I think of myself at their age, watching my own father crying for his lost mum.

I am writing again, but once more it's unfocused. I complete a short instrumental suite for Ronnie that no one will ever hear and I try to move my head into a "writing space." I have a lot to write about, but I'm confused about the direction the music should take. This time my writer's block has more to do with the fact that I'm feeling unfashionable and distant from the current music scene. Rap is big now, and songs, as I knew them, seem to be disappearing. Tim Pierce and I get together with writer/producer Bob Marlette and experiment musically with a new direction my writing has taken. Over the next few months we write and record songs that I would never have come up with on my own. They are very groove oriented, with drum loops and quirky guitars.

I decide to release it in Europe as a band concept album, so the three of us briefly form Sahara Snow for the purpose of releasing the record overseas. Fans from the U.S. buy it as an import, but it doesn't really do much. The musical climate has storm clouds overhead for us musicians raised on rock, and radio doesn't know where it's going. I return to acting again and film a couple of Movies of the Week for TV but nothing worth mentioning. Wow, is this 1978 again, for Chrissakes?!

We muddle along.

Then I get a call from my acting agent. He's really my touring agent, but I'm not touring, so he's my acting agent right now. There's a TV series ready to go and they're looking for me. They want me to play an ex-cop (how original) who now owns a surf shop (okay, that's kind of original) and all he wants to do is surf (now that's original), but his little brother wants to be a private detective and keeps getting my character involved in karate-kicking, girl-chasing, bad-guy's-ass-whupping, naked-chests-on-the-beach and girls-in-skimpy-bikinis-type action. The original title for the show is (cringe) *Surf and Protect.*

In one of life's weird sidesteps, I was originally up for the David Hasselhoff part in *Baywatch*, but I thought the script was so lame that I wasn't interested. Now that *Baywatch* is a huge hit, they want me for the *new Baywatch*. I know these shows are just excuses to parade hot girls around in their bikinis. I'm not saying that's a bad thing, by the way. I'm all for a show that parades hot girls around in their bikinis now and then; I just didn't think I'd be part of the team. But they offer a lot of money. So I take the gig, and they say that we're going to shoot the first season in Australia. Okay, cool. No, wait . . . Australia is too expensive. New Zealand's cheaper; we're going to New Zealand instead. When I grow up and have kids, I'm never moving, remember? Well, guess what? "Kids, we're moving to New Zealand." And as my old mum had done so many years before, I try to add a little history and perspective to the new destination for them. "Hey, did you guys know that the Maori name for New Zealand is 'Aotearoa,' which means 'Long White Cloud'?" They don't really care and ask if they can bring their video games.

We are all actually up for the move and B and I could use a bit of a getaway right now. Traveling and reading were always my prime educators anyway, so I get the tickets, buy our boys some books, and away we go. So what am I thinking at this point? Why am I so ready to jump on board this show and go halfway around the world to film it? Mr. D would fucking well like to know!! He loves the house we're living in now. It looks like the place we sold, only it has smaller windows and more tree growth around it so it's dark and gloomy in here. Sunbeams don't reach very far inside this "house of shadows," and my Darkness likes it that way because it tends to keep me down longer. "Why are we moving?" he asks, but I know it's a rhetorical question.

I'm still disillusioned and lost with my music. My focus is now on making money (never a good place for me to operate from), and acting has always been my back-pocket go-to gig when I'm feeling financially challenged. I love music and my muse so much when I'm writing and playing that it would feel like I was whoring her out if I let money rule me there. I never have and I never will. I am, however, okay with whoring out what acting talent I possess. I have always been okay with that (see: the *GH* years). I'm worried about my family's security now that my finances are so precarious. And I need a friggin' break. We all do. The prospect of living abroad is actually pretty exciting, and my family is eager for the journey. Mr. D says he's staying in LA, and that is *so* okay with me that I offer him the use of one of our cars, the surly bastard.

And so I inch toward building my second fortune. I figure if I could do it once, then a second time should be easy. I also get some well-timed advice from one of the richest guys I know. He says to me, "Always sign your own checks, and always deposit your own checks." I do that to this day. And I've learned a lesson: no one cares about your money like you do.

The scripts to *High Tide* (as it is now called) are fairly good for the first season of the show. They're funny, and the action zooms along from car chases, to houses being blown sky-high, to bedding bodacious babes, to kicking bad-guy butt. George Segal plays our boss but refuses to learn his lines, insisting on cue cards instead, which is a bit distracting when you're in a scene with him and he keeps searching madly off camera for his next line. The production values aren't great and it's pretty poorly shot, as most of the guys responsible for *The Lord of the Rings* are still in grade school or pooping in their diapers at this point.

The crew we use are a bunch of misfits and loonies from around New Zealand. The focus puller, who looks like he's never had a bath in his life, picks boogers all day long and drops them onto the director's unsuspecting bald head. The lighting guy is a cross-dresser who often shows up on set in full drag and makeup. Then there's the uptight, sexually repressed sound man who shouts "No good for sound" after every take and makes us have to shoot the whole fucking scene again. And if we ask the crew for fifteen minutes extra at the end of the day to finish shooting the scene we're right in the middle of, they refuse on the grounds that the pubs will be closing in an hour.

The director is an East End cockney who lucked out and married a baroness and now insists we all call him "the baron." He makes the sweet New Zealand production company jump through hoops to get him a bloody Rolls-Royce so he can tool around on weekends in style. He's a hilarious storyteller, though, and some of his tales are even true. He was Cary Grant's wingman for a while and was on hand to perform services such as standing lookout while Cary banged Sophia Loren behind a sand dune on some movie set. And then there's the beautiful Czechoslovakian girl the producers cast as a beach babe in every third episode because she's so amazing-looking but whose husband keeps turning up on the set to yell at her and tell her to put her clothes back on and come home.

I beat what I've always considered to be a healthy fear of man-eating sharks long enough to try surfing at Piha, one of the primo surf locations on the globe. The New Zealander who happens to be the current world surfing champion pushes my board into the waves trying to teach me how to ride the thing. It's kind of the "surf" equivalent of having Andre Agassi lob tennis balls to you so you can practice your crappy forehand.

But the best part of the trip is that Barbara, the boys, and I are together as a family. And I don't cheat once! Fucking whoopee! It's kind of pathetic that I feel like I should get a medal. You mean I'm supposed to act like a human being with a conscience? It's expected? A change is as good as a rest, and B and I are feeling stronger and more connected now that we're in a new, "clean-slate" location and away from anything that reminds us of the shit we've just been through. She is the mom and caregiver and I am the mammoth-slaying breadwinner. It's very clear-cut, and right now simplicity is good. Our boys settle into school pretty well, and unlike me as a kid in England, where I was the Dork of the Century, my sons are from the U.S. of freakin' A. and are hipper than next week's haircut.

We have a beautiful home right on the beach outside Auckland with the Fuji-shaped island of Rangitoto as our morning view and the constant waves of the Pacific beating at the edge of our front lawn. It doesn't suck. To my dismay though, Mr. Darkness has changed his mind and hitched a ride to this fair island. He's missed me. And by the way, he totaled the car I lent him. Occasionally he'll chime in as I'm sitting in the makeup chair getting ready for a day's shoot. "You're looking a little tired there, pal. You can't do those late nights like you used to when you were young, huh?" But I'm working twelve to fourteen hours a day on this show and I don't have time for him. The long arm of the Screen Actors Guild doesn't reach as far as New Zealand, and we are not getting union breaks. But we are excited for the show and up to the task.

Yannick Bisson, my Canadian co-star, is a really decent actor with a wicked sense of humor. He has two young daughters around the same age as our two boys. We all think it's pretty safe here in good old New Zealand, where there are no guns, sheep shearing is big news, and crime is infinitesimal compared to the States. That's why it comes as a bit of a shock when my youngest son Joshua—then four years old—is abducted while walking along the beach with Barbara and Liam. I'm running the opposite way down the same beach with my headphones on when a very out-of-breath Liam stops me (he's been chasing me for five minutes) and says some guy has taken Josh.

The world does one of those camera moves where I stay in place and the background zooms out surrealistically. I take off at full speed after my precious son. For ten minutes I live every parent's nightmare. I reach Barbara, who is screaming and pointing along the beach and rocks. I run on. This isn't happening. You only read about this stuff; you never actually go through it. I have only one thought: *God, let him be okay*. I ask the few people along the way if they've seen this guy with my son. They all point in one direction—farther down the beach and farther still away from me. I keep running. My wife has called the police from one of the nearby houses on the beach, and I see a chopper in the sky already, circling.

I turn a corner running at full speed and almost trip over Josh. He's casually making his way back to where he'd last seen his mom and brother. I scoop him up in disbelief and kiss his eyes, nose, and ears (we've always loved his ears). I ask if the guy hurt him, and he says no. We meet up with Liam, who's taken it upon himself to go after his little brother. The three of us head back to their mom. He is our beautiful boy again, and not some tragic memory we can never erase. A cop brings a stuffed toy lion around to our house and gives it to Josh. Josh calls the lion Hairy. He calls the guy that grabbed him "a dickweed." I would have to agree with that assessment.

Apart from the odd abduction, the trip to New Zealand is energizing and healing. The country is spectacular, life is simple, work is plentiful, the weather is beautiful, and the people are caring and soulful (except for the fucker who tried to steal our kid). What's not to like? We spend two weeks filming on an island called Pakatoa and every evening, after the shooting ends, I grab one of the dirt bikes the stunt guys are using and put little Josh on it, and we ride to the top of the island to watch the sun set over the Pacific. We are all sad to leave New Zealand when shooting is completed. We know that the second season won't be filmed here because the producers are already talking about San Diego.

The upside of shooting in San Diego is that it means we return to Malibu, which still feels like home. They replace Oscar-nominated George Segal with a "Playmate of the Year" who can't act, but whose boobs are bigger than George's. I know by this move that *High Tide* isn't long for this world. It becomes a "babe of the week" show with actors like Lucy Lawless and Denise Richards doing their best with the dialog from the ever-worsening scripts. The producers of *High Tide* are great at selling a show, but they suck pretty hard at quality control. We end up with a fairly successful show in South America and certain parts of Europe, but one that is relegated to the wee hours of American TV, where the only people who see it are lonely insomniacs and the occasional bored night watchman. I want out. Unfortunately they have sold one more season and I am contracted to it.

Then pale blue eyes peer at us through the fence of a dog adoption center one fine morning and my animal spirit comes home. Barbara names him Scooby and I name him Gomer. I tell everyone that he's so awesome we had to name him twice. He is the coolest. Friends tell us he reminds them of Ronnie. Not in looks, because he is a brindle pit bull mix with eyes the color of Paul Newman's, but in his vibe and his connection to me. We film the final season of *High Tide* in Ventura, so at least the locations are getting closer to home. And Gomer accompanies me everywhere I go. I think he especially likes the bikini-clad girls, who ask if they can walk him on the beach during lunch breaks. The *High Tide* scripts get worse. Barbara and I are renting a house in Malibu and flying to different parts of the country to see if there's anywhere else we would prefer to live.

When we walk out one morning and see a "For Sale" sign in front of the very house in which we are currently living, Malibu wins by default and we decide to buy the house we've been renting. It's a modest three-bedroom family home set in a spectacular canyon in a family section of Malibu, and when we make an offer on it, our landlord—an ex-FBI agent who drives a Rolls-Royce and also owns a yacht (?)—says that he thought we were looking for a mansion! He didn't even consider we might want to buy this place. But we do. We remodel. And our kids beg us never to leave it. So we don't. It's a soulful home and we know it. There's something that resembles a "good spirit" around this house. It's already been the backdrop for some healing for me, and the size of the place allows for room to breathe, but visitors don't get lost and we don't need an intercom to find each other.

I'm trying to write again now that *High Tide* is on its last legs and my focus is shifting, but I can't seem to finish a single song. I've been working full-time as an actor over the last few years, but I'm still a musician at heart. I'm just having trouble finding my way back to it. Halfway through every song I'm writing, the Darkness confirms what I fear: each song is shit. I have never been so blocked. Since writing songs is at the core of my identity and in recent years has been the wellspring for what little self-worth I have, this inability to compose even one song erases most of the gains made in New Zealand. Plus, now that we're home I'm back on the "playing field" and starting to feel some of the old pressures. So I reach for the phone to call Robert Stein, my confessor. But my friend and keeper of all my secrets has died of cancer and taken everything I ever confided in him to his great and well-earned rest.

I am desperate for help and don't know where to turn now that Stein is gone. I read a book about a new pill. It's called Prozac. I go to a psychotherapist and he says I am a classic candidate for it—and that'll be $350 please, thanks so much, shut the door on your way out. He says I have what he calls "clinical depression" and prescribes twenty milligrams. My Darkness, of course, has a word or two to say about this doctor's diagnosis. "You think a fucking pill is going to keep me away forever? Not a chance, Rickyboy. Oh, as a side effect of Prozac your dick may not work. Yeah, that oughta keep your wife happy." I'm not at all sure what I'm expecting to feel on this stuff, but I am a little concerned that it'll turn me into some kind of permanently high pill-popping happy freak. What I do feel is that, for a while, it puts Mr. D in a closet and shuts the door so I can finally finish a song. Prozac blows the black cloud away, and I focus on the things I can do something about, rather than the things I can't. The drug allows me to still have my emotions, though; it hasn't turned me into a non-feeling automaton and it doesn't blow away *all* the bad stuff.

Now that we're home owners in Malibu once again, I start getting recurrent feelings of shame and inadequacy about losing our first house in such a typical, rock-star new-money, clueless-about-what's-really-going-on kind of way. But I'm also feeling strong enough to try to do something about overcoming this self-flagellating regret, powered either by my strengthening spiritual path or the vitamin P I'm dosing myself with—or maybe a combination of both. So I get in my car and take a drive by our old house to see what happens. I've always been big on confronting a problem head-on, and I think this is what I'm aiming at with the drive-by.

I enter through the old canyon gate, past familiar streets we used to walk with Liam when he was a baby. I pass our once-upon-a-time house. So many memories here—so much pain still associated with it that I can't seem to get past, no matter how I try or how much better everything else seems to be. This is where I failed as a man, and my family suffered for that. I think about how my dad never put us, his family, in such a position: moving because of financial troubles. I am ashamed again. This house was also the material proof that I had made it. I could look at it every day and see the validation of all my struggles and my persistence. Here it was, in one big three-dimensional representation. For all the world to see. It was the only concrete illustration of fame that mattered to me. Not all that shit I listed for myself around the swimming pool that morning: the platinum albums, awards, financial gains, sold-out tours.

Revisiting the scene of the crime doesn't help. I turn the car around and head back up the road to the highway, disappointed that I still feel such overwhelming pain. I don't know what I thought I'd find in here, but it certainly doesn't resemble any kind of closure. All I feel is a deep sense of loss and failure as I drive away.

I am half a mile from where the old street empties out onto Pacific Coast Highway when suddenly a huge hawk, with a three-and-a-half-foot wingspan, swoops down in front of my car and, staying ahead of me by about ten feet—neither changing direction up, down, or sideways—guides me out of the neighborhood for the final two hundred yards. Near the mouth of the street, he veers to the left and is gone. My heart is hammering in my chest and I have to pull the car over to the side of the road. Did that just actually *happen*? I sit there for minutes rerunning it in my mind. I think back on the hawk that came to me when Ronnie died, caught in the flue of a fireplace, and know that this was no coincidence. When I start the car up and hit the highway, something in me has been healed.

CHAPTER SEVENTEEN

A BETTER DESTINATION

IN THE STUDIO AND ON THE ROAD

The '90s

This recent visitation by the hawk has left me with the renewed understanding that there is more to our existence than I can possibly perceive through my five senses. There's something out there in the hard, bright cosmos that's bigger than just we humans, who live, breed, ponder, and die on this little ball floating in space (the Rock of Life). Our world has been witness to some amazing stuff, not all of it powered by us hominids. And this latest memo from the hawk is all the confirmation I need. I've drifted in and out of this conviction for most of my life, but moments like this make me wonder why I ever doubt at all. And I think the signs all started when the hangman's knot came unraveled that morning in the shed. I've always felt that I was singular, unique, destined for something special—as we all are. It's just that at times, some of us (yes, that would include me) gravitate more toward fear than faith, and fear and faith cannot occupy the same space at the same time. But it's in our power to choose. So if it's a choice between believing and not believing, then I'd rather believe. And that's my decision at this point in my life—to believe.

Prior to this, I have intelligently (by my own reckoning) looked at the facts, rationally thought them through, and come to the conclusion that God cannot exist. He just doesn't stand up to reason. Which makes sense, because having faith is, by its nature, an irrational act. But now

I'm done with being the discerning snob who's superior to the ignorant, faithful masses because he's figured it out. So it's with open arms that I decide to believe again: I embrace God and accept every little miraculous sign I've been fortunate enough to witness. From here on out, my heart and mind will be open to all the very real possibilities. I feel like a dry and empty lake bed as the first drops of a monsoon rain hit its baked, cracked surface. I think this is what Stein was helping to push me toward. My faith and the Prozac seem to be keeping Mr. D at bay most of the time, and I'm curious to find out if I can do it on my own. But I'm not ready to get off the "vitamin P diet" just yet.

This "flooding of my parched soul" brings on songs. And I'm suddenly scrambling to write them all down. As far as songwriting goes for me, it never rains, but it pours. The songs I write are, to varying degrees, about my spiritual surrender. "It's Always Something" is the first song I finish, and it's an acceptance that no matter how great things are, shit will generally follow and, thankfully, vice versa. I mention my sweet old man for the first time in a long time, and his firm and abiding belief in me is finally put into a song:

When I was a kid, the teachers and the priests said,
"Why you let him run around like that?"
My father said, "If the boy wants to play the guitar, I say we let him"
Through the hard years he was my rock when I just could not win.
So it goes, you know my father died just before my leaky ship came in.

The years-long break from touring has enabled me to put some distance between myself and the problem of my sex habit. (When I was seventeen, I don't think I could have envisioned putting the words "sex habit" and "problem" in the same sentence.) It has been a healthy break in that respect, and I'm hoping that when I do start touring again, I'll be able to keep my focus and not jump back into the nightmare of fucking every girl I can (again, the seventeen-year-old me wouldn't understand this dilemma). But the prospect of touring again sometimes feels like an abyss ready to suck me back into it. "Prayer" is a song I write and it is a prayer I send.

And now I feel all I can do is not enough
My Rome is burning and I'm standing at the deep abyss
But every passion started with an act of love
And every act of love started with a single kiss
Father, father, your gift was this world of light
And I've betrayed you with a single Judas kiss
I've been my own executioner, but it's not just me anymore
Now I send a prayer to heaven for the chance to be
A better man than the man I see—

I make a commitment to be that better man.

Barbara and I are doing well, and I'm writing love songs about her again. She jokes that "Ordinary Girl" is a kind of backhanded compliment because it professes my love and need for her deep, nurturing side. She wonders where all the songs about our hot sex went! You just can't please some people . . .

As I finish writing more songs, I become eager to record again. I have to smile sometimes at my occasionally indomitable spirit. In the face of all the crap I've been through, my inner seven-year-old starts pogoing every time we get the chance to make a record. Go figure. I call Bill Drescher, who recorded most of my '80s songs with me, and tell him I want to make an album and that I'll pay for it, then turn around and sell it to a label. The music business is changing faster than record companies can fire their overpaid staff, and the internet is opening up some new possibilities—none of which have actually made anyone any money yet, but there's hope—and as things are looking better for me financially, due mainly to *High Tide* and some adroit investing, I'm not as worried as I might be about taking on the cost of funding my own record.

Jack White, my longtime friend and drummer, is doing very wel thank you. Katey Sagal is at the height of her *Married . . . with Children* fame when, in 1993, she and Jack meet and marry. Jack now has a bigger house than I do. I'm happy for him and his relationship, which has produced two beautiful kids. Jack has a studio in the garage of his new home and offers it to us to cut the record. Everything goes great. Really, really great. For two weeks. Then Jack and I butt heads. It's happened before, of course, but it was mostly over girls and the blood was left on the hotel walls. Now, the face-off is at his home, and it's about territorial pissing. Jack feels that we're abusing the studio he has kindly offered to us by finishing too late at night and not cleaning up after ourselves. I tell him I can't make a record if I have a curfew every night and that, yes, we are cleaning up after ourselves and if he doesn't like it he can take a flying fuck at the moon. We confront each other around the pool. (Maybe there's something about mid-sized bodies of water and things coming to a head in my life.)

The repercussions of us duking it out are more significant now. We are "men" with families. We should behave with more maturity. So we tell each other, "It's very clear you're an asshole, man," and I bail to another studio to finish the record. My new main man/dog Gomer is there for every session, just as Ronnie was almost twenty years before. When the record is finished, I name it *Karma* because "Prayer" is too Western-sounding and I want the title to announce that the songs are about aspects of my emerging spirituality. (See, we really do think these things through.) And once the record has found a home at a new independent label called Platinum, who do you think calls me up to get a band together and go on the road? Ladies and gentlemen . . . Jack White. Our friendship still stands.

The bond that I've found with other musicians is the strongest I've ever known. We are all still fifteen-year-olds at heart, committed to the path of "girls, guitars, and glory." I am a musician in my soul. We are cursed/blessed with this love of making and playing music, and it's a worthwhile journey, even though we've always been considered one step below hookers in social standing. At least we get our hookers for free, motherfucker.

You may have guessed by now that I'm a bit of an obsessive personality, so it should come as no surprise that I've been a "seminar junkie" since attending Lifespring in 1979. The newest and biggest one on the radar right now is from Anthony Robbins, so I head off to an Anthony Robbins Fire-Walking Weekend to try to get a new and better handle on myself. I'm often recognized and occasionally cornered at these types of events, but I also enjoy reconnecting with people once we get past the celebrity thing. And I find it both scary and exhilarating to open myself up in a public forum, where we're all encouraged to talk about our fears, doubts, and self-destructive issues. As I've said, these "self-help" symposiums are all based on the precepts Napoleon Hill first put forward in his 1937 book *Think and Grow Rich* . . . oh, and before that, the Bible, right. I'm reminded again of stuff that I already knew but have forgotten.

Seminars like this always push participants to "write things down" and read and reread books that speak to us because, at the root of all this, we're just dumbshit, eat/sleep/fuck protozoa that have only recently crawled out of the muck at the edge of a stagnant pond. We need to hear about the true direction and path we should be on again, again, and a-frigging-gain. Of course, if God wants to send me an e-mail that says, "I am proud of the battle you wage," I would be as happy as a bivalve mollusk. But so far I haven't received anything that clear and direct. Though the hawks were pretty cool. Thanks for that.

After this seminar I toss away the Prozac . . . so far, so good; I'm feeling strong. Now it's meditation vs. medication. What a difference one little letter makes. I'm meditating fairly regularly now (with no downtime for forced naps), and I come to understand why the Darkness was making me go unconscious when I tried this before: It's because meditation is the only time I am truly at peace and present in the moment. And with no future and no past, there is nothing for Mr. D to fuck with me about. And he disappears completely. He ceases to exist. He buggers off! Of course, as soon as I finish my meditation, he's sitting there right next to me picking at his scabs impatiently, but I can now make him vanish anytime I choose. This is startling news and something I was not expecting from meditation. In fact, I don't know what I was expecting. I assumed it would take the place of prayer in my life, but it's something else altogether. When I meditate correctly and reverently, it's true peace, I'm not asking/begging for something, fearing, doubting, looking for an answer, wondering if I'm heard. I'm not seeking. I just am. And because Mr. D disappears now when I meditate, he loses the power to put me to sleep.

I still vacillate up and down, high and low, in and out of feeling good, now that I've released the steady foot on the gas pedal that is Prozac, and I still pray for those I love and (will it never end?) things I want! I understand God as less a literal figure than a presence, an essence. Okay, it's something I'm still working on. A birthday card from Tim Pierce to me once read, "May God grant you some of your mountainous wants." Dude. Is it that obvious?

The album *Karma* is released. Jack and I put a touring band together and we hit the road. It's been years since I've toured in any real way, and I'm anxious before the first gig. We're playing a new venue in Las Vegas because it puts us close to home. The date is sold out, but I think to myself, How much of this audience is just wanting to see whether or not I weigh 350 pounds now, or to confirm that I have indeed not died from a drug overdose? I don't know what to expect. I have so many questions: How will I feel when I'm onstage? Do I still "have it" or has "it" taken a hike? Will it feel natural to me, playing and connecting with an audience again, or will it feel forced after so much time away? Do I even have the stamina for a ninety-minute show? How will the audience react? Will they sit fairly subdued, fondly recollecting the old songs, or will they still have the energy I remember? I expect they are probably wondering some of these very same things.

We hit the stage and the audience immediately explodes. As far as I can see, no one sits down again, either. I'm standing onstage after years away from touring, and the seven-year-old has at last been let out of his room. But I don't know how the crowd will react to the new music, and as the band launches into "It's Always Something," I'm watching the audience and listening for signs that they aren't getting it. At the second verse I sing the line: "My father said, 'If the boy wants to play the guitar I say we let him . . . '" and a roar goes up from the crowd. I look around to see if something has happened onstage that I might have missed, but the audience is still looking my way. I realize that they've just shouted their affirmation of my dad's words. I'm warmed and strengthened by the crowd's vocal support and their obvious agreement with my dad's belief in his young son's choice of a career, despite the lack of support from anyone else. My champion gets a nod . . . and, it seems, so do I.

I accidentally smash one of my $3,000 guitars during a hot minute, but I'm okay with it. I have faced a moment of truth and proved to myself that my passion for playing is still alive and well. My guitar tech, who was with us through the '80s, says laughingly, "It's like I went to sleep in 1980, woke up, and everything's still the same." It's a relief, and the seven-year-old in me is beside himself. He's missed this intensely. But offstage, away from the happy frenzy of performing, I have to face the sexual temptations that lurk out here on the road. They wear short skirts and they smell good.

Love is spiritual, sex is biological. But Stein always insisted that there was something spiritual I was looking for with all the fucking around. He said (true to Jungian philosophy) that there was a god behind my sexual stuff. He would talk about Eros and that I needed to honor him. At one point I tried to tell myself that this meant he thought I needed to get laid more. He meant I had to direct my sexual energy toward the god and not the women I was nailing in the name of Eros; to use *sublimation* and direct whatever powerful sexual energy Eros was representing to a more constructive pursuit—for example, writing songs with that passion, which I guess has happened from time to time when I was denied the sexual gratification I wanted (thank you, Gary's stained-glass-making girl).

We also delved into the fact that I was seeking validation from women: that I'm okay, meaning desirable. There's a lot of that in my drive to succeed as well. If I could do this, screw her, reach that, then it proved I was worthy, right? Well, that only lasted as long as the distraction that came with seeking lasts. Once I was no longer distracted, then I was left with the hard fact that the girl wasn't screwing me, she was screwing an idea, a fantasy projection, this famous guy: RS. And that didn't contribute to my self-worth in any way. Hence the whole collapse by the poolside that morning when I realized that all the career achievements didn't translate to me being worth anything more.

The sexual issue had also become a habit just because I'd been doing it for so long. I never felt better from it, or higher, or less depressed, I just did it because it was "what I did." It's a little like what drinking is for confirmed alcoholics—only more fun (sorry, I didn't just say that). It also booby-trapped me when I came home to Barbara, the one person who truly loves me for me. The person who fell in love with me, was okay with the man I was then, and with whom I had such great sex before I had any fame and fortune. The one who sticks with me through losing our house, my depression, and my infidelities, and the one who bears our children. In short, the one person who could truly give me the validation I seek. Stein had said I'd possibly blocked B with my single-minded pursuit of success and my ego-seeking screwing around. And that she is the one true soul who is in my corner and could help me transform and develop the self-worth I'm so desperate to find.

He wondered also if it was true (and I had always had an inkling of this) that perhaps I had hurt my life and career by having too much sex. He meant sex unconnected to love. You know, just mind-distracting screwing. He likened it, in its destructive potential, to drinking too much alcohol or taking too many drugs. Overindulgence in sex could be just as harmful to my spirit and sense of self-worth as any other obsession. I think he was onto something. Again I miss the connection we had and the knowledge and understanding of me that died with him.

We start to tour the U.S. and my old demons are right there looking for action. Let me be clear: I don't mean that I see hot women as demons. It's the demons in me that want me to abuse my sexual need and damage myself, my family, and my life if I may employ a drug term—by using. At times it's a battle, but I do okay.

The band gets tighter through the tour. The crowds get crazier. The seven-year-old in me is a very happy boy. The adult me, not as much. Although I love playing live, my desire to push it further is kicking in heavily and I want more and more of this, even though by normal thinking, things are going pretty fucking great. And so I get to feeling unsatisfied with things as they are. The problem with being so driven, always wanting to do better and be more and reach farther, is that it's not possible to fulfill and satiate this completely. I know that as long as I'm not truly happy, the Darkness will be with me. I know that as long as the Darkness is with me, I will feel inadequate. And as long as I feel inadequate, I will be driven. And as long as I'm driven, I'll never be truly happy. Do you see my dilemma?

So does Mr. D. "We've been through a lot of shit together," he says. "And most of it is your fault." He has a way of putting things that make them hard to argue against. During VH-1's *Behind the Music*, I mention my battle with depression publicly for the first time. The Darkness is ecstatic. "All *right*!" he says. "Now *I'm* famous, too." Because I've done my best to take sex off the table as a viable option, I begin to drink more heavily than I ever have before. Never alone, thank God, but I certainly overindulge at dinner before a show. It makes playing the show a little riskier for everyone, band and audience, because I get sloppy. So our live shows can flip from being really great and tight to being loose and unfocused. This is not what I came out on the road for.

It's not an easy life sometimes, with all the traveling and time away from home, but it's ten times worse with a hangover. I've always been able to reel in my drinking when I felt it was getting out of hand, but it's harder now that I don't have the sexual free-for-all to run to after a show. The only relief I get now is from alcohol. I know I need to get a handle on all this red wine consumption, but I think I'm waiting for "the wall." You know, the wall we hit when things get too far out of hand. It's painful, and it can really wreck your front end, but it does tend to stop you in your tracks. And mine is in my future.

Deep inside I understand that I'm just trading one dependency for another, but I think to myself, "It's only red wine, for God's sake, so what's the big deal? It's not like I get so blasted I can't perform or can't have a life. And the only one I'm hurting is me." Now, this is a big point. Because I've been so ready to hurt myself, my family, my life, and my career with my sexual stuff, it seems like a step in the right direction that I begin to damage only myself. The Darkness thinks it's a capital idea and even gets people to buy me drinks. I have begun to self-medicate. It will take me a while to get a handle on my drinking, but I'm only minimally aware of the danger it holds for me and my family, and I'm not prepared to do much about it for now.

Barbara and I are feeling some tension between us now that I'm back touring, and of course she has very reasonable concerns about me and my fidelity. I understand her fears and can't blame her, based on my past. It's difficult to live with her suspicion day in and day out, though she has stood by me when millions wouldn't have—I decide I owe her some leeway, for Chrissakes. So who should call when I least expect it and I'm in this still-precarious state? Las Vegas: home of hot showgirls, almost-legal hookers, and the fabulously self-destructive motto "Whatever happens in Vegas stays in Vegas."

Right in the middle of my tour, Las Vegas picks up its golden telephone and calls me. The big show at the MGM Grand is a $60 million audio/visual assault called *EFX*. Michael Crawford has been the lead since it opened two years ago, and now he's leaving. MGM wants to know if I would like to take his place. I fly up to meet the producers and see this musical that looks like a Broadway show on acid. It's an almost incomprehensible, startling, dazzling, special effects–driven spectacular featuring forty-foot-tall fire-breathing animatronic dragons, giant spaceships landing from the stars above, huge sets that rise up through the massive stage floor and swing in from the sides, the biggest Vari-Lite system in the world, explosions, fireworks, and a cast of thousands. It also has lots of singing, acting, and dancing. I've done okay in the first two endeavors, but dancing is a bit of a reach. It's a year-long commitment at least, and I'm really enjoying getting back into writing, playing, and touring, so I pass. And anyway, Broadway is calling, too. And they only want a month.

Smokey Joe's Café is the Broadway show featuring Jerry Leiber and Mike Stoller's great catalogue of songs. I play "the white guy" in the cast of brilliant, multitalented freaks of nature that seem to inhabit every nook and cranny of Broadway. I sing and dance (yep, dance) my way through songs like "Jailhouse Rock" and "Stand by Me." "Spanish Harlem" almost gives me a heart attack on the second night of the run.

It's my solo on a classical guitar—and there are no fret markers on this type of instrument. Us boys raised on RedFenderStrats aren't used to this, and we need guides for our nimble fingers, so I put little marker dots on the top of the neck where the usual fret markers are. In the middle of the song, in front of a packed house, I pick up the guitar for the solo and see that some overzealous stagehand has cleaned the freaking guitar and wiped off my marker dots. I don't know where to put my fingers. *Holy shit!* I have to think fast: so I close my eyes, tell myself I don't need bloody dots, I relax—and I play the solo without a mistake. It's a very real example to me of what letting go and trusting can achieve.

Barbara and our boys join me in New York for a week or two, and I'm happy as any singing, dancing fool could be. B does laugh herself sick at my dancing, though: it's a fair cop.

My album *Karma* does okay, but the company goes under in the middle of the launch . . . again. Is this 1978? After my stint in *Smokey Joe's* comes to an end, I go back on the road and continue touring. Then, Vegas picks up the golden telephone once more, and this time, they make me an offer I can't refuse. And for a guy like me, with my sexual issues, what better place to go than Sin City?

Whooooo-hoooooo!

CHAPTER EIGHTEEN

HOW BAD COULD IT BE? PRETTY FUCKING BAD, ACTUALLY

LAS VEGAS

2000–2002

There are still some details of the Las Vegas deal to be hashed out, so I sign on for a two-episode arc in *Suddenly Susan*, the Brooke Shields sitcom that is a big hit at the moment. We shoot in LA and I meet a young and gifted comedic actor named David Strickland, who's a regular on the show. The last scene we film at the end of my second episode is an ad-libbed thing where I play the guitar and David goofily rocks out. Then everyone breaks and goes home for the weekend. Except David. He drives to Las Vegas, books into a motel room off the Strip, and quietly hangs himself, miles from anyone who cares or could help.

His personal Darkness wins one for the "team," and it's a sad mnemonic of what could still be my possible end. It also reminds me that while Vegas is a town of hyped high times, it's also a town of less-touted lows—a haven for more depraved instincts that can bring on our Darkness. I will soon be residing in this asylum by choice, this place that draws desperate souls like bugs to a zapper. Am I one of them? I become a little afraid. *My* Mr. Darkness, however, is ecstatic. He's confident that I'll buy into the whole "What happens in Vegas" mentality, and he's pretty sure he can get me to crash and burn for him out there.

Barbara and I have some heart-to-hearts and finally decide that since the Vegas gig is only for a year, we won't drag our boys out of their school and drop them into some Nevada desert academy only to pull them out again in a few months to come back home to Malibu. I'll go to Vegas alone and commute. The plane flight is only twenty-five minutes from Vegas to LA, and I'll spend three days of every week here at home. What could go wrong? Really? I mean, hey, c'mon. Don't assume that because I've gone through years of therapy and have come to some understanding regarding my straying ways, I'm no longer capable of tripping over my dick and seriously screwing up? (You don't? Oh, okay, thanks for the support.) But my intentions are good, and I continue to thank the gods a thousand times for B, this amazing woman who has graciously agreed to accompany me through life and has stuck by me in good times and in bad.

The internet has arrived, and I have an active website as well as a fan base that is a growing online presence. "Reach out and touch someone" may have been a line used to plug a phone company, but it is waaay truer of the World Wide Web. I'm evidently easier to track down than ever. And so I'm contacted via the ether by a few enterprising girls, one of whom I knew (in the biblical sense) back in the '80s. She starts sending some fairly sexually explicit e-mails my way. There is nothing physical between this girl and me anymore, but I can appreciate that there are degrees of unfaithfulness. One is virtual.

For weeks, Barbara and I have been edgy around each other, courtesy of the looming Las Vegas gig. One afternoon all the smoldering mistrust (hers) and wounded resentment (mine) come to a head, just as I'm reading one of the e-mails from my freaky online girlfriend. An epic argument ensues, spiked by the powder keg of all the unspoken pain and resentment and lit by the fuse of this e-mail that I shouldn't be opening, much less reading. The fight is not pleasant and is entirely my fault. No one hits anyone, but there are flying objets d'art here and there, and our furious, screaming argument pushes a well-meaning visiting relative who overhears it to call 911. Things get quickly out of hand, and before you know it there's a cop car outside our house and, like my Australian convict forefathers before me, I am slapped in irons and taken away.

I will tell you everything about myself, but I draw the line where protecting my girl's privacy is concerned, so imagine what you will: it's probably way better than the real thing anyway. I'm taken to jail, booked, fingerprinted, and stuck in a cell. The cops who take me in do mention that I can "thank O.J. for this." Evidently the post-O.J. rule is that if a report of domestic violence is made, someone is going to the pokey.

Around the same time that I'm sitting my arrested ass down in a cold cell, across town in a pretty swanky restaurant, the good folks from the MGM Grand Hotel are waiting for me to show up to discuss the final points of our contract regarding yours convictedly starring in their multimillion-dollar show, *EFX*. I would love to have seen the looks on their faces as someone stepped up to inform them that their guest of honor for this evening was, at this very moment, sitting in a holding cell at the local lockup with fifty of the most discerning members of the press lined up outside, ready to froth over and film the latest celebrity fuckup. It had to be a killer moment.

No felony charges are filed against me for spousal abuse, but they say I have to go to counseling for my temper. I take it up the ass and sign on for the counseling. Everyone loves a train wreck, and the only thing better than watching someone succeed is watching them fail. And what a pity I don't have a new album out now, because the press coverage is excellent. There are helicopters buzzing over our cute little canyon home, and my young boys are afraid to go out and jump on the trampoline because of them. The ground-based press is also relentless: at my door, at my neighbors' doors, and taking photos through the windows of our house to see if they can catch me in the act of beating my beloved wife to death with O.J.'s bloody glove. I think back to when I first came to the States and actually believed that the press was here to respectfully and earnestly help me further my career. Guess I'd been wrong about that too. Hahahahahahahahahahaha.

Eventually someone kills someone else by forcing them to choke on the Hope Diamond or something, and the fresh blood lures the vultures away. Our boys can again go and bounce on their beloved trampoline. And all those press ass wipes can suck my dick.

I do have some penance to do, however, and I swear off the unfaithful e-mails. And it sticks. I'm also inspired to back off drinking, since the whole argument was, of course, alcohol-fueled, so the bust isn't a total loss. I have truly put my wife through hell in my time, and I am again thankful for what an amazing person she is. I'm also trying to figure out what I did that was so great in a previous life to have found her in this one. At this point we've lived in Malibu for fifteen years, and 95 percent of the couples we met when we first arrived have split up. Most of them seem even less happy now. There is something to be said for swimming across the river of shit in a marriage hand in hand, so that when you get to the other side, you have someone to hose you off and together you can enjoy the last rays of the setting sun.

I get ready to go back out on the road. Then Las Vegas calls again to say that all is forgiven and would I like that job after all? Barbara and I talk it over and she says to go for it, and I do. With misgivings. So in Las Vegas, Sin City, the only town that *really* never sleeps, I go into rehearsals for the "big shew."

I am ensconced in one of the high-roller penthouses at the top of the MGM. It has a winding staircase that Scarlett O'Hara would feel at home on, a butler, a private elevator, three huge bedroom suites, a mammoth wall of fifty-foot floor-to-ceiling windows providing a view of the million and one lights of the Las Vegas strip, a free Apple computer, and Carrot Top living two doors down. We go into rehearsals with *EFX*, and I quickly realize what a giant monster it is—one we need to get on its feet in a month and a half. It's exhilarating to be part of a leviathan enterprise like this: so much bigger than the biggest traveling concert tour I'd ever been on, and the people are all talented, the food is great, the work is challenging, the location is exciting and has undeniable electric energy, the money is good, the songs I write work well in the new show, the stage sets are staggering, and, yes . . . the girls in the show are all pretty smokin'.

I am excited and full of trepidation at the same time. My family comes and goes, and Barbara loves the seemingly thousands of world-class restaurants in Vegas. Josh digs it all, too, and will soon be my regular companion up here once the show begins its run. Only Liam doesn't have much time for the place. He does like the video arcade that's the size of a three-story Wal-Mart, however.

I immediately figure out that the only way to make money in Las Vegas is to work here. I stay clear of the gambling halls. It's enough that I'm potentially gambling with my sanity, my marriage, and my life up here.

The show opens, and the audience and press alike seem unanimous in their verdict that it's the best incarnation of *EFX* yet. I'm excited to be a part of such a dynamic spectacle. Having been locked up inside the MGM for three months now, I need to get out and feel some fresh air on my face, so I move from the hotel into a large house on the golf course of a private gated community off Tropicana Boulevard. The area, called Spanish Trails, also houses Las Vegas luminaries like Siegfried of Siegfried and Roy, Andre Agassi of Andre and Brooke, and some oil-rich Arabian dude who built a giant house here and then imported all his furniture from the homeland only to find that the couches and cushions contained large communities of rats, which, given the ample food supply in Las Vegas, went into reproductive overdrive and took over his house. He shut the place down, never having lived amidst its gold-plated sinks, solid gold toilets, and acres of expensive marble, and took a permanent hike. Oh, and thanks for the addition to the rat population, putz.

Once I move into the house, I start bringing Gomer up with me. I can't fly him, so he has his own car and driver to take him back and forth from LA to Vegas every week. Clearly I'm getting into the Vegas spirit of goofy excess, but I love my dog and he's more than worth it. He comes to all the shows and hangs out in the dressing rooms and workout areas, walking from dancer to dancer before the show, to get his scratches, pets, and massages. Dogs are good for everyone's spirit.

Josh flies up with me and stays for a week at a time, school permitting. We are supertight until he meets Kris, the boy who plays young King Arthur in *EFX*. They discover a mutual love of video games and it's hasta la vista, Dad. They are friends to this day.

I also bring my recording equipment to Vegas and set it all up in the living room of this big empty house. *EFX* is basically an evening gig, so I have plenty of free time before and after the show and I'm determined not to misuse it. I'll make this time count: I will write songs. So I sit in my large and lonely house, ten minutes from the Strip, and wait for inspiration to come. The first year ticks by and the show is running like clockwork. I wake up at midday, get breakfast, and eat outside in the sunshine while Gomer sniffs around the pool area where the squirrels have left their annoying, dog-baiting stink. We take a walk, and then I noodle on the guitar and keyboards for a while. At around five I have a shower and get ready for the show. I have a light dinner, work out for a half hour, then hit the stage.

The show is a freaking spectacular that is a roller-coaster ride from the word Go. The $60 million spent on production, effects, lighting, stage sets, animatronics, sound systems, computers, costumes, and talent is evident from start to finish. We all take our bows amid exploding air cannons and a rain of confetti and streamers, then Gomer and I head back home, where I sit and noodle some more on my guitar and keyboards before going to bed. Everything is just fucking super, thanks for asking, but I'm in a bubble and experiencing nothing. Where is inspiration for writing to come from if everything is just peachy? I can't write when I'm on this fat and happy, contented, regimented schedule. I worry again that maybe some of my best songs have come from hard times and struggle. And Darkness.

Barbara and I are in stasis while we wait out the year that this show has to run. It's more difficult than we thought it would be, and we aren't seeing each other enough to work through the issues, so instead we go into a holding pattern. I haven't been drinking at all while I'm here in Vegas and I work out every day at *EFX*'s gym, so I have never been in better physical shape. I'm pleased to have avoided the obvious philandering, but I am stuck again with my writing and don't know what to do about that. I feel like things need to be shaken up. Even the mood of the whole country is all "Happy days are here again," with the stock market flying, real estate booming, people working, spending, and traveling, and not a lot of drama for us here on the home front. Then someone decides to change the game.

Marni O'Doherty is an investment banker in New York City. She's a smart and funny thirty-one-year-old with a successful career and a loving husband. She is also an RS fan. On a Tuesday morning like any other, she's at work in her office building in Manhattan and takes a moment to post a comment on a Yahoo! Rick Springfield message board. It's the last anyone will ever hear from her. A few minutes later, 300 tons of commercial aircraft plows through her office window overlooking Manhattan, and 9/11 has begun.

I'm sleeping in our home in Malibu when Barbara wakes me up crying to tell me that terrorists have just flown planes into the World Trade Center. Our complacency vanishes. We walk out into the morning and feel an eerie silence from the skies. No planes are flying. Everyone is wandering around in shock. I drive to the store. It all feels completely surreal. Like a dream. I call Las Vegas to find out what's going on with *EFX*, and even Vegas has come to a standstill—there are no shows tonight. Planes are grounded for days while America tries to get a handle on the threat, but life must go on, and MGM is saying it wants to start running the show again starting Wednesday, so I drive back up to Vegas. Being so far away from my family at such an uncertain time is unnerving for us all, but I am my father's son and I must not shirk my responsibilities.

The first show, the night following the attacks, is the toughest performance I have ever been involved in. There is a weight hanging over the room that we can't lift no matter how hard we dance, sing, joke. We do drop a huge U.S. flag at the end of the show, which is a way of sharing the grief, and I have a guitar made with the stars and stripes across its body, but the flag waving is short-lived, and the pain and loss that we all feel are laid bare. Traveling suddenly feels much more dangerous, flights are cut, the economy nosedives, and so I sign on for another year with *EFX*. B and I continue to live separate lives, and the strain grows greater for both of us.

Then halfway through *EFX* one night, a safety rope breaks on a beam that I'm supposed to be hanging from during an *Indiana Jones*–type fight scene in the show. The huge stage resembles an aircraft carrier deck, complete with elevators, trapdoors, and a very solid, unyielding, all-steel surface. I feel the rope break loose while I'm swinging twenty-five feet above this stage. The fall seems to take forever. I have time to think what I might do if I survive. When I hit, the world goes fuzzy like a TV set that needs tuning. I leap up, glad that my legs are still working. "Hey, maybe I'm okay," I think as I run to the H. G. Wells time machine I'm supposed to jump into so I can fly away as the earthquake hits and the giant stage sets rock. Then I see the curtain coming down and think that maybe I'm in worse shape than I first supposed. As I try to change my clothes for the next scene (still unaware that the show has been stopped), a sharp, jarring pain shoots up my left arm and I realize it's broken.

The emergency crew enters the backstage area as I'm being helped to my dressing room. The cast and crew are giving me the "Oh my God, it's the Elephant Man" look and I am wondering if maybe I have fucked myself up pretty good this time. As the ER guys strap me onto a gurney and begin asking me if I know where I am, what my name is, and how many fingers they've showing me, I remember thinking, a while back, that "Things need to be shaken up." I'm carried out, now with a scary-looking neck brace attached, to the waiting ambulance and loaded in amid hurried shouts and admonitions of "Don't move—just lie still." I begin to think that maybe I should have been more specific as to exactly how things should be shaken up.

Hey, wait a minute! Aren't I now in a very enviable position? Millions would kill to be in my shoes, wouldn't they? Because I have just severely injured myself while working at a Las Vegas casino . . . and it's the casino's fault!! Casinos are really, really, really, really rich, if I'm not mistaken! Well, MGM hired themselves the right guy when they signed me on, because when the bosses call the hospital to see how I'm doing and how much it's going to cost them, I let them off the hook right away. I have a broken left wrist, broken left arm, and (again) rib damage, but my brain, braincase, and spine are all good. I tell them to relax, there won't be any lawsuit, just pay for my hospital stay. They do that and send me flowers, too.

I won't say who, but one of the guys in this show before me hurt his back, sued, and won against MGM, scoring himself a cool $40 mil. But my dad raised me in the belief that the only true way to earn money is through your own righteous endeavors and that no good will ever come from "easy" or "blood" money. The fall was an accident. No one wanted me to get hurt, so why should I make someone fund the rest of my existence? Especially since I'm still walking around with all my faculties. I come to the conclusion that it's hard to kill a Springthorpe. A three-story free fall to a steel deck is usually a recipe for a wooden overcoat and a permanent dirt nap. Someone was watching over me that night. And I think I know who.

I take three weeks off to heal, and then it's on with the show! Whoo-hooo!

CHAPTER NINETEEN

DARKNESS AT NOON

THE TWO SIDES OF LAS VEGAS

2002–2003

Unfortunately, my dad never gave me the benefit of his views on relationships with women who aren't your wife. I'm sure it would have helped. There are two female relationships I form up in Vegas. One is chaste, the other not so much.

The chaste one

Her name is Sahara. She is seven years old by the time I begin *EFX* in Vegas, and she's a bright and burning spirit. Amy, her mom, has been bringing her to my concerts for a couple of years now, and I have such an instant bond with this sweet little bean sprout of a girl that the only explanation for me is: our relationship was predestined. I've experienced this before—a deep connection to another human being that can't possibly be explained by the brief time we spend together in this life. I know this was most definitely the case when I first laid eyes on my sons as I stood beside Barbara in the delivery room and watched them enter this world. I experienced it with B the moment I laid eyes on her. Occasionally I've felt it with strangers I have met and later loved. The feeling is spiritual more than worldly, so it's not really possible to convey in mere words that anyone other than Shirley MacLaine would understand . . . oh, and Arthur Conan Doyle. Mostly it feels like recognition. And there's a sense of relief whenever this connection—or reconnection—is finally made.

There are times when I have almost missed an encounter with someone, destiny made it happen, and it later turned out to be a fateful meeting. These seemingly chance meetings aren't necessarily for the better, although the ones I mention here certainly are. It's a beautiful mystery. So, Sahara was five years old and standing in a long line for a meet-and-greet after one of my live shows the first time I "saw" her. I was doing the "Hello, how are you, nice to meet you" thing and I looked up to see how much longer the line was going to keep me there before I could go back to my hotel room and crash, when I caught sight of this little angel face with bangs and a big smile about twenty people back, bouncing in and out of the queue like she didn't have a lot of time to waste and could we please get to the "meeting" part. She lit up the room, and everyone stepped back to let this little Energizer Bunny have her moment with me. She said, "Hello," then jumped straight to "Do you want to hang out later?" And this is not precociousness; it feels more like familiarity.

I see her a couple more times at different shows, and when I move to Las Vegas, Amy and Sahara come to visit often. The town is a great match for Sahara's energy, and she falls in love with Vegas—and Vegas with her. And of course she loves the fact that there is a Sahara Hotel and a Sahara Boulevard here. Amy is a good woman and has been a fan since she was Sahara's age, but she's not at all starstruck, having worked for Scotty Moore (Elvis's guitar player) for a few years in Memphis, where she met celebrities by the dozens. She is enjoying reliving her childhood though her spirited daughter. We occasionally all hang out together at the Hard Rock Café after *EFX* is done for the night, and Sahara and I play our favorite game, hangman. She is smart, funny, and—if ever there was one—an old soul.

I fall hard for this sweet girl and make room for her in my life anytime she and her mom visit from their home in Cape Girardeau, Missouri. I even drag her up onstage during *EFX* to dance with the cast. And it's not just me: this reaction to Sahara is universal. Sue Packard, my assistant during the run of the show, isn't exactly child-friendly, but Sahara manages to draw my kid-resistant right-hand woman into her corner. Sue later says to me, "If I could be guaranteed a daughter like that, I'd have one in a heartbeat." Although Sahara has no idea who Tony Curtis is when he comes backstage to say hi, she smiles like a champ for a photo with him. And she is a *hell* of a hangman player. We go to lunch, make fun of the cheesy Elvis impersonators on the street, and hit the video game megastore regularly. Having a relationship like this with such a big-spirited kid makes Las Vegas seem positively homey. But living up here is making me feel increasingly disconnected from my real home, so it's probably not surprising to anyone that there is also:

The unchaste one

It is a year before I even begin *EFX* that I meet her backstage, amidst the controlled frenzy of yet another post-concert meet-and-greet. At twenty-one she is barely a woman and still looks like a girl. I give her a quick hug as we're introduced and she starts crying. I assume she is a serious fan and just overcome. She says she's sorry and seems genuinely embarrassed; she doesn't know why she's crying. I'm instantly attracted to her vulnerability, and as I let go of her hand, she lingers at the final touch and looks me in the eyes but says nothing more. She is gone. I think about her that night. I was deeply turned on by the odd mix of signals: fragility and boldness. Erotic, vulnerable, maybe a bit of craziness somewhere there in her eyes, but with an innocence and softness that begs to be saved. (Oh, no. The worst thing I could possibly do is think I might save someone.)

Some weeks later, I see her again. She's standing behind a chain-link fence as I enter the gig. She calls to me and I jog over like an eager schoolboy, which, at fifty-one, I am most certainly not. She asks if she can come backstage, and I set it up through my crew, something I never do for a stranger. I see her in the audience as we play that night and I feel like I'm playing for her. She doesn't take her eyes off me. Backstage after the show I'm feeling like I used to back in the '80s when I'd scan the backstage group for the perfect candidate to share the night's activities. I haven't done this for years. It's exciting and troubling to be feeling it again. How quickly I could go back to my old ways; I should know better, I tell myself.

We meet for the third time. She tells me briefly about her incredibly dysfunctional family and her desire to become an actress or a dancer. It's all pretty unfocused stuff she's saying, but my focus is crystal clear and on her: She has flawless skin; a young curvy body; and sad, pale-blue eyes. Although she isn't particularly beautiful, smart, or mature, she possesses a disarming mixture of innocence, vulnerability, confidence, and damage (uh-oh). And she has a wicked sexual presence. That sexual presence is the bait I will soon lunge for like a witless barracuda, pretty much unaware of the hook imbedded in the soft, tempting flesh.

Before she leaves backstage, she surprises me by kissing me full on the mouth and whispers "I'm horny" into my ear. I feel a thrill course up and down my spine.

I expect to run into her at the bar in the hotel that night, but she's nowhere to be seen. She is taunting me. Even though she's so young, she seems to be fully in control through her sexual innuendo, her looks, and her touches. I have some experience in this area, but she's running rings around me. And this obvious and overtly erotic attention from such a young girl is a little unsettling. There is also a wildness and recklessness about her that begins to feed my chimera. She is like a contained explosion at this point, but I sense there will soon be a full detonation. I secretly hope that I am inside the blast zone.

Late at night, as I hang on the edge of sleep in a strange bed in a lonely hotel room miles from home, my Darkness tells me that I might really be worth something if I could fuck this girl. "Not that she'd be really interested in an old dog like you, though," he adds. And this is his real point.

I start to think about her all the time. Even though I suspect that Mr. D is lining me up for a very, very hard fall, I choose to ignore my own internal warning signs. And I have a sad suspicion as to what's behind this sudden attraction. At the heart of it, I want to be young again.

In a first real step over the line, I give her an address where she can write me, a PO box reserved for business. And this is business. Monkey business. She writes poems that she asks me to read and sends them to my PO box, which makes the local post office suddenly take on an air of forbidden fruit every time I walk through its once-sterile, government-regulation doors. I'm already in over my head.

The long wait that I have to endure between seeing her and maybe consummating this thing is adding fuel to the fire of my compulsion for this girl. She comes and goes and is not making it easy or, in fact, possible for me to do anything about my reptilian-brain impulses. I think that I've completely lost my fucking mind. And still no sex. I'm seventeen again, trying my damnedest to get laid, and the more it's denied, the more I want it. I am out of control. And confounded.

I eventually give the unchaste one my cell number and we talk sometimes. I pretend our calls are fun and innocent, but they are a betrayal. We talk on the phone like we're a couple of teenagers, and it reminds me of all the missed times in my late teens when I *wasn't* talking on the phone with girls and being just generally goofy and giddy. It's something I missed out on in my very dark, screwed-up teen years: this mindless, not-a-care-in-the-world, swoony, frivolous boy-girl phone chitchat. Because of the connection I have with her, this relationship is going in a different direction than if we'd just had sex one night . . . not that we have.

Although there are ads in every paper of every town about this new *EFX* show I'm starring in, I call her to tell her I'm in Las Vegas in case she wants to come up and hang out. "It would be cool," I say and I sound like an idiot to myself. I try to seem casual, but by this point I'm on edge every time I hear her voice on the line. She comes to Vegas eventually and finds me lonely and dispirited. I take full responsibility for what happens between us and honestly don't know how it could have gone any other way. My desire to have her is very strong. And the longer the wait, the more it grows.

She comes to the show, and afterward, backstage to my dressing room. I expect her to run into my arms, but she sashays in, mock-fanning herself dramatically, as though in a sweat after walking by all the hot young bodies of the male dancers backstage. She actually tells me she thinks one of the other actors in the show is sexy. Again, small voice telling me . . . *opposite direction . . . run fast . . . don't look back.* But I just stand there and tell her I've missed her. She kisses me deeply and asks if there's anything to drink. I go look. As I am rummaging through my dressing room fridge, the warning bells are ringing loud and clear, but I am wearing my super-silent earplugs and am singing "La la la la" as loudly as I can to drown out anything I don't want to hear.

I agree to meet her later in her hotel room. As I make my way up though the elevators and corridors, I look at all the video cameras everywhere, watching me, tracking my betrayal in low-def video for the whole security department to see. I make brief "love" to her this one night. It's not great, and I don't know what I thought it would be, but I have time invested now and I am left to my own fantasies, doubts, and fears when she goes home, back to her life, and gets consumed by it.

I stop hearing from her. She won't return my calls. She is not following the time-honored rules of sex on the road—and neither am I. She is supposed to now be under my sway, and I'm supposed to not think very much about her. It seems to be the reverse.

This is probably the wrong time and I am the wrong guy to try to quote the Buddha, but there is something to what he says about lust and desire: that like a weed, it will persist until the root itself is dug up and discarded. I think I've trimmed the leaves and branches back quite a bit on my desire/lust plant, but the root is definitely very much alive and sucking up nourishment from the black earth of my wounded soul. I have been vain in thinking I could manage all this.

When we finally do speak again on the phone, she says she's seeing other guys. This hurts like a motherfucker, but I have no leg to stand on, nor do I want to put myself in the position of questioning or challenging her unfaithfulness. I can understand why I was drawn to her in the first place, but what's keeping me hooked on her now? It makes no sense, but my initial attraction has mutated into a sanity-threatening obsession. If I could just figure out the real "why" of it, maybe I could release myself from what is beginning to feel like a curse. Understanding eludes me. There is no "why." It just is. And I know it has to end.

Once I stop calling, she starts calling again at my house in Vegas. I sometimes just sit there in the living room, staring at the phone as it rings and rings and rings. I hear her voice as she leaves a message and my heart races. I know this is not love, because I know what love feels like, and it's back home waiting for me—I hope. But whatever this is, its pull is strong. I feel like I'm losing my mind. She calls one day when I'm feeling weak, and I pick up.

"Hi," I say.

"Oh God, I'm so buzzed."

"What are you on?"

"Hello?"

"I'm here."

"You won't believe what I just did."

"What?"

"I just had a foursome with three guys."

"You did?

"Yeah . . ."

"Wh . . . why?"

"I don't know, I guess I was drunk. They were pushing me."

"I thought . . . didn't we have . . . I mean . . . I thought . . ."

"Hey, you're married. What am I supposed to do?"

"That's crazy."

"What's the difference?"

"I . . ."

"I'm a skank."

"No, don't say that."

"I'm just a slut."

"No, no, it's . . . where did it happen?"

"At this guy's house. We drank a bunch of beer and we just . . . I don't know . . . one of the guys didn't want to do it, but I said it's okay and he . . ."

"I gotta go."

"What?"

Click.

What was I hoping to find in this insane relationship? Not this. I know it doesn't matter that I stayed away from temptation for so long: it happened in the end, and it makes all the resistance meaningless. I feel like the alcoholic who abstains for a couple of years and then goes on a lost weekend to end all lost weekends. Not only have I fallen off the wagon, I've nuked the fucking thing.

And I've hit absolute rock bottom.

I am so bitterly angry at this girl, at myself, and at my damned obsessions, and I'm confounded by the giant step backward that I've taken. For me there has been no healing in therapy, only recognition and understanding. Healing will take a spiritual path and the abandonment of many desires and needs. It is, in itself, a pretty friggin' tough nut to crack.

As I get ready for another performance of *EFX*, the Darkness looks back at me from the bathroom mirror and shakes his head in mock disapproval. "Nice one, jerk." There's a slight upward curve to the corners of his mouth. He knows he got me, and I know it, too. Down I go to that familiar place where I'm worthless, needy, and vain and where Mr. D keeps a warm bed for me with a cup of hot cocoa on the nightstand. I go to a local doctor and he prescribes lithium for me, but it makes me crazy and unsteady on my feet sometimes and I fear for my life while walking atop some of the huge sets during the *EFX* show. I switch to sleeping pills, and they work for a while. At least I can get some peace when I'm unconscious at night.

I miss my family. The Vegas gig is starting to feel like a life sentence, and I'm in such a sorry state that I need intravenous fluids and vitamin B12 shots every night now just to get through a performance. One evening after a show, I sit down by the fireplace in my home away from home, furious that I've wasted a whole year and a half up here and betrayed my family and myself as well. It's midnight. "I'm not getting up from this chair until I've completed a song," I say out loud. My voice echoes through the empty house. It feels pretty lonely. I know writing is the only way for me to get a perspective on all that has happened. The only place (other than the now-unavailable security of Stein's study) where I'm unswervingly honest is in my songwriting.

I think of all the time I've let slip by, my giant fuckup with this affair, how desperately I want out of this gig, and how much I've hurt my girl B and my family with this duplicity. The time I've spent here now seems like a terrible, ruinous waste. The song that comes out first is—appropriately—one I call "Wasted." I have a focus for my writing now. I am hurt, lonely, and angry, and what could be better fodder than this for writing a few happy-go-lucky pop tunes? At last I begin the wonderful and at the same time horrible process of songwriting. It is the only way I know to get these caustic emotions out in the open and look at them objectively in the cold light of day. I need to purge myself of all this shit. And the music that comes out of me in the following months is a cry from my wretched soul.

Once I'm past the shock, it is the anger that comes through in the first songs I write. Anger at the situation, anger at this girl for not choosing me, and anger at my own feelings of never being enough, most pointedly brought to light by this recent fucked-up relationship. "Perfect" is one of the first songs I complete.

I tried hard to be the perfect one
But it's not enough

It's not enough. [. . .]
I wish I was perfect for you.

And from "God Gave You to Everyone":

You make me feel I don't mean anything to anyone.

I'm as pathetic and broken as I sound in these songs. But I'm not the only one who is treated honestly in them . . . she is, too. From "Will I?"

Cause you gave it away like it was nothing at all.

And sometimes I just want to tell her in language she may understand. From "Idontwantanythingfromyou":

But everything you gave to me
You went and gave away to anybody else
With a dick.

And if that wasn't plain enough, I combine the two themes in "God Gave You to Everyone."

God gave you to everyone
Cause I'm not enough.

As the writing of the songs progresses, I acknowledge my own part in it, too. From "Beautiful You":

You took me down on my own knife.

Even feeling as lost as I do, I can see the irony of the situation.

My resentment and pain are pretty raw in these first few songs, and I can still hear it in my voice and in the angst of the guitar work when I listen to this CD now. I don't listen to it very much. I think I may have been trying to chant my way out of my desperate feelings in "Idontwantanythingfromyou" when I sing:

I don't hate you
I don't hate you
I don't hate you.

It might have been true at this point, but I suspect the opposite.

Gradually the writing of the songs and the releasing of the emotions begin to work. The anger dissipates—or crawls down a sewer or goes wherever anger goes. Through the process of songwriting, I come to terms, to a degree, with the situation and find what has been so elusive: acceptance. To my surprise I even find some compassion for this girl who has tormented me for so long. From "Your Psychopathic Mother":

I know why you give yourself away
Cause they make you feel special
But you never feel special enough.

And yes, the same could be said for me.

At last I get through it enough to take a hard look at myself and my life. "My Depression" is the result. An abbreviated inventory of my life so far. I'm not happy with what I see:

Looking in the mirror and thinking how it used to be.
Don't like the skin I'm in
Caught in a tailspin.

And more to the current point:

Oh my God
It's my life
What am I doing kicking at the foundation?

That's right
My Life
Better start looking at my destination.

And focusing on my destination is what I do next, in a song that points me home to Barbara, the place I should have been all the time. From "Eden":

Monday morning in the garden of Eden
Looked over and I saw your face
Never felt what you made me feel
Never felt so out of place
The sinner sleeps with the angel
I heard you breathe my name
Stumbling through the gates of freedom.

And since I'd put my life into the three-minute pop song, "My Depression," I try to narrow it down to two lines. I think I come pretty close in "Eden":

I've wanted so much in my life, desired everyone I knew
Now I would not take it kicking and screaming, the only one I want is you.

Once more I have to atone somehow for my betrayal of Barbara, and I recommit myself to never letting this betrayal happen again. Writing is my way of healing and dealing with this garbage I have just made us both endure. The only real question is: Will B still have me? I can't ask her directly. Not yet. Right now all I can do is put it into the songs I write. I know they won't be easy for her to hear. I only hope that in the end she'll see where my words finally lead. These songs are my way to own up, confess, and to begin my long journey back home to her.

Thank God Gomer is with me in Las Vegas, or I would probably disconnect entirely. I think about my love . . . no, I guess "passion" would be more accurate . . . for dogs. They are the true constant in my life. My dog makes me feel loved without any doubts or whispers from the Darkness. I am seven again when I look into my mutt's eyes. I'm running through the bright, promise-filled morning fields of Broadmeadows with twenty hounds slavering at my side every time I commune with a dog. It is pure, and there is nothing to confuse it (Dog/God). I often feel I might have been happier in my life if I'd been a veterinarian. But I probably would've had to be a famous one . . . with a TV show . . . and who girls wanted to sleep with. Jesus, is there no saving me? I keep writing, and thankfully *EFX* finally grinds to a close. I now know why the shelf life of a Broadway or Vegas star in any given show is usually no longer than two years. After that, the alternatives become either to consume massive amounts of alcohol and painkillers or to shoot yourself in the face.

I head home, like a wounded soldier, for some R & R. How did I ever think I could survive this stint in Vegas without going off the rails? Mr. D had high hopes for much worse, possibly something fatal. But he's satisfied with what he got. It will take me a year to get through all the feelings I have about this abortive relationship, and the ripples from it will last even longer. But I must get on with my life and my work, and I cannot mentally afford another sabbatical. I know that for my own sanity I must pursue putting all this emotion into the songs that will now carry it all for me. And this simple act is liberating.

CHAPTER TWENTY

HEALING TO DO

BACK HOME

2003–2006

Since there is no rest for the wicked, after a week at home I start recording my twelfth album. It is incredibly cathartic to have finished these songs and to begin recording again, to turn all that pain into something productive that releases my inner fears and doubts. I'm able to put the affair in Vegas behind me for now because I actually get some immediate healing from these songs (seventeen of them), and thankfully, being in the recording studio puts me into the mode of thinking of nothing but the record I'm making 24/7. Again, it's a pay-as-you-go venture, but my new band is killer and I am turned on to cut these songs, which all have strong hooks and are under three minutes long. Again, if you don't like this song, please keep your seats because we have another one coming rrrright up.

This is also my way of fighting back. Of standing up and not letting the episode crush me. I am back and doing the only constructive thing I know how to do with all this shit I'm feeling. The whole writing process I went through in Vegas has been a better and faster restorative for my soul than anything I could have achieved in therapy, but a thousand silent, nagging doubts and fears remain: I haven't confronted my betrayal in my real life or begun to make amends with Barbara. I've put everything on hold to complete this album.

Mr. D is not thrilled, as he never gets much of a peek in when I'm recording. If he shows up, it's just to whisper that he thinks the new songs are crap. I've entered into a co-owner studio venture with my new drummer Rodger Carter (Jack White has health issues that have sidelined him from touring), so I'll finally be making a record in my own (co-owned) studio. The good news is that the songs are all strong (so the Darkness can go fuck himself); the bad news is it takes eleven months to record the album. Rodger will eventually kick me out of the aforementioned co-owned studio business, claiming that I've spent too much time making this album. He has plans to rent it out to other musicians so he can make some money. And I don't fire him from my band for evicting me because, well, he's right: I *have* spent way too much time recording these seventeen songs. This causes the coining of the phrase "Man, what do you have to do to get yourself fired from this organization?" (We use it to this day, whenever it's appropriate.) Gomer hangs hard at the studio with me. Rodger, being similarly dog-obsessed, names the studio "The Doghouse," so how bad can he be, even though he's covered in tattoos, has a piercing at every curve and fold of his body, and has just asked me to vacate the premises? Until I do, Gomer has Rodger's many mutts to play with.

With song titles like "I Don't Want Anything from You," "Your Psychopathic Mother," "Jesus Saves White Trash Like You," and "Every Night I Wake Up Screaming," it's pretty obvious what the overall vibe and energy of the new record is.

Now that I'm recording again, Barbara and I don't see a lot of each other, but at least we sleep in the same bed every night, and there's a lot to be said for that. I'm feeling a little better and I think she is, too, although we still haven't sat down for the air-clearing talk we need after Vegas. We're committed to our life together, though, and sometimes it's best to simply shut up and live, so we do just that. She is troubled by some of the new songs she hears and realizes that I'm keeping her at arm's length about them. This album will become her least favorite of all my records—and rightly so.

If I could just pull you out of the narrative and chime in here from 2010 for a second, I would like to state my case regarding my sweet girl Barbara and myself, inasmuch as I am a jerk and she is an angel and a very private person who is putting up with me airing some rather sordid laundry throughout this book. I'd also like to address those perfect souls who are reading this and saying to themselves, "Why is this masochistic woman putting up with this asshole?" I'm happy that your life is so unruptured that you can make such a distant judgment call, so I'll only address the humans *in the audience. B and I are together forever and made that commitment a long time ago. Though I have broken the faithfulness clause, I would never want to live without her, or she without me. She has forgiven me more than I have forgiven myself, believe me. I don't take her forgiveness as a reason to do as I please, although to some it may seem that way. I have struggled with this sexual stuff; I hope the struggle is evident. B is not happy with me telling some of this, but she knows I've always been truthful when I write and that my life is what it is. She is the best person I have ever known and I have been and will continue to be her much-soiled knight in rusty armor as long as she will allow me. We have had our battles and our surrenders and victories and are still very much in love with each other. We have both seen friends who were couples break up over much less and be more miserable apart, so we have made a vow to be together at the end. There are limits, of course, and I have pushed these and pray to God that I will push them no more.*

Barbara knows I confess, express, and fantasize in the songs I write. Although most of them have been about and because of her, she does know when sentiments other than my love for her are voiced in rhyme.

Unfortunately—at this point, anyway—my job, as I have defined it, is to write songs about my life that are truthful. What's the point of doing it if it's just a bunch of made-up shit? It is art, after all, and art must be free to express itself, no matter what level or form. And that is what I do. It doesn't make it right or fair or even "okay," but she married me and I married her and we will work it out one way or another.

I name this album *Shock, Denial, Anger, Acceptance*, a corruption of the Elisabeth Kübler-Ross phrase for the emotions that accompany dying. My spirit has come close to dying more than a few times in my life because of my poor choices. This Vegas affair feels like the closest I've come to spiritual annihilation.

The record is released on my own Gomer Records label (you were expecting another name?) and in the next few months I build my own studio (screw you, Rodger) and marvel at how the record business, after all its success and excess, has returned to what it was at the beginning—a cottage industry. Because I've always been "the boy who loves monsters," I name my studio The Black Lagoon, and Rodger isn't allowed to record in it . . . ever. Our friendship still stands, which is what I love about musicians, especially drummers. Although, theoretically, drummers aren't really considered musicians.

Hahahahahaha.

My spiritual path has seen some serious neglect up in the wastelands of Las Vegas, so when Richard Page, my friend, former '80s background singer, and Mr. Mister alumnus, gives me a copy of a book entitled *The Tibetan Book of Living and Dying*, written by the master who he and his wife Linda follow, Sogyal Rinpoche, I latch onto it hungrily. It is the first Western view of Buddhism I've ever encountered. Barbara and I begin going to the Pages' house once a week to meditate with their group, even though I haven't been involved with a spiritual gathering in many, many years. It's a great way to reconnect with B through doing something together that's good for our souls, and I also reconnect with my meditation.

We sit in a circle and one of us leads the group. It's a different meditation technique than TM, in which a mantra is repeated. Master Rinpoche encourages completely freeing up your mind through focusing a little on breathing, a little on relaxing, but mostly on just being. It's difficult at first with my monkey-mind chirping in every two or three microseconds: *How big a jerk was that guy who cut me off on the freeway? Man, wouldn't a cappuccino be great right about now . . . hey, I forgot to pick up those jeans from the dry cleaners . . .* but when peace arrives, I feel utterly free. We all connect, and that alone is good for B and me. This is truly the only way I find peace in my life, no matter how great things get or how high I climb or how much I acquire or how many women I have sex with or how much money I make or how much my dog loves me (wait, strike that last one) or how loud the applause—it all comes down to me, alone in my room, communing with God. It sounds so simple; why don't I live there? I try, but life keeps getting in the way.

We start up a new tour. I have residual concerns about my faithfulness on the road, but I'm feeling like I've learned a hard lesson from my major screwup in Vegas. It has taught me something after all. And aside from that rather huge exception, I've been doing okay regarding abstaining from the "musician's life." Vegas is also the reason I am no longer drinking heavily, as twisted as that looks in print. I'm no longer getting laced before a concert, and our gigs get better and better. All hail the resilience of the human spirit.

At one show, a persistent fan tries to shove a bunch of roses in my hand while I'm playing a guitar solo. I yell at her over the sonic boom of the band, "I'm busy, dammit." She keeps it up, shoving and poking me with the roses. I grab them from her and windmill them against my guitar strings in frustration. The red petals blast across the stage like they've just hit a wood chipper and the audience reacts. The first ritual "rose decapitation" has occurred, and our stage will be showered with rose petals at every show from that moment on as fans come forward with bouquets and I happily comply by guillotining the petals on my guitar strings, becoming kind of the Morticia Addams of the guitar world.

The concert tour is going full-throttle, with the new, more aggressive album making it safer for guys to show up as well. Eventually we take the show to Japan, where the audience is 95 percent male. It's a new energy for me. We ask one of them why there are so many guys at my shows now, and he says "Back in the '80s the girls kept us away so we couldn't go. Now we buy the tickets first!" Through the passage of time, meditation, and a new commitment to the right path, I finally begin to change, so the whole twisted sexual draw of Japan is now pretty much a memory. I think it's been so long since I've been involved in the sexual excess of the road that I've gotten out of the habit. A lot of it was just that, in the end. Habit. That whole "this is just what I do" thing is gone. And I play better, too. And have more time to see the sights.

I sink a bunch of my own bread into the promotion of the *Shock* album (as it becomes known for short), but radio is in even more of a mess and hip-hop has a stranglehold on the charts, so there's still not much room for rock and roll. The album does end up at the top of a few "Best of 2004" lists, but that's about it.

I'm fired up again to get things rolling and working smoother so I can enjoy them more. I sign on with a new manager, Rob Kos, who turns out to be the first real music manager I've ever had. He is sharp, tough, and well versed in the business, and he's also a musician himself. Things start to take a turn for the better immediately. Wonder of wonders, *General Hospital* calls after twenty-five years and asks if I'd like to come back for a story arc on the show. Did you guys lose my number or what? I think about it, and Rob and I decide to do it and see what happens. The press is big around the first episode and the show goes to Number 1 in the ratings that week. I guess a lot of people were curious. The writers bring my character back as an alcoholic—was someone trailing me for the last four years taking notes?—and the scripts aren't as bad as I remember.

It's bizarre to see doctor's scrubs hanging in my dressing room again with a "Noah Drake" tag attached. And the first scene I have with Jackie Zeman (my *GH* love interest twenty-five years before) is positively surreal, because our characters discuss how we both have grown kids now and how much time has passed—and in real life, enough time has passed that we both really *do* have grown kids. A soap is the only type of show I can think of where an actor gets to play a scene pretending twenty-two years have passed, and twenty-two years actually have. One of the freakiest acting experiences of my life.

GH even creates a second character for me to play: a (you guessed it) rock star. This is something I wouldn't have done back in the old days, as it would have smacked of sellout right when I was fighting for my identity as a musician, but radio and the whole music business are in dire straits and everyone is looking for a new way to get their music to the people. Bands are now fighting to get on TV shows like *GH* for the exposure. The character the writers of *General Hospital* come up with is a rocker named . . . Apollo Love. Wow, just when I was starting to have a little faith in soap writing, too. Huh. So I say I'm not playing a modern rock guy named Apollo Love. I suggest Eli Love, because I know from experience that writers are married to the names they concoct and won't go too far astray. My strategy works and they say okay. There is no time during a shooting day on a soap to do drastic makeup changes to make this "Eli" guy look different from the "Noah" guy, so I give Eli an Australian accent. This really messes with my head having to jump back and forth between the two characters at the breakneck pace that is insisted upon by the directors and producers of a daytime drama.

I start playing more dates with my band. The shows are becoming something of a mutual communion between the audience and the band and me. It's pretty amazing to see the great connection—part shared wealth of memories, part new experiences—that are the soul of our live show now. Our touring has gotten to a very manageable place as well. We fly everywhere (no buses ever, ever, ever!) and we go out for a few days, then come home for a few days. It's the best of both worlds. On the road the performances stay fresh and exciting for us, and back home our families treat us like returning heroes every week. Barbara and I are doing well, to the point that if I get on her nerves, she'll joke, "Aren't you supposed to be going on the road soon, for Chrissakes?" It's a warm place to be, even though Vegas still hangs from the corner of the room like a ninety-pound spider.

I'm feeling much more secure about my life on the road, keeping a handle on my sexual garbage and playing music for the sheer joy of it.

My band is brilliant and we all actually really like each other and have such a great time on tour that when we play with other artists, some of their band members send requests: "If you ever need a [guitar player/drummer/keyboardist], here's my number." I'm having real fun again without the guilt and torture of sex and self-doubt. Yeah, that feels really weird to say, too, "the torture of sex." Wow, never in a million years would I ever have thought I'd write that, but I've earned it, the torture of sex, through my bad use of it and the way I have hurt the ones I love. It's still something I have to watch out for.

I go back into the studio and record a CD of songs I wish I'd written. They are covers of hits by other artists from the '70s and '80s because I need a break from writing after the fairly painful *Shock* album. It's 2005, and cover records are a hip thing at the moment. Since I didn't write any of these songs—with the single exception of "Cry"—I don't have the same parental attachment I do with the songs I write myself. It's a nice change to be in a studio without constantly worrying about whether the songs are good enough or not. It's actually fun. Richard Page comes in and duets with me on a cover of Mr. Mister's big song "Broken Wings." We like it so much, we release it as a single.

Just before we start touring for the album, I happen to go to a Los Angeles Lakers game and they put me on the Jumbotron screen and play "Jessie's Girl." I want to say, "I've written other songs, y'know," but I'm actually proud of the path this song has taken once I let it go. This is something I never could have imagined: the life this song would take on once it was out of my hands. Back in 1997, "Jessie's Girl" was placed in a pivotal final scene in the movie *Boogie Nights*. A band called Frickin' A has a hit with its JG cover. It turns up in TV shows like *Friends* and is featured in the films *13 Going on 30* and *Keeping the Faith*. The song gets me invited to one of Stephen Colbert's early *Colbert Reports* to take part in a skit in which he forgets the lyrics to "Jessie's Girl" and I prompt him from the side of the stage. For reasons still not clear to me, my photo permanently adorns his studio-set wall. Not only didn't he pay me for my appearance, the cheap bastard, but years later he tried to sell that photo on eBay for $350,000 after the market crashed in 2008. If I wasn't such a fan, I'd be upset.

Where was I? Oh, yeah, *that* song. In the web comic *Penny Arcade*, Gabe literally gets away with murder (a jury acquits him, finding his actions justified) after he proclaims "Jessie's Girl" to be the greatest song ever written and kills a friend who is musically inexpert enough to disagree with him. *Rolling Stone* ultimately pronounces it the Number 1 requested song in the karaoke world (not quite sure what that means), and it's one of the two most requested '80s songs at clubs around the U.S. (the other being Journey's "Don't Stop Believing"). I frequently hear it blasting out of the amps of cover bands in clubs from city to city. More recently, "Jessie's Girl" has turned up in the Vince Vaughn movie *Couples Retreat* and in the Robinson-Cusack-Corddry comedy *Hot Tub Time Machine*. The bloody song seems to be having better luck in films than I've had so far. And lately, in TV. Recently on the hit TV show *Glee*, Finn had occasion to sing it to his ex-girlfriend who had since become—coincidentally—Jessie's girl.

I think that's enough about "Jessie's Girl," so let's move on.

I'm happy to report that by the time I record *The Day After Yesterday*, that album of covers, Mr. Darkness has been hanging out but keeping his distance for the most part, just giving me little self-deflating pokes now and then, the swine. Gomer is happy to have his own record label. Liam is at an art college studying acting, while Josh is getting ready to move to USC in a year. And Barbara and I are sound asleep when, in the middle of the night, we hear a knock at our front door.

The last thing I want to see at my door at 2:30 in the morning, having just been roused from a deep sleep, is a brace of young, buff sheriffs who look like they're still in high school. But that's who is there to greet Barbara and me when we finally answer their incessant and, at this hour, spooky knocking. And it scares us, with all that it portends, to have police at our house in the early hours of the morning. They apologize for waking us, then jump straight to the business at hand. "Do you know a Liam Springthorpe?" one asks. "Yes," B and I answer in unison, "he's our son."

"He's just been found bleeding and moaning on the side of the road," is the official reply.

The world stops turning for both of us, and the moment is frozen forever. The sheriffs don't have much more information than what we've just heard. They're locals, and all they've received is a radio call. Because they were in the area, it fell to them to deliver the news. They add that our boy is, at this moment, lying unconscious in the emergency ward at the Henry Mayo Hospital in Valencia. They can't tell us if he'll make it or if he's on the brink of death. Barbara and I both go into survival mode. Our sole, shared purpose is to save our son. I run to my car and take the longest ride of my life, to Valencia, about an hour from where we live. I've left Barbara at home with only a few words said between us. We know what we have to do. I go to him, she calls everyone she knows who can help—doctors, friends, nurses, anyone who may give us an edge in saving Liam's life.

In a desperate tragi-comedy of errors, when I get to the hospital I'm in such a state and the signage is so bad that I can't find the emergency entrance. I have to stop and ask a Chinese guy walking his dog (at four a.m.?) where the ER is. Struggling to keep a lid on my panic, I take his barely articulate directions and eventually find my way into the emergency entrance. The doors swish open and I run through to the check-in desk. A nurse leads me into a room veiled by sterile nylon curtains and I see him. Our son. He's lying on his right side on a gurney with the covers pulled up to his chin. All I see is blood.

"The doctor will be in shortly," the nurse says. Liam is unconscious and hooked up to all kinds of life-function monitors that surround his bed like sentinels on a deathwatch. He looks like someone has beaten his face with a baseball bat. Caked dried blood is everywhere. His left eye is swollen shut; black, red, and purple and the size of a tennis ball. His hair is matted with dried blood, which covers the left side of his face, runs down his neck, and stains the blanket that is tucked in around his chin, cozy-baby style. His lips look like they've exploded from the inside. He is ashen and, save for all the damage, looks like our three-year-old baby boy, fast asleep in his crib where nothing and no one can ever harm him. It's all I can do not to lose it.

I call B on my cell phone and tell her I'm here and he's alive, but that we don't know much yet other than that his left eye is in bad shape. She says she's on her way. The local police who found Liam come in to talk to me. They amend the earlier news and tell us he wasn't found lying by the road; he was discovered in the bushes outside an apartment building. They tell me the name of the building. "That's where he lives," I answer. I think of the kid who has the apartment below my son, a drug addict/dealer with whom Liam has exchanged insults in the past. I tell the cops and they leave to check up on this. The doctor comes in. "Your son looks like he's been beaten very badly," is what I hear from this man.

"Is he going to live? Does he have brain damage? Is his eye any good? Will he be okay? Can we save him?" I have a million questions.

"We don't know anything yet. We'll need to do X-rays and a CAT scan to see if there's any bleeding in the brain. And we'll also check for any spinal damage. We should try to pry that eye open to see if he still has any sight left in it. It looks like it took a pretty bad whack."

"Well then, get on it, for fuck's sake!!!" I want to scream, but I know that won't help my son. Instead I tell the doc I'll stay with Liam and ask if they would please come and get us when they're ready for the tests. Some nurses enter the room to help me hold my son down while the doctor tries to separate the bloodied swollen eyelids of his damaged left eye to ascertain if there is any vision remaining. My son screams in pain through his delirium. The doctor finally relents and says that the swelling is too great. They will get him into X-ray. They all go to set this in motion and I'm left alone with Liam. I kiss him and tell him I'm here and that everything will be okay. He doesn't hear me. I feel like I should be doing more than just sitting there holding his hand. I'm torn between wanting to drive to the drug dealer's apartment, break down his door, and kill him, and to sit here with our boy like a good daddy should.

A nurse comes into the cubicle and says we're being moved to a private room so we won't be bothered. I take this as a sign that everything else will be handled quickly. I'm wrong. We are in this "private room" for twenty minutes and Liam is getting restless. His arm is obviously badly broken as well and he is moaning in pain. He still hasn't spoken a recognizable syllable. Finally I allow the thoughts into my head: What if we lose our boy? Or he is crippled or brain-damaged or blind? I jump up and storm out to the front desk like the harpy who will destroy anyone to defend her child. The doctor says he's been looking for us and didn't know we'd been moved to a different room. They run their battery of tests, and I don't leave my son's side. Barbara arrives with information from our good friend Leonne, who is a psychiatric nurse and deep in the medical system. They've already got Liam cleared for transfer to the UCLA Medical Center to see Dr. K (as he is known), the preeminent eye surgeon there. Barbara is in shock at the terrible sight of her precious firstborn. We sit in silence with Liam while the test results are compiled. It seems to take forever. All we want is for him to live. We'll deal with the rest as it unfolds.

The local cops return and ask me if I would step outside. In the hall of the emergency room, they want to know if my son has ever tried to hurt himself. This is so unexpected that I do a double take. Liam is passionate about the actor's life he is entering, loves his music, has a good circle of friends, is connected to his family and his home, and gets plenty of interest from the girls he meets.

"How do you mean?" I ask.

"Has he ever shown any suicidal tendencies?"

Wait, is this my son or *me* that we're discussing? The Darkness chimes in, "The apple doesn't fall far from the tree, if you get my meaning." I hate this line of thought and push it out of my head with all the strength I have left. I listen, unbelieving, as they tell me they checked on the kid/dealer in the apartment below and he was not involved in any way, but that the screen on Liam's third-floor bedroom window was pushed out and there is blood on the cement pavement directly below it. My son fell three stories to a rock-hard sidewalk, obviously landing on the left side of his face, and he's still alive? The cops are focused on this as a possible suicide attempt. I've heard stories of parents being blindsided by their kids' hidden issues—finding that their daughter has OD'd on a drug the parents had no idea she was even on, or walking into the garage to discover their "happy-go-lucky" son swinging from a crossbeam. I have a moment of doubt, but then quickly realize this can't be the case with Liam.

"He didn't jump," I assure them, but I want to go to the scene of his accident and try to understand it for myself. I know my son, and maybe I'll see something the police missed. I go back inside and tell Barbara that it looks like he fell from his bedroom window and that I'm driving to his apartment to take a look. She stays with our still-unconscious and bloodied boy. We are desperate to ask him questions. We hope he will eventually be in a condition to answer them.

The apartment building is ten minutes from the hospital. I park and walk around to the back, where Liam's apartment faces out on to the hillside. I look up and see that the wire-mesh screen has indeed been pushed out far enough for someone to exit through the window. It looks so high from where I stand. How did he survive this fall? What could have possibly made him jump? At my feet is a large puddle of dried blood, already soaked into the porous concrete. From the amount of blood I can see, he must have lain where he fell for an hour or more, in the middle of the night, without anyone near enough to know or care or help, while we slept on, oblivious. I stare at the dark stain for minutes. We still don't know how much of our son is left. I drive back to the emergency ward with all my questions.

The scans and X-rays reveal no bleeding in Liam's brain, his spine is okay, and it looks like his eye is still there, although we won't know if he has sight until the swelling goes down enough for the doctors to open it. His left orbital socket is badly cracked, which is not good, and his right arm is broken in three places. Again I think, "It's hard to kill a Springthorpe." We stay with him through the day until he's taken to UCLA. B rides in the ambulance, I follow. He begins to regain consciousness, but he's confused and disoriented. Family and close friends fill our son's room at UCLA all through the night and the following day. Some break into tears when they see the condition of his face. Others go silent at the sight of him, damaged, semiconscious, immobile. Slowly he comes back to us. He begins to refocus and the story is finally pieced together over the next few days, and this is what is revealed.

Liam is fast asleep in his apartment when, in the middle of the night, he's awakened by the loud and very obvious sounds of someone breaking in. He hears footsteps outside his closed bedroom door and sees the light suddenly switch on beneath the threshold. Still half asleep, confused, and believing he's at home, where his bedroom window opens out onto a small tiled roof, he pushes out the screen and steps through the opening onto that roof. But there is no roof, and he drops like a stone, three stories to the hard pavement, landing on his left side, breaking bones, and knocking himself unconscious. Blood pools around his face from the wounds he receives and he lies there untended until the police arrive, summoned by a neighbor who tells the cops he's been hearing moaning outside his window all night.

I momentarily want to kill this guy for not reacting faster, but I know this won't help our boy now.

Some days later, once he is at UCLA, one of the first phone calls Liam can take himself is from his good friend David, a fellow actor at college. Liam tells his concerned classmate the story of his accident, beginning with the person breaking into his apartment. "I think that was me" is the unexpected response from the other end of the line. Six months earlier, because David lives at his parents' house far off campus, Liam had given his friend a key to his apartment and told him anytime he wanted to crash, just to let himself in. Of course by the time our son was awakened by someone he had mistaken for a bold and noisy burglar, he had forgotten this pertinent piece of information. A slightly inebriated David had let himself in that fateful night, slept his buzz off on the living room couch for an hour, then decided he could make the drive to his parents' house after all. He headed back out, using the only route that did not take him past Liam's unconscious form lying on the blood-soaked concrete, and therefore remained completely unaware of the chaos his late-night visit had just caused. For Liam, this must get filed in the "no good deed goes unpunished" category. I've always believed the Buddhist phrase "Everything is a blessing." I'm still struggling to find where the blessing could be in this.

The doctors finally tell us that our son does have sight in his left eye but that the socket must be rebuilt or the eye will slowly drift out of alignment. Dr. K is an eccentric but genius eye surgeon, and he will perform the incredibly delicate, high-tech procedure on our son. Liam will wind up with a titanium eye socket along with bone grafted from his skull to make sure it all heals well and strong. Before he is wheeled into the operating room for the three-hour surgery, a nurse writes the word "yes" on his left cheek so that the correct eye will be operated on. A low-tech precaution to thwart a potential screwup, but better safe than sorry. Liam goes under the knife. The outcome is by no means a given, and we pray for the recovery of our boy as we hang in the waiting room, which is filled with families in similar straits regarding their own loved ones. There is a closeness born of silent understanding in this room.

Three long hours later a nurse comes to us and says everything went well. We are relieved but unsure what exactly that means. We hurry to post-op to see him. He is still out from the anesthetic, but Dr. K assures us his should be a good result. We'll know for sure in a week or two. The next day we take Liam home and I leave for the road. I've cancelled a handful of dates to stay with our son, but it's time I get back to my commitments. I call every hour on the hour to see how our boy is doing but it's maddening to be so far away. When I get back home, he is on the couch looking miserable. He has a white gauze patch over his damaged eye. He lifts the patch to show me that his left eye is no longer tracking with his right eye. His vision is poor and he thinks he looks like a freak. "I can't focus properly on anything. How can I be an actor with *this*?" he tells me in anguish, pointing to his damaged and wandering left eye.

I call Dr. K, furious about this result. I'm sure this deeply respected, even revered senior surgeon isn't used to being yelled at by an unhinged musician. But he takes it well and tells me our son's eye should soon come back on track. And sure enough, several weeks later, Liam calls to tell me that his eyes are tracking together again, and his vision is 100 percent. Looking at him today you would never guess what his face has been through. Having come so harrowingly close to losing him, B and I are more overprotective of him now than when he was little. And we've learned the hard way how fragile and resilient our kids really are.

I decide that Joshua needs a break. He and Liam are so close; Liam's accident and hospitalization have been rough on him, too. And I could use a little R & R myself. We decide to go fishing. We ask Liam to come (B isn't into fishing), but he declines, since he's so relieved to be recovered and back in the flow of his art college. I tell him if he won't come fishing, then the three of us are all going white-shark cage-diving sometime soon. And he agrees.

Josh and I head to the deep interior of Alaska. There are no roads and no cars, and the only way to get anywhere is in a floatplane, which takes off and lands on the many lakes that dot this pristine wilderness. Once we touch down on one of these inland seas and have unloaded everything from the plane, we hike each day, along with our guides, to the nearest stream to fish. Josh and I are both avid fishermen and this is the ultimate fly-fishing experience for us. We are absolutely in the middle of nowhere and glad to be away from the stress of the nightmare we've just lived through. It's so great to be with him now as he reels in a giant salmon, screaming and hollering like he's at a Lakers game.

It's a healing trip (not as much so for the salmon we catch, but hey), and we stare in awe as great brown bears come out of the undergrowth and walk by us, not twenty feet away. It's kind of like I imagine white-shark cage-diving will be, but without the cage. As a huge bear comes within munching distance our hearts beat faster and I ask which one of our guides has the gun. They say they don't carry guns and tell us to raise our arms above our heads every time a bear comes too close, and shout, "Ho Bear." "You're fucking kidding me," I say. But this silly move actually works. I'll be damned. And no one gets eaten (except, again, the salmon).

Thanks to the years I spent off the tour circuit helping to raise Liam and Josh, the bond I have with each of our boys is strong and deep. It was so worth it. The only job that I am confident I've done my best at is being their father. And it is the one I've gotten the greatest joy from. Josh and I head home after three weeks of frontier fishing and scary big-bear moments. I've had time to clear my head up in the chilly North, and I prepare to do what I've known all along I have to do.

For our life together to be what we both want it to be, I must face B with my deceit in Vegas. The only meaningful prayer is for forgiveness. And that is what I pray for. She is furious with me and hurt that I would break her trust yet again. I owe my life to this girl. To grant her some privacy, I won't go into the details of our consequent discussions but, needless to say, they are intense. Over time we heal and we stay together—and not in a resentful way, because there would be no joy in remaining in that kind of partnership. We know that there is no way to live together unless we can ultimately be honest and accept each other, warts and all. Even if I am the frog with the warts and she is the princess. And she is.

Life goes on. And so does touring. We shoot a new concert video, the first since 1985's *Beat of the Live Drum*. We film at the beautiful Coronado Theatre in Rockford, Illinois. It's the very first show for my new guitar player George Bernhardt, and he's pretty anxious about it. He is a brilliant player, but thanks to a bad case of nerves brought on by the fact that his first show with the band is being recorded in a high-definition, eight-camera shoot, he screws up "Jessie's Girl." Rodger asks again, "What do you have to do to get yourself fired from this organization?" The funny fucker. But even this is apparently not enough to get someone canned. We do the song again for the cameras. George hasn't messed that song up—or any other song—since. Then, in Atlanta, on a beautiful summer day while we prepare for the first of two nights in an outdoor venue called Chastain Park, I get a call on my cell phone. It's one of those moments I could have lived my whole life without.

CHAPTER TWENTY-ONE

BIG BOYS DO CRY

CAPE

2007

I hear silence. Then there's an odd, muffled sound. My first thought is that it's either a fan who found my cell number and then got cold feet or a telemarketer who's really slow on the draw. I'm about to hang up when I hear a wrenching sob. I look at the ID on my phone and see that it's Amy, Sahara's mother, calling. I get a chill. She's crying so hard she can't speak. Every time she starts a sentence, she chokes up and begins crying anew. I wait on the line and I know that whatever is coming is not good.

Eventually she gains enough composure to tell me the terrible news: Sahara (only twelve years old) has just been diagnosed with stage 4 brain-stem cancer. It's the most aggressive form of cancer a child can possibly get. And it's inoperable. I can't think. I want to rewind the broken conversation we've just had and make it come out a different way. I can't accept this information. Maybe I'm dreaming. It certainly feels like it. I have that light, floaty feeling as if all the blood is draining from my head. "What?" is all I can say. Amy repeats what she has just told me. But even before she is finished I know it is so.

I try, mentally, to put the image of our little Energizer Bunny—who loves to play pranks, have thirty "best" friends, travel the continent with her *Harry Potter* backpack filled with Juicy Fruit gum, lip gloss, ink pens, notepads, disposable cameras, and snacks, and who loves to hear the swish of a "nothing but net" basketball shot—into a hospital bed with a tumor on her brain. I can't do it. No child should be dealt the diagnosis she's just been handed. But it's true. Amy has to go; she just wanted to reach out and tell me, knowing how much I love her little girl. I tell her I'll talk to her soon; we'll figure this out. Will we? She says good-bye and hangs up. My first thought is, "How could God let this happen?" Spent and breathless, I sink to my knees in my hotel room and offer up a "passenger-on-a-crashing-plane" prayer to save our girl. "Dear God, whatever it takes, don't let her die."

The picture that Amy just painted couldn't be any bleaker, but if anyone can beat the odds, it's Sahara. This is the girl who ate octopus sushi to win a $5 bet from me; who had an entire rock band and its crew catering to her every whim; who always took the side of underdogs at school and defended them with all her heart; who answered "I'll do it," when a little boy showed up at her school with the handcuffs (but no key) he'd stolen from his mother's bedside drawer and suggested that they handcuff someone; who could climb into the hearts of people that didn't even like kids; who loved to dress her obstreperous cat Semo in a variety of Build-a-Bear outfits; who (with Amy sitting beside her in the classroom) once queried a DARE officer who had asked if there were any questions, following his anti-drug lecture, "Do you think my mom is cute?"; who loved Las Vegas and who wasn't afraid of anything.

My thoughts turn to Amy and her husband, Shannon. Having recently come so close to losing Liam, I have an idea of how they must be feeling. But there's a slow-motion horror to a terminal diagnosis like this, much different from the heart-pounding emergency that B and I faced. Amy texts me later, "My heart is broken—my faith is shattered." She says the doctors have told them that there is no hope. They tell her to take Sahara home and make her comfortable until she passes. But compliant acceptance is not Amy's style. She dives into the world of malignant glioblastoma tumors with a tenacity born of mother love. She will do everything she can to save her girl. She goes online, talks to doctors, asks friends, searches for solutions both medical and alternative, and seeks answers from mothers whose children are similarly afflicted. We all have a vague belief that there is a cure for cancer out there somewhere—something they're just not telling us. We've heard it's experimental; it's herbal; it involves stem cells, apricot pits, fasting, eating meat, being vegetarian. Jesus Christ, she's twelve years old. Won't someone save her?

The Darkness doesn't screw with me on this one; it's dark enough as it is. Maybe for once it's even too dark for him.

The band and I must remain on tour, but I stay in close contact with Amy, Shannon, and their girl Sahara. My first phone call to Sahara after the diagnosis is full of phrases like "We'll kick this thing in the ass" and "We're gonna beat it." She sounds bright, responsive, and positive, and she says, "Yes we are." She is sure it's just a matter of time before this is all behind her and we're laughing and having fun again. I tell her I love her and that I'll come and see her. She never loses her belief that her cure is just around the corner. A few more treatments away. One more journey. In the end it is decided that Sahara will undergo radiation and chemo, just like my sweet old man did over a quarter of a century earlier. Cancer has stolen so many people I love. It will not take this girl. Not on our watch. And so Amy, Shannon, and Sahara move forward to face the medical gauntlet that is the treatment of cancer in our lifetime.

My fans are good people. Really good people. I let them know about Sahara's battle through my website, and they take up her cause like it's their own, creating fund-raisers: charity auctions, sales of T-shirts and bracelets bearing Sahara's name—anything that will make money to fund her treatment. It offers hope to all of us that the "official" exercise of charity fundraising will directly translate into saving her life. It's all we can do. We can't offer healing or medical expertise, so we raise money. Money equals success, right? We also offer up prayers by the millions.

My manager Rob, my agent Jim Gosnell, and I arrange to put on a benefit concert at the arena in Sahara's hometown of Cape Girardeau,

Missouri, to show our support and help defray the costs of her mounting medical bills. She is beside herself when we announce this: she has always wanted us to play in "Cape," as she calls it. We all wish it were just a normal gig. Because she is an avid and really excellent basketball player, her dad has taken to calling her "Hoops." Her jersey number is 21. Remember that. We advertise the show as the "Hope for Hoops" concert. Sahara and Amy move into the Ronald McDonald House in Houston. Typical of Sahara, she wins everyone at M. D. Anderson Hospital over to her side and even sends Shannon out with her own birthday money to buy crayons and coloring books for the "sick kids" in the ward, not yet fully realizing that she is now one of those kids. The chemo begins and it makes her ill. While throwing up into the toilet one day, Sahara looks into her distraught mother's eyes and asks, "Are you okay?" That's the kind of kid she is. Amy waits until Sahara is asleep before she allows herself to cry.

When the band and I visit the Energizer Bunny in Houston a few weeks later, she has lost a lot of weight and her balance is off, but she's still her vibrant self. She even comes to the show we're playing in the area and is clearly looking forward to the benefit concert. The oncologist takes head X-rays to see how she is progressing, and Sahara is crushed to learn that the tumor is still there. She thought it would be gone in a month or so. We "grown-ups," on the other hand, are thrilled that the tumor appears to have stopped growing. I guess it's all a matter of your expectations.

By the time my band and I arrive in Cape Girardeau, everyone there is familiar with Sahara's condition and her battle to win. The whole town shows up: the press, the mayor, her school, her basketball team, and her biggest fan: me.

Sahara is frail and thin at this point, but she tries her best to be our little Energizer Bunny still. I bring her up onstage and she gets a hero's welcome from the crowd. Her favorite song of mine is "Love Somebody" and I jump off the stage to sit with her during some of it. She smiles like a star and takes it in stride. The audience cheers. They are cheering for her. The show ends, and at the meet-and-greet afterward she makes the time to take photos with fans and whispers to me, "Now I know how you feel." She tires quickly.

Sahara goes home, and I go back to my hotel room and sit on the end of my bed. We did manage to lift some spirits and rally the town of "Cape" to our girl's aid, but my Darkness, in the wee hours, reviews the evening a little differently. He tells me that it was all just a big letdown. The show is over and nothing has really changed; everything is still the same—the prospects of her survival, the therapy she is undergoing, the hospital she will soon return to, and the late nights where it all comes down on us. "What did you change?" is the question he poses to me as I struggle for sleep.

We go on with our tour and Sahara goes back to Houston to the realities of "last-ditch" therapy and her slowly deteriorating young body. The fan auctions continue, the plastic bracelet sales climb, and Amy and Shannon continue to pour their hearts and souls into saving their baby girl. The next time we get together, Sahara is confined to a wheelchair but still wants to come to the show we're doing in nearby Tunica. The drugs that are helping her chances of survival are also making living painful for her. Her weight has now gone in the opposite direction due to the large doses of steroids that are part of her regimen. Her pale skin has multiple splits and tears because the drugs are thinning the tissue. And she won't go out without one of her many hats now that her once-bouncy auburn hair is patchy, curly, and orange. The tumor is messing with her speech, and she's having trouble being understood by anyone but Amy. Yet I recognize her words when she calls and leaves a message on my cell phone: "I love you," she yells down the line to me. I wish I'd kept that recording.

One day, not long after, I log on to her website to catch up on the many messages family, friends, fans, and even supportive strangers have posted to her, and I read the following from her webmaster, Pamela: "I've started this blog at least ten times and hit the delete key, unable to find the words that convey what is in my heart and what is about to take your breath away: Sahara died this evening." And it does take my breath away. How can she be gone? My natural instinct is to blame someone or something for depriving her of living her full span of years. Years that, I'm sure, would have yielded some amazing things, considering the powerful spirit that resided in her.

But instead of looking for someone to blame, I think back on moments that now seem beautifully guileless and precious beyond words. To the time, not too long ago, when Amy was making jokes about Sahara wanting to go shopping for a training bra. How she was starting to be aware of boys. Had, in fact, raced into the house one afternoon and dragged her mom outside into the backyard to confess "I kissed a boy today." Now she is forever thirteen. The Darkness speaks softly to me one night after Sahara passes. "So much for all your cheerleading and fund-raising, huh? You really couldn't do jack shit for her in the end, could you, jerk?" On this particular night, I would have to agree with him.

On the evening of Sahara's death, Barbara and I are in the kitchen. We have a floor-to-ceiling window that looks out onto the entrance to our house. Both of us keep seeing a shadow darting to the front door. Not just once, but several times. I know it is Sahara. And we're not the only ones. My band and I are playing in New York and Amy comes to visit. She is in Central Park taking photos when suddenly she sees a man walking toward her wearing a blue T-shirt with the word SAHARA printed across the chest in huge white letters. He stops, turns around, and goes back the way he came, but not before she snaps a photo on her iPhone. I've seen it.

Later, Amy and I are walking down 48th Street looking at guitar stores, something I love to do anywhere. We come to a small store that has one guitar in its main window. It's an old and very vintage one from the '60s. I notice the guitar is called a "Sahara" and Amy notices the price: $2,100. Sahara/21. Things like this happen again and again. Amy is with Sue Packard, my assistant from the Vegas days, seeing *KÀ*, the show that took over the MGM Theater after *EFX* closed. It's hard for them not to think of Sahara when they're together again in the town she so loved. They're being seated when Amy hears someone a few rows back yell "Twenty-one" at the top of his lungs.

Eventually, months after Sahara has gone, Amy finds a videotape in her camera that she had no idea was there. It's Sahara, self-filmed on the day she heard her initial diagnosis. She has the camera trained on herself and says into the lens, "When you see this I will be eating all the cheesecake I want." She loved cheesecake. It was her favorite food in the world, and she would eat it all day long if she were allowed to, which she wasn't. Our powerful little Energizer Bunny truly seems to be reaching out to us. There are messages from her on Valentine's Day and Christmas, and her number 21 still keeps showing up. We all like to think our girl is letting us know that wherever she is, she is okay.

Her service in her hometown, a tearjerker of mammoth proportions, finds the church packed to the bell tower. Amy and Shannon, looking shell-shocked and frail, red-eyed kids, solemn parents; players from the Lady Comets (Sahara's favorite local women's basketball team) sniffling into Kleenex; local members of the government with platitudes in their pockets but heartfelt looks in their eyes; and some of my band and me sitting quietly in a row. There are photos of Sahara in the full power of her youth, smiling her familiar, thousand-volt smile; wreaths and vases of flowers; a video screen showing a slide show of even more photos. I can hear one of my songs, "Celebrate Youth," playing softly over the house speakers, and at the center of it all, a small, bright-pink box of about the size that might hold a pair of kids' shoes. It is her ashes. The ashes of a thirteen-year-old girl named Sahara. It is unfathomable.

I flash back to the moment, years and years ago, when I am standing in our living room in Australia and seeing my own father's ashes being handed across the threshold. There is a terrible finality in the act of cremation, which I have felt is both healing yet at the same time incredibly disruptive. It is, in a way, an acceptance that they are gone, returned to the cosmos, the earth, the sky. But it is also a huge mind-fuck to see a loved one suddenly reduced to a tiny, ordinary box. It's impossible-seeming, and yet what are we in the end but this? My reminiscing also takes me back to the minute I first saw Sahara bopping in and out of a backstage queue as if she had too much to accomplish and not much time to do it. I understand that now.

People speak at her service. A young girl stands and delivers a beautiful and sweet poem she wrote for her lost friend. I struggle tearfully through "Free," a song I'd written about dealing with the loss of a child, for the parents of a young boy from our neighborhood who'd drowned several years earlier. Despite my bright and shiny pop-star image, I've written a lot of songs about death.

Some of us take the long, silent drive back to Sahara's home after the service. We sit in her bedroom and tell stories, while Amy clutches the *Harry Potter* backpack that was her baby's traveling bag of choice when they would go on the road to Disneyland, to Palm Springs, or to see me. The stories and the shared grief help momentarily, but everyone knows it will be a long, hard journey to the far shore of any healing.

A few days after she'd left this earth, I had gone to my computer and put down some thoughts. A few sentences on losing her. Writing has always been my way of seeing the forest through the trees. It's my soul's compass, my way of dealing with things that are tangled up inside my brain. And I need to do something for her. Something good and pure that speaks of who she was and what she meant to me, like I did for my old dad years ago. I want to build a memorial to Sahara, but I am no stonemason or sculptor or builder of any sort. I am only a writer.

A few weeks after the service I have a melody to a verse and chorus of a new song I am thinking of calling "Saint Sahara." I have no words for it yet because I generally write lyrics last, but I'm lost as to how I should phrase my feelings for her and her death. I don't want it to be maudlin or soppy—she wouldn't want that. And Amy herself had recently said to me, "If you write a song for her, please don't make it a dirge." I know what she means. On the computer I see a document titled "Miss S." That was my nickname for her. I open it up and the words I wrote almost a month ago are there before me and they fit the melody I have written so perfectly that I am actually stunned. I've never had this happen before, ever. I lay the newfound lyrics into the first verse and sing it out to her in my music room:

Come on, close the book and turn out the light
Put your plans aside tonight
Yeah I know it's not wrong, but it sure isn't right
An angel bids a last good night to us
Come on Sahara, give us a smile
You've walked this far with us, let's walk one more mile
Hey Saint Sahara, beautiful child.
You left us all wanting, you left us beguiled.

And life goes on.

CHAPTER TWENTY-TWO

WHERE IT ALL BEGAN

RETURN TO OZ

2007

I take a trip back to Oz for my first shows there since I left in 1972. I play a bunch of dates in Australia's six main cities—Brisbane, Sydney, Hobart, Melbourne, Adelaide, and Perth. Not a lot has changed, as far as your options to play a gig go, in the almost forty years since I left Australia's brutal shores. We play the local arenas and I try to find something I recognize in the land where I once lived, dreamed dreams, fell in love, learned to play the guitar, and received a neighborhood whipping. I expect a few past issues may arise now that I'm back *performing* in Australia instead of just visiting my old mum's house, but I'm not prepared for the onslaught of emotions that surface in me once the shows start in the "Great Southern Land."

Working here makes all the difference to my mental state, and it is my first truthful and solid re-bonding with the place where I was raised. I'm no longer just a casual visitor, the boy in the bubble, removed and distant, stopping by for a quick reminisce before I head back to my home in the U.S. I've forgotten a lot of what I felt back in the days when I lived here and options were few. But now it rises up in me, and I begin to understand just how much pain and longing I really associate with this country. Feelings that had waned with time or that I'd suppressed are suddenly front and center. They've been waiting for me to return and make a real connection with Australia, my home. As I travel around the country, I am thrust back, against my will, into memories and forgotten issues that have been buried alive for more than thirty years in the rich, black, clotted earth that is my distant past here.

The first big town we hit is Brisbane. It's the same city I journeyed to in 1969, straight out of Vietnam, in my lurching, uneven pursuit of a musical career. Two women I recognize are in the meet-and-greet line after the arena show. One is a middle-aged woman who was once a seventeen-year-old goddess I loved for a while, or believed I did, back when I was nineteen and playing in the inauspiciously named Wickedy Wak. Her name comes back to me—Gaye—and as our eyes meet there is a flicker of doubt and embarrassment, as we each must wonder what we look like to the other after all this time. A moment of disorientation while we take that mental trip back thirty-five years to when we last saw each other.

I am almost sixty and so is she, and what we meant to each other for a brief time in 1969, when we were both teenagers looking for something to hold on to, is all there is between us. I also recognize the woman with her, Anne, and remember her as a young blond surfer chick back in the day when the Beatles were still a recording band. I feel like I owe these two. All those years ago they were the first to claim fandom and friendship with a young unsettled Ricky and let him know he was okay. I associate them strongly with my first success as a fledgling musician and the beginning realization that I might actually be able to pull this dream off. Seeing them fills me with gratitude, pride, and yearning. But they are gone—whisked out along with the rest of the meet-and-greet line—before I can think this through, much less express it.

Next stop is Sydney. It is the hedonistic capital of Oz. Beautiful and perverted.

My early journeys through Australia, back when I was living and gigging here, were the beginnings of a lot of the sexual shit that I have had to deal with later in life, when it shouldn't have been all about fucking. We all got into as much sex as we could back then. It didn't matter how young they were, or even how old they were, or if they had husbands or boyfriends, were virgins or hookers. A lot of it seems like normal young-guy stuff and to a degree it was, but I was never able to shed the obsession as I grew older and should have been letting much of it go. The habit of a sexual path is as powerful as any habit. And I picked up a hell of a habit. It's been hard to break. It's never good to have as much as you want of *anything*.

Walking around Sydney one afternoon makes me feel the same claustrophobic feelings I used to experience in this place. This was the biggest Australia had to offer? It wasn't big enough. But what was I really searching for? Certainly not physical size. LA always feels too big. I e-mail B every day. The only good thing about being away from her is that we both focus on what is important—us. And all the garbage that has accumulated throughout our relationship just falls away.

We travel to Hobart. The big town of Tasmania . . . where Errol Flynn was born. And that's pretty much it for Tassie. There is absolutely nothing else Tasmania is famous for except its early and punishingly hard penal settlement in the 1880s. (A prisoner escaping with another fellow lifer got a bit peckish after a while and killed, cooked, and ate his companion. "He tasted like chicken," he is quoted as saying on his reapprehension.) Obviously I have always avoided this place. I stay in my hotel room until the show to make sure I don't get killed and eaten.

The next city we go to is Melbourne, where most of my demons were born and raised. I'm pretty certain Mr. D is from around these parts. There is suddenly so much unresolved stuff here for me to deal with, I can't even begin to assess it. I guess I've avoided it on my previous visits by going straight to my old mum's house and consciously or unconsciously keeping myself sequestered there until it was time to go back to the U.S. *All* of my dark teenage stuff is here. Now that I'm out and about and interacting with this place, it's impossible to avoid it. The memories are lurking in the dim alleyways of the local pubs, in the angry finger flipped out of a moving car window, in the gray cinderblock schools that still look like the prisons they were to me as I served my time there, and in the sharp twang and drawl of the down-home Aussie accent that I associate with such buzz-kill phrases as "Are you a fuckin' queer, mate?"

On a day off in Melbourne, I take a side trip out to 13 Subiaco Court, my old home. The street seems much smaller than I remember, but the house still looks the same. Sharp-edged cream brick, lawn struggling for life, and bushes screaming for water. I see my front bedroom window facing the street. I was a tortured little motherfucker inside this house, and the present occupants are completely unaware of all the history that is here for me. They can't suspect I'm standing outside, full to the brim with emotions, looking at this small suburban battleground that was the center of my teenage universe.

It's in this house that I tried to hang myself by the neck until I was dead, that I beat my face in anguish and torment until it bled, that I gave up on school and wondered if I had ruined my life, that I obsessed over the girls I couldn't approach and masturbated several times each day out of sexual frustration, teenage angst, and something a little deeper and darker that wouldn't surface as a serious problem until I was in a committed relationship years later; where I built guillotines, gallows, and fire pits and tortured schoolteachers and shopkeepers in my dark imagination; where I learned to play the guitar; where I met Pete Watson, the man who delivered me from an academic hell, named me "Rick Springfield," and set me on the musician's path. It's the house out of which I sneaked late at night to sit in the car while my friends robbed convenience stores. The house where I forged my strongest memories as a young teen. It all happened while I was within those so-familiar walls. So much life lived in this place: it's difficult for me to absorb it all as I look upon it so many years later. How can a simple, nondescript, cookie-cutter suburban house have so much hoodoo, so much energy, the residue of so much pain and so much innocence lost? So much *life*.

A few stops down the line from here is the Richmond train station, where I was beaten by a gang of drunken older boys while I was trying to get home one night carrying a bad case of blue balls after rubbing up against a teen temptress at a local dance. “Are you a fuckin’ Sheila, mate?” came the rhetorical question from the group of toughs as I stood begging for the late-night train to arrive and usher me into the safety of its brightly lit womb (“Sheila” being the derogative term for a *girl* back then). Of course my hair was longer than theirs and my slight frame made me an easy target. I was smacked across the face and beaten for my insolence in not answering. I arrived home aching and angry, and I stole into bed so no one would see me or the damage done. I fell asleep thinking that in the final analysis, I was indeed “Howard the Coward.” I couldn’t fight back to save myself.

This wells up in me now, this shame and remembrance of my helplessness, my loneliness. And it’s lumped in with all the other moments I felt weak and unprotected in my teens. It seemed these bastards were everywhere: challenging me, telling me I couldn’t go to this party, that dance, get on this train, have my hair that long, be younger than them, walk down a deserted street with a girl, live where they lived. *Those fuckers will pay.* The phrase jumps into my head like it’s been waiting for me to get here and face this. That’s what I want. I want to hit back. It amazes the part of my mind sitting back and taking notes (something writers always do) that this reptilian-brained auto-response would ring such a big bell in me. *Hit the bastards back, hard.*

The next night, after the show in Melbourne, the band and crew go to a local dance club, and of course I drink too much. People are getting loud and some are saying stupid shit, and I’m in the bathroom when a guy walks in and says something I don’t like. I don’t even remember what it was, but it’s enough. *Hit the bastards back.* It surfaces in me like a breaching shark. I boil suddenly with long-suppressed, long-simmering anger. With all the teenage angst I can muster, I slug him in the face and he goes down hard, bleeding from his nose, like *I* did so many, many years ago. *Fuck you, asshole!* Of course I instantly feel remorse once the adrenaline is absorbed back into my system, and I want to make him feel okay. I let him know it was nothing personal. I am fighting back for the young man from ages ago, with the androgynous look, who wasn't strong enough to fend for himself in the land of the Tough Guy. Of course I don't say this to *him*. But even I am surprised by how volatile being here has made me. The strangers I am bound into close contact with on this Australian tour—the crew, the other artists, the audiences, the promoters, and assorted tour personnel I work with—remind me of the people (both positive and negative) who helped raise and shape me as a kid, a teenager, a young adult.

B has always accompanied me on previous trips to Oz, and I think it's partly because she isn't with me this time to remind me of who I am now that I'm feeling this bond with my origins, and all the stuff it stirs up, much more strongly. I hadn't realized how this view of Australia as a bully state during my later teenage years had affected me. Maybe some of this is a skewed distant memory from a tortured and powerless teen, but it didn't come from nowhere. Being home in Australia as a full-fledged adult male is like waking up one day with Spider-Man powers. And all those young guys who used to threaten and intimidate me at local dances, lonely train stations, and brightly lit pubs look like youngsters themselves now. Part of me wants to hug them and tell them it's okay, don't be so afraid of this world, we're all struggling, too. And the other part wants to fuck them up so bad their mums wouldn't recognize 'em. The need to be more than the limited view that I felt some of these people projected onto me, combined with the inherent feeling that I would never achieve my full potential in this place, is, I think, what drove me from this beautiful land and a life that could have been.

I was raised as a musician in a time in Australia when any artist that came from overseas, be it the U.S. or England, instantly received more attention, more money, more kudos, and more respect than the Aussie acts, even if the visiting stars sucked ass, and it made me feel even more inadequate than I already did. It proved to me that if I really wanted to make a mark, stand for something, join the world stage, I had to leave this land. I wasn't the only one who felt this. Other bands and singers would leave Oz to seek greater fortune elsewhere.

I could write a whole book about my connection with Australia—my homeland. It truly is my small town that I love/hate. It has breathed life into me, raised me, scarred me, taught me, taunted me, given me hope, given me dreams, caused me harm, taught me to survive, taught me to feel shame, built my faith, and shown me that my faith is worthless. I am forever tied to this harsh, inhospitable, dry, barren, unique, spiritual world, and I can only hope that one day my ashes will be spread upon its unforgiving and beautiful red desert. So much is inside me, wrapped up in these emotions, that I think I drink to numb it all. I'll deal with it later.

The Darkness is on tour as well. Like me, he was born here. He chimes in now and then with words of wisdom and is clearly enjoying his homeland resurgence. The morning after I drunkenly punch the guy in the bathroom of the club, Mr. D stares back at me from the beloved hotel bathroom mirror and tells me that he's proud of my unfettered feelings, and by the way, one of the girl singers on the tour would really like to get me high and fuck me. But his main reason for popping in is to have me understand that I am now and forever an outcast, an expatriate, an unfavored son, the visitor I thought I always wanted to be. But there is a neediness in me that so wants to belong to this land, these towns, these people, that I switch back and forth between the high I get from playing shows here to the fear that I have left behind a huge part of who I am in this country when I moved to America. It's something that I will probably never shed, this feeling of what could have been, a life not lived and a future never realized. I'm sure it's why I've stayed away so long from this place and resisted a real reconnection: I can focus on everything I have, and not everything I missed out on.

It's the last date of my tour. I'm playing in Perth, the most remote major city in the universe. It is staggeringly beautiful: an ocean-side city where women have that lean, willowy beach look, sunburned men drink and fight, and sharks take the lonely swimmer. It is 3,000 miles from the nearest large city. And who lives here now? Hank B. fucking Marvin, the man who inspired me, as well as a legion of British guitarists that you know and love, and the original owner of the very first REDFENDER-STRAT!!! The man I first idolized as a twelve-year-old weasely would-be guitar player back in sweet, dying England of the very early 1960s. This man was the first-ever English-born guitar hero.

Up until Hank, it had been the Eddie Cochrans, the Duane Eddys, and the Scotty Moores who had the monopoly on the guitar-star thing. Hank and his band the Shadows became superstars throughout Europe, Asia, Africa, and Australia in the late '50s and early '60s, though they were never able to crack the U.S.—and that was just the way it was. Back then (before the Beatles) there was only one way for music to travel across the Atlantic—from the U.S. to Europe. It simply did not go the other way. If you weren't American, you had a hard time getting any music played in the States. And we knew it and felt humbled and a little intimidated by that fact. Occasionally a British or Australian song would be a U.S. hit for a few weeks, but it never amounted to anything lasting or any real American career for the artist.

Hank suddenly made being a homegrown star cool. *He* was cool. He looked like Buddy Holly and played an American guitar—the only Fender guitar on this side of the Atlantic at the time. He inspired all of us snotty-nosed English kids (yep, at this point I still considered myself a Limey) and made it seem possible for all us non-Americans to aspire to something magic. And he was and is a brilliant player, with a tone that guitar players still refer to as the "Shadows" or the "Hank Marvin" sound. He was a veritable giant in 1961. Now in 2007 I have been e-mailing him for a few months prior to the tour, and I finally call him when I get to Perth. He is gracious, and we arrange to meet at a restaurant in the part of Perth where he now lives. (Maybe being able to meet your childhood idol is the *third* good thing about being a celebrity. Remember? First, getting good restaurant reservations and second, occasionally helping your kids in their school life. I'm pretty sure there is no *fourth* thing.)

Now, honestly, think of the person you believed was a god when you were a little kid. The artist/singer/actor/writer/cartoon character who you would have given anything just for the privilege of lying down upon the street in the rain so they wouldn't have to get their celestial feet wet . . . now invite them to dinner and have them accept—that's how I feel about the prospect of getting together with Hank. Every English guitar player owes an allegiance to Hank B. Marvin: Eric Clapton, George Harrison, Jimmy Page, Jeff Beck, Brian May—truly, the list is endless.

I've reconnected with my old school mate John Kennedy in the intervening years and am pleased to find that he has not ended up in prison. In fact, he has a good life and a great family. And because he and I became friends over our shared love of the Shadows and specifically Hank B. Marvin, I invite John to Perth on this day so we can both be fourteen-year-olds together again while we pretend we are adults and chat jovially with Hank B. It is a stunning moment in time, and dear Jesus I wish we could have somehow known this was going to happen when we were little tiny "nuts haven't fully dropped yet" boys and longing to be guitar stars ourselves. I wish for anyone who is a fan of someone to have such a meaningful meeting with their life hero. It is everything fourteen-year-old Ricky and fourteen-year-old Johnny could have ever dreamed of. And God bless Hank for being such a stand-up human being to see the love and fandom blazing pathetically in our eyes but still carry on a conversation as if we were all equals. It's not very often that our heroes measure up to our expectations, which is why I usually don't like to meet people I am a fan of. And we are all fans of *someone.*

I return to my home in the U.S. of A. with a guitar signed to me from "Hank B." Gomer doesn't care much about the guitar, but he is *real* happy to see me. And I, him. My girl B has a question in her eyes. It's the result of me being away from home for so long, and I tell her I am hers now. I know you may be thinking that I am a dickhead to ever have given her cause to doubt me in the first place, but let me just say in my own defense . . . you are correct: I am a dickhead. It is behind us now and I intend to never have it be a question in her eyes again.

CHAPTER TWENTY-THREE

IN OVERDRIVE

HOME

2010

The first song I complete when I get home is to my girl B: "Venus in Overdrive." The goddess of love in full force. A metaphor for Barbara herself and the constant love she has brought into my life. I am a lucky son of a bitch.

Here's me thinking love can never survive
You showed up Venus in Overdrive
Sex just got me buried alive
Turn on
Venus in Overdrive

I begin recording my new album, having written all the songs with my band's bass player, Matt Bissonette. This is the first time I've ever collaborated on the writing of a whole record. It's something I've resisted previously on the grounds that if you write a song with another person it becomes a "song by committee" and therefore loses some of its personal charm and depth. I'll add a caveat here and say that the great songwriting partnerships of the world—Lennon and McCartney, Rodgers and Hammerstein, etc.—defy this concern, but they're pretty rare. The kind of connection they achieved doesn't happen very often.

I've heard some songs Matt has written and I like them. Because we're around each other so much on the road, we just gravitate toward this songwriting partnership, and I'm excited by the results. Something happens with our songwriting together that maybe wouldn't have happened if we'd written separately. Matt is one of the most brilliant musicians I've ever met (Matt, send the check to my home address), and we have a mutual respect of each other's strong points as far as the craft of writing a song goes. Plus he's possibly more driven than even I am when it comes to getting a song finished. Matt has just lost his mom, and we are in similar places in our lives with regard to family relationships, things we no longer want to be involved in, things we hope to achieve, dreams we hope to fulfill. And we are both deeply affected by Sahara's death. The album we write is full of her soul.

We record *Venus in Overdrive* in less than thirty days at my cool new "no drummers allowed" studio, the Black Lagoon. This is a far cry from the almost eleven months I labored over *Shock, Denial, Anger, Acceptance*. Gomer has a bed under the console and another one in the corner of the control room. There's his water dish and a bowl for the special "people" food that Matty Spindel, my studio engineer, brings in fresh every morning. The backyard is just beyond the studio door so "the Gome" has ready access to a place where he can stretch his legs, check for bastard squirrels, and pee and poop in close proximity to his main man, me. I'll know I've truly beaten my demons in this life when I come back in my next life as my own *dog*.

This time the songs we record are more along the lines of *Working Class Dog*: power pop with strong hooks and most no longer than three minutes. We cut two more new songs about Sahara—"Oblivious" and "God Blinked."

But there is a short break while we conduct the annual Malibu "pack-up-your-real-important-shit-and-run-for-your-fucking-lives" fire drill. I wake up one morning ready to head to the studio when Barbara comes rushing into the bedroom to tell me there's a big fire and it's headed our way (not good). I have just bought one of those gasoline-powered water-pumps (good) that you drop one end of into the pool and hose down the house with the other, but I've neglected to read the directions on how to operate it (not good). So with the fire storming over a ridge of the not-too-distant mountain (really not good), I fill the pump with gas, find all the right connections for the hoses and get it running (good). I toss all the outdoor furniture into the pool (which makes it look like the aftermath of the *Titanic* sinking), then grab some of my vintage guitars and put them in my car (also good) before realizing that I now have a half-container of gasoline sitting by the house (not good), so I figure I'll put it in my car, since the car is filled with gas anyway, so how much worse could it be? (good?) and then remember I've just put some of my treasured vintage guitars in that car (really not good), so I unload the guitars from the car and put them into my son Liam's car (good), but he says, "I'm not leaving. I'm staying with you to fight the fire" (not good).

All this time, B and my old mum (who is visiting us from Australia for a few months of recreational fire drills and shopping) are loading the dogs, photos, and home videos into her car and getting ready to head for the hills—at least those that aren't on fire (good)—while the cops are driving up and down the neighborhood broadcasting, "This is a mandatory evacuation!" (not good). But then I realize that there is no such thing, because they can't force you to leave your home (good . . . I guess). I then run into the house and grab some of my more valuable *Star Wars* figures (extremely geeky) and put them in Barbara's car. When she comes out, she asks me what's in the big box that's taking up all the room in her backseat (could go either way). I say "It's my *Star Wars* stuff." She rolls her eyes and goes back into the house for more photos of loved ones (okay, good). Then she grabs my old mum and they head off to the local safe place. I crank up the pool-pump thing and start hosing down Liam's car (with my cool guitars inside it) and he says, "Dad, what are you doing? Spray the HOUSE!" (smarter), so I do. And when I walk out into the street again it is eerily quiet. A few neighbors are standing beside loaded cars and trucks and we all look at each other and offer tight, strained smiles. It's kind of like we're waiting for the flesh-eating zombies to come, as monstrous billows of dark-gray smoke suffocate the horizon.

Eventually the capricious winds change, the fire heads the other way, and we're all spared again (really good). My lovely mother and the very patient B drive back home, and we unload Gomer and his two sisters Molly Moleskin (a schnoodle) and Piggy the incredibly pudgy pug, plus all the crap we loaded into the car in the first place at the onset of this yearly oh-my-God-we're-all-gonna-die ritual. We're all tired, happy, and in need of a big, fat glass of red wine. Later, I drive around town. There are blackened mountains everywhere, and it seems like we live on the moon (but a moon with a really nice beach). Thankfully the ocean won't burn. Well, maybe after a few more oil spills it might.

I have an uncomfortable suspicion that my *Star Wars* stuff may secretly be sold online in the coming weeks, so I go to my website and alert certain fans to watch eBay and make sure my super-neato space toys are not heartlessly sold off. There are some really commando, hard-core superfans who will watch my ass on this and alert me if certain very, very, VERY rare one-of-a-kind *Star Wars* 3½-inch plastic figures show up online. I have paid some serious money for these really badly molded and painted, dopey, cheesy plastic figures, and I do not intend to lose them, goddammit! Yes, that is the *Star Wars* toy–obsessed part of me that still lives in my mum's basement and hasn't kissed a girl yet.

Soon of course the rains will come, now that the fires are gone, and acres and acres of newly denuded, precious topsoil will be washed into the ocean to choke the fish. I'm pretty sure that somewhere in Malibu, a new-money numb-nuts asshole has built himself a big fancy house on top of Chumash Indian burial grounds. How else do you explain all the fires, mudslides, floods, and earthquakes? There are even too many fucking frogs here! Pestilence, anyone?

We get back to finishing the new album. I send Amy the three tracks about her girl to get the okay. She leaves a sweet and tearful message on my cell phone that they are all good with her and Shannon. I'm glad. The monument is built, and we release the album *Venus in Overdrive*. It debuts on the U.S. charts higher than any album of my career. And the first single, "What's Victoria's Secret?" gets more attention than my last three albums combined. We hit the TV and press circuit and then take the new album on the road. In my hotel room again, late at night, I realize I am doing this for the right reasons now. I'm not purging myself of guilt or having to own up to any bad conduct in these songs. They are all basically positive and about the true and good side of my love and passion. I am playing and performing for the absolute joy of transmitting this new music. It's a powerful feeling.

B and I are closer than we have ever been and the bottom line is, we still turn each other on. She is more crucial to my existence than ever. I am never more content than when I am at home, feeling safe, and she is busy moving around the kitchen, cooking something brilliant for her family. She has become my spiritual center, my soul-compass: the one who keeps me turning in the right direction. Her love for me has been strong enough to keep her by me while I worked through my shit and tried to be better for her. She, more than anyone on the planet, understands me and has given me room to write publicly about our life in song and in prose. She makes it work. She is the reason we are together. She is also the best person I have ever known. And we have built a life together that continues to grow.

Mr. D is still with me, of course, and he chimes in now and then. "Hey, Sport. You're just one slipup away from this all turning to shit, y'know?" And I *do* know. He's right. So I meditate. I pray. I focus on my work. I give thanks for my girl B and my family, and I occasionally go on vitamin P when the Darkness gets too in-my-face. It's not a perfect solution, but I'm still very much a work in progress. I feel kind of like an idiot savant sometimes: pieces of me are really messed up, but there's a part that has a gift. A glimmer of potential and promise amidst the flaws.

I record a CD of the lullabies I wrote for my sons when they were born almost twenty-five years ago. We rent a cruise ship and begin the annual Rick Springfield and Friends Cruise, playing and partying down to Key West, Cozumel, and back to Miami. Eventually, in our third year, our cruise goes to the Bahamas. We head to Japan again and again with no dark shit at all, and Mr. D is pretty bored and pissed off about that. Suck it, fucker! We go to Europe for the first time in years and play outdoor festivals.

I'm determined to get back into my acting career as well, and I am cast in a four-episode arc on the TV show *Californication*. This is a very risqué show about sexual addictions (typecasting?), and it's the first show for which I've ever had to sign a "nudity and simulated sex" waiver (where you agree that you are *okay* with indulging in simulated carnal perversion on cable television) before beginning work. Now, hold on a second here. Did I just say "nudity, sex, and *work*" in the same sentence? Well yes, I did. And halfway through the filming of these shows, which are brilliantly written and a blast to do, I drop my pants and have "sex" with a young stripper. And I don't have to get a divorce, I don't end up on the evening news, my kids aren't ashamed of me (in fact, they're quite proud), and I get *paid* for doing it! Maybe *this* is the direction I should have been going in all along—*acting* all this crazy shit out! Acting is much more fun and a greater reward for me since I'm older and have a certain amount of life experience under my belt. I'm turned on by it now like I am by music, and I look forward to playing more sexual deviants.

Okay. I'm going to drop one final name here, so watch your toes. I'm a music fan first and foremost, so consequently I'm a fan of other musicians. When I was in my teens, Paul McCartney became *the* guy. Seeing the Beatles was a life changer and Paulie was the one I singled out. He was the one I most wanted to be like. His were the songs I dissected and tried to emulate. His hair was the style I tried to comb my unruly mass into a sad simulation of. I had such a boy crush on him. I kept his photo in a notebook otherwise reserved for my sacred but quite dopey poems, atrocious song lyrics, amateurish drawings, and other artsy-fartsy stuff. At some point I left the notebook behind, but my fanship of Paulie has only grown. It's been a lifelong dream to meet the man who was the object of my teen worship. I get my chance early in 2010 at a pre-party for the Golden Globes. I know he'll be there and, in truth, it's the only reason I attend. A mutual friend has arranged an introduction. In my mind, it's just Paulie and me. Mano a mano. I step up to the meeting and I'm shaking like a little girl. Paul eyes me warily, perhaps trying to decide if I'm a stalker or just another avid fan. (I'm the latter, but I probably come across as the former.) And of course I'm sure it's a thrill for him to meet yet another Beatle freak, but it all goes swimmingly. Afterward I send the resulting photo of the two of us to everyone in my e-mail address book with the advisory that they "suck it . . . hahahahha . . . here is a photo of me with my new BFF Paulie." And in some bizarre way, my life now seems oddly complete. I love being a fan. It puts life in perspective and there is always more to aspire to when you're looking *up*. And everyone is a fan of *someone*. Paul is a fan of someone, I am a fan of Paul's, and someone else is a fan of mine.

I love music and being a musician. For all the poor choices I've made in my life, I've made some very right ones. I'm glad I took the chance and bailed on school when I did (Liam and Josh, if you're reading this, it's all bullshit). I'm glad that I decided to travel and play and write. I love guitars. I have them all over my house: on walls, in stands and corners, everywhere I look. They're beautiful, individual works of art, and each one has as much soul dripping from it as Howlin' Wolf's sweaty brow on a hot night at Silvio's Lounge on Chicago's West Side.

And I'm beginning to feel that maybe, just maybe, I am enough. Though every now and then, when I'm feeling good and I start humming to myself or thinking a thought that makes me smile, my old adversary will chime in, as he often has in good times before. "Yeah, everything's just fucking peachy, isn't it, dipshit?" hisses my Darkness. Which of course will switch my focus to everything that *isn't* peachy in my life and my world. I know he will never let me go. And maybe I deserve him. I continue to do my best and to live well: to be the man Gomer thinks I am, my sons believe me to be, and Barbara is pretty sure I am in my heart. I still feel guilty over the pain that my past actions have inflicted on those I love—particularly B—but I try not to wallow in it, no matter how much my Darkness thinks I really should. My focus is on the present and the future as I watch out for booby traps on the path ahead. And the Buddhist phrase I most need to have tattooed backward on my forehead so I can read it in the bathroom mirror every time I look, is: "Each morning we are born again. What we do today is what matters most."

On good days I love my life, my girl B, my family, my music, and my career choice. On bad days I want to drive straight into a fucking tree. And most days are spent somewhere in between. I think back to "Gary's Girl" in my old stained-glass class and the "million-dollar snub" she gave me, and I'm thankful I don't always get what I want. Proof that something wonderful comes with every slice of shit we are served.

So what do I believe?

I believe in the path I have chosen and the emptiness of celebrity. I know that identifying the demons that drive me is a good start, but it's only that: a beginning. Analysis and psychotherapy are instructional, but not a satisfying end in themselves. The battle is lifelong. Certainly recognizing the things that propel and pursue me is a major step, but it is not a cure. There is no cure. The drug addict knows this. The alcoholic knows this. The sex addict knows this. And I know this. The Darkness is the shepherd of all my negative thinking, drives, passions, and weaknesses. And I will take the fucker to my grave. I continue to wage a daily crusade not to let him take me over.

The things that changed me for the better are obvious to me. Barbara is my light and my love. She is the one true soul life who wants to be my companion through this life, and I hers. She has incredible depths that I am still discovering. Those fortunate enough to know her, love her for her selflessness, her passion for others, her hopeful view of the world, and her benevolence. Not to mention her awe-inspiring burritos.

My precious sons Liam and Josh, who made me realize I am *not* the most important person in the universe: *they* are. And I thank all that is merciful that I get this. It took a giant load of pressure off me. Plus I get to hang with these two most amazing beings. I seek/pray for a true and hopefully lasting spiritual connection, something I am exploring on an hour-to-hour and minute-to-minute basis. I may never know the truth until it looks me in the eye at the end.

Speaking of the end, this isn't it! There will be volumes II, III, and IV in this autobiographical series. ("Oh no," they moan in unison.) I have a lot of living left (I hope) and still too much to learn. And I don't know how it will end, thank God. Hey, speaking of God and faith, it's good to have someone who believes in you to guide you from time to time. My dad was there, both physically and spiritually, with a hand on my elbow to steer me back during the times I wandered off my path and headed for the cliff. He's with me still. I inherited my old mum's persistence and "school-of-hard-knocks" fighting spirit, but it was from my dad that I learned to love others, never shrink from kissing the face of a dog, and periodically get down on my hands and knees and humbly thank the gods. When I meditate and connect to God, he/she most of the time wears my dad's face. This is amazing to me, since it was my father's death that originally caused me to question my faith so many years ago. I am incredibly lucky to have had that sweet guy as my father and as a constant believer in me; I always hurt for anyone I meet who doesn't have a good "old man" connection the way I did. I'm doing my best to forge that same kind of good bond with my two sons, and as I've said, I think I'm doing an okay job of it. Mostly.

I realize now how important family has been to me, both my own and those that adopted me when I was most in need. I couldn't have survived without them during those times when I was adrift in a foreign land. I am eternally grateful for the few who stepped in and filled that void. It's usually something only blood relatives can do. I thank all that is meant to be that I found B and that she found me. Our connection is irreplaceable. *She* most certainly is. And I completely embrace how important it is for me to be an honest and moral person, to accept all the shit I am saddled with and have created for myself, to write with veracity and passion, and to be able to absorb a good hard kick in the balls now and then when the world doesn't go the way I want it to. Also to be a good shepherd of the small furry animals.

And speaking of small furry animals: My sweet main man Gomer is about to check out and go home. I wish we could be together forever. I look at my dear old boy, silver-muzzled, tired, at the end of his good journey. The only beings I have had a pure relationship with, and with no regrets, are the dogs in my life. There has never been a moment when I have wished anything but to be with them. My beloved companion Gomer has been with me for fourteen years now. He is so deep and amazing that he waits for the two months I have off from touring before he says good-bye. Over these precious weeks I hang with him, lie with him, breathe him in, take mental pictures that will last a lifetime, kiss him, cuddle with him, and share him with all those who love him. As his legs weaken, I carry him around the house from dog bed to dog bed, inject water into his mouth with a syringe so he doesn't go thirsty, feed him cat food, raw steak, chicken teriyaki, and Gelson's chili by hand—anything that will entice him to eat. I hold him upright out in the grass so he can pee.

We're all bracing ourselves, but there is really no way to prepare for the end. I have said good-bye to so many beings I love. Gomer is the hardest, because he's woven into the fabric of our daily lives. He is part of our family, has local friends, distant fans, and a presence that is forbidding and mighty. I fear the giant black hole he will leave. I don't want our connection to end. I see him lying there and I don't want to let go. We all know his pain and the look in his eyes that truly says, "I'm only hanging on because you bastards won't let me leave." We're trying to find the courage to say good-bye.

And as sure as winter, the fateful night arrives. He is breathing too hard; it looks like it hurts him. His eyes are unfocused, yet they still catch our movement around him as he lies on our bed. The vet arrives. We come to the decision. He gives our boy his shot and we hold him, talk to him, tell him over and over that we love him, and kiss him until he takes four deep breaths and is gone. He is gone. *He is gone.* May the starlight guide you home, my sweet boy. We all crumble into one another's arms for support. That night I am missing him terribly and he comes to me in a dream. I wake with the phrase in my head—"It is the *way* of things." And I understand that it is.

I take him to be cremated at the place I took Ronnie many, many years ago. I have more peace with Gomie's death than I did with Ronnie's. We gave him all we could. We sent him home with love and tears. He died well. I have no regrets. And he will always be our boy. I take his ashes (that too-small box, again) to the grave site where we eventually buried Ronnie's ashes, and I pray that they are together and will wait for me. I don't look for a sign, but I know there will be one. As I rise and walk back to my car with my furry boy's ashes under my arm, I look up. I see two hawks circling lazily over the grounds. Only two. Gomer and Ronnie together. Spirits.

I know every story should have an ending, though thankfully my life is still going on, but I'm thinking about my own mortality lately. I hope for a painless crossing when my time comes, but whatever it will be, it will be. Not that I deserve a free pass or that I'll have a say in the matter, but I'd like to suggest that the first thing I see when I cross over is a big-ass sign that reads "All is forgiven." My dad will be there, and my mum (though it's not a certainty that she'll go before me; as I have said, she's made of extremely tough stuff), and my sweet mutts will be there, too. The best line about what awaits us is the one Will Rogers said: "If there are no dogs in Heaven, then when I die, I want to go where *they* went." I wholeheartedly concur. Ronnie will be running to me with Gomer at his side, both smiling as only dogs can smile, along with Cleo, my only friend in adolescence, and way, way in the back, running to catch up as fast as his legs can carry him, a scruffy black-and-white terrier from a long time ago . . . my long-lost and abandoned boy . . . Elvis.

ACKNOWLEDGMENTS

From the Touchstone side:

Stacy Creamer: ace editor, publisher, and friend (who, disguised as Supergirl, fights a never-ending battle for truth, triathlons, and the literary way)

Lauren Spiegel	David Falk	Stacy Lasner
Martha Schwartz	Rob Goodman	Stuart Calderwood
Cherlynne Li	Marcia Burch	Mark Speer
Joy O'Meara	George Turianski	Mick Wieland

From the RS side:

Barbara, Liam, and Joshua: my heart and soul

Mum and Dad: thanks for the rude awakening

Rob Kos	Julie McCarron	Jay Gilbert
Alana Mulford	Steve Fisher	Ken Sharp
Jim Gosnell	Kym DeGenaro	Kim Jakwerth

Last and least: my Darkness, without whom none of this would have been possible—the bastard.

otograph © Tom Kelley/Ventura, CA